**SECOND EDITION
UPDATED 2007**

Fit for Real People

SEW GREAT CLOTHES USING ANY PATTERN!

BY PATI PALMER & MARTA ALTO

Design by Linda Wisner
Illustrations by Jeannette Schilling,
  Kate Pryka and Diane Russell
Photography by Pati Palmer
Styling and Sewing by Marta Alto

Edited by Barbara Weiland

Acknowledgements

Without our students, we wouldn't have had a "living research laboratory." From our early days running a sewing school at Meier & Frank (a May Co. department store) to 15 years of traveling with fit seminars, and now to our sewing school at the Fabric Depot, in Portland, Oregon, a hearty thanks to students worldwide whom we've taught and from whom we've learned.

We also thank those who graciously volunteered to be models for this book in hopes of sharing their own challenges so you could benefit. They volunteered their time and often helped with the solutions: Anastasia Alto, Olga Anderson, Debbra Demissee, Lila Duff, Dorothy Jacobson, Brittany Kaza, Kathy McCullock, Patty Myers, Laurel Nugent, Marty Palmer, Sharon Takahashi, and Catherine Welson.

Some of the models are Certified Palmer/Pletsch Instructors who were taking workshops here in Portland while we were writing this book. Thanks to Connie Hamilton, Janice Langan, Karin Larson, Joyce Lockyer, Marcy Miller, Denise Paulson, Sandra Willoughby and Gretchen Youngstrom.

A special thank you to former Palmer/Pletsch traveling associates Lynn Raasch, Karen Dillon, Leslie Wood, and Barbara Weiland, who not only contributed fit ideas over the years, but so graciously allowed us to reprint their photographs on page 59. At that time, we were all 30-something and sewed with a size 10.

Susan Pletsch, Pati's business partner in 1975 when they coauthored *Painless Sewing*, didn't want a chapter in that book on the "boring" subject of fit, so issued the ultimate challenge to Pati then: "Write something I would read and that's easy to understand and fun." Well, the book ended up having 30 pages on fit. We thank Susan for her initial request.

During our research on sizing, we talked to a lot of interesting and helpful people: Bruno Ferri, President, Wolf Form Co.; Dr. Ellen Goldsberry, Director of the Southwest Retail Center at the University of Arizona; Bill Rankin, Owner, Dress Rite Form Co.; the late Betty Brown, a costume designer with a huge historic pattern collection; Nicolai Tamburino, Vice President Tailoring at Neiman Marcus; Ardis Koester, former Extension State Clothing Specialist for Oregon; Carol Salusso, Ph.D., Associate Professor of Apparel, Merchandising, and Textiles at Washington State University. Thanks also to Whitney Blausen for including a Palmer/Pletsch pattern in the sewing and patterns history exhibit she coordinated for The Fashion Institute of Technology in New York. And to Kevin Seligman, Professor, School of Theatre Arts, Northern Illinois University, for trustingly sharing with us his large historic pattern collection to photograph for this book.

We thank all the technical experts from the pattern companies who gave us information vital to this book and with whom we shared our fit philosophy: Karen Burkhart, Simplicity Pattern Company (Pati had previously worked with her at McCall's and at Vogue before that); Pat Perry and Janet DuBane, Vogue/Butterick Pattern Company; Sid Tepper, Carl LaLumia, Emily Cohen, and Kathleen Klausner, all from the McCall Pattern Company. A special thanks to the technical people at McCall's who are helping Pati build fit information into the tissue and guidesheets of the Fit For Real People patterns: Benhaz Livian, Charlotte Schulze, Christine Carballeira, Pamyla Brooks and Stacy Wood.

Several people read the book one or more times during its gestation including Marty Palmer, Jack Watson, and Connie Hamilton. We thank you for caring.

Without our talented production team and their long, intense hours of work, this book would not exist. Our artists, some of whom we've worked with for 20 years, often even made samples to test the instructions. Our most sincere thanks to Linda Wisner, Jeannette Schilling, Kate Pryka, Diane Russell, and Sarah Oaks.

Lastly, a thanks to our hard-working staff, and to our loving families who've been so supportive over the years and especially during the three full years spent actually writing this book.

Cover photo by Carol Meyer
Copy editing by Ann Price Gosch

Copyright © 1998 by Palmer/Pletsch Incorporated.
Second Edition copyright © 2005 by Palmer/Pletsch Incorporated.
Second Edition Library of Congress Control Number: 9780935278651
Published by Palmer/Pletsch Publishing, 1801 NW Upshur Street, Suite 100, Portland, OR 97209 U.S.A.
Seventh printing July 2010 — printed by Journal Graphics, Portland, Oregon, U.S.A.

Second Edition ISBN 978-0-935278-65-1

Table of Contents

About the Authors

Marta Alto

Marta's career as a sewing expert began during her summer "vacations" from studying at Oregon State University, when she sewed costumes at the Oregon Shakespearean Festival in Ashland. That led to a job at San Francisco State University teaching drama students how to sew costumes. As a result, Marta learned how to sew without patterns and to fit many actors' figures.

Marta's unconventional problem-solving approach to fit grew out of this experience. Pati used to cringe at Marta's less-than-technically-correct solutions to fit. Now Pati enjoys Marta's creative problem solving, including the coining of new fit terms such as "smooshing out a dart" and "taking a little here and putting a little there."

After five years in San Francisco, Marta returned to Oregon in 1972 with her 4-year-old son and became a custom dressmaker at a major Oregon department store. She sewed for designer-clothing customers who couldn't find the right silk blouse, for mothers of brides who wanted a special dress that fit, and for people wanting outfits out of that wonderful "new" fabric, Ultrasuede.® Marta then became an assistant buyer and later managed the store's sewing school. After the birth of her second child in 1977, she "retired" to teaching sewing in Portland, then Seattle. In 1981 Marta joined Palmer/Pletsch, and traveled throughout the United States, Canada and Australia teaching Ultrasuede, Fit, Tailoring and Serger seminars.

In 1986 Marta became a Palmer/Pletsch corporate workshop educator. She is also co-author of **The Serger Idea Book** and **Sewing Ultrasuede** and has made four serger videos and one on Ultrasuede. She currently teaches at the Palmer/Pletsch school in Portland and does writing and research on sewing trends.

Pati Palmer

Fit has always been Pati's specialty. After she earned a degree in clothing and textiles from Oregon State University, one of her first jobs was to start a sewing school at Portland's Meier & Frank department store. That was only the beginning of her experience fitting thousands of women. As a result, she has developed workable techniques that any size sewer can use with commercial patterns.

Pati is billed as the "Fit Expert" in the McCall's pattern catalog, which has featured nearly 100 of her designs. Besides conceiving the designs, Pati and her staff write the sewing and fitting instructions themselves.

Palmer/Pletsch was formed in 1973 when Pati and her then-partner, Susan Pletsch, merged their writing and speaking talents. After co-authoring four books, they traveled throughout the United States and Canada teaching seminars based on the books. By 1980, nine Palmer/Pletsch associates were teaching 900 sewing seminars a year.

Pati and Susan approached Vogue Pattern Co. in 1975 and became a licensee, the first time an educator signed on with a pattern company. Five years later, Pati and Susan switched to The McCall Pattern Company. Now McCall's president Bob Hermann tells Pati she is the company's longest-running licensee, beating out the previous title-holder, Marlo Thomas!

In 1986, after buying Susan's portion of the business, Pati established four-day workshops in Portland, Oregon. Sewing enthusiasts have come to the workshops from around the world to learn the latest techniques. In 1990, Palmer/Pletsch added teacher training and in 1994 initiated a certification program, the first to be developed for sewing instructors. To date, more than 140 teachers have graduated and more than 80 have become certified.

Pati and her husband, Jack Watson, who helped hand-collate her first book, reside in a lovely historic home where they entertain sewers during the workshops. They are also parents of a 12-year-old daughter, Melissa.

Foreword

Marta and I have been through it all. We've been involved with computer patterns, the "never-have-to-buy-another-pattern" basic pattern designing kits, drafting, draping, measuring, sewing muslins—you name it. After 25 years of hands-on teaching and fitting thousands of DIFFERENT bodies, we've found a way to teach fit that really works. We have also been training teachers from around the world since 1990. What they tell us is that "IT WORKS!!!"

I have been designing for American pattern companies since 1975. I am truly a believer that pattern companies do an amazing job in providing good designs, sewing instructions, and standard-ization. I've had the unique experience of being able to ask questions firsthand. I've learned *why* they do things and how they constantly improve their products.

People often criticize pattern companies with-out understanding why decisions were made. For example, someone criticized one of my McCall's designs for having an "unnecessary" seam. Well, the reason for that seam was that the style couldn't be efficiently cut out in a size 22 without it. That doesn't mean WE can't eliminate the seam if we want to. Always remember that **the pattern is the manu-script; YOU are the editor!**

Another favorite statement is that one pattern company fits better than the other or that they are all so different in their fit. In this book we will attempt to show you that there is no need for those fears. You can sew suc-cessfully with patterns from ALL pattern companies. READ ON!

Fit is a process. Why? You must first really get to know your body. It is some-times a rude awakening, but is always empowering. Then you must understand grainline. In well-fitting clothing, the horizontal grain is parallel to the floor and the vertical grain is perpendicular to the floor,

except for bias cuts. This concept will be a useful tool as you learn "tissue draping."

Fit is fun! If you can think in 3-D, you will marvel at your ability to solve fit puzzles. You will love the clothes you sew that flatter your figure because they fit. If you are a dressmaker, being able to fit means dollars. You can charge a lot more if you can create clothing that fits! Good fit is worth the time it takes!

Read the first part of this book to understand the WHYs of fit. We've used art where it will most quickly help you understand a concept. We've used photos of real people whenever possible, because there are very few "standard" figures.

Once you understand fit basics, look to the sections that address specific fit challenges. As you sew for yourself or others, keep this book beside you as a reference and you'll be well on your way to experiencing the rewards of fitting-as-you-sew!

Sincerely,

Pati Palmer

Authors Marta Alto (second from left) and Pati Palmer (third from left) join Behnaz Livian, Head of Patternmaking (far left), and Sid Tepper, Design Director (far right), at The McCall Pattern Company.

photo by Carl LaLumia

5

CHAPTER 1

The Palmer/Pletsch Approach to

- **IT'S EASY!**
- **IT'S PRACTICAL!**
- **IT APPLIES TO *ALL* PATTERN COMPANIES!**
- **IT'S NEARLY MEASURE-FREE!**
- **THERE'S NO NEED TO DRAFT EVERY DESIGN FROM SCRATCH!**
- **THERE'S NO NEED TO MAKE A MUSLIN!**

Does this sound too good to be true? Marta Alto and Pati Palmer have developed this method by fitting thousands of women during the past 25-plus years. Now for the first time in a book, they share what they've learned with YOU!

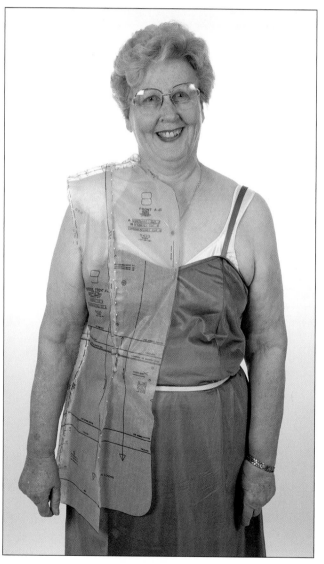

1. Buy the right size pattern.

2. Tissue-fit the pattern.

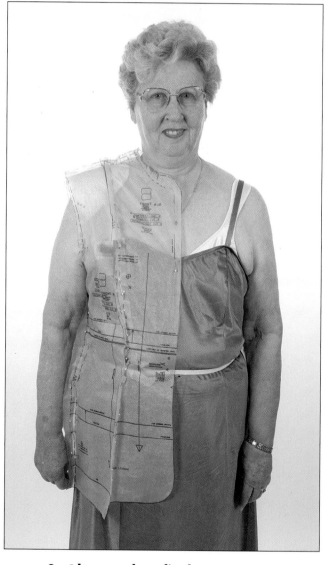

3. Alter and re-fit the pattern.

Fitting—Successfully!

Learning to fit is a process. The more you do it, the better you get. The best fabric and the finest workmanship cannot compensate for poor fit. In fact, 25 percent of your sewing time should be spent fitting.

In this book, you will learn this fitting process. We will show it to you in several ways so that you can really absorb and understand it, then apply it to everything you sew.

4. Pin-fit-as-you-sew.

5. Enjoy the final garment.

How This System Was Developed

Measuring Didn't Work

During the '70s, Marta and Pati used a full set of body measurements to determine size and alter a pattern. Then they decided there must be an easier, more accurate way.

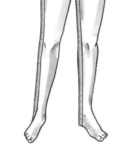

Muslins Were Tedious

They tried making and altering muslins. Students complained that this took TOO much time! They wanted an easier way.

Pati and Susan Chose to Work with Commercial Patterns

After toying with the idea of designing their own fit pattern, Pati Palmer and Susan Pletsch decided that it would be better for sewers if they put their ideas into commercial patterns. In 1975, they designed Vogue's fit pattern and in 1980, one for McCall's.

Today, all American pattern companies are using this system created by Palmer/Pletsch in their basic fit patterns.

Their Goal Was to Make Fitting Easier

To make altering easier, Pati and Susan added the concepts of outlets and "in-case" seam allowances (larger than necessary in case you need them) to their patterns. They decided against multisizing in their fit pattern for better accuracy; they preferred to have stitching lines printed on the pattern and to have wider seam allowances to allow for more room if needed.

If you squint at the pattern tissue, look at only the dotted lines and eliminate the outlets, you have the "sloper" that the pattern companies use to design their patterns. Once you fit a basic pattern, you will have a "road map" to fit any fashion pattern.

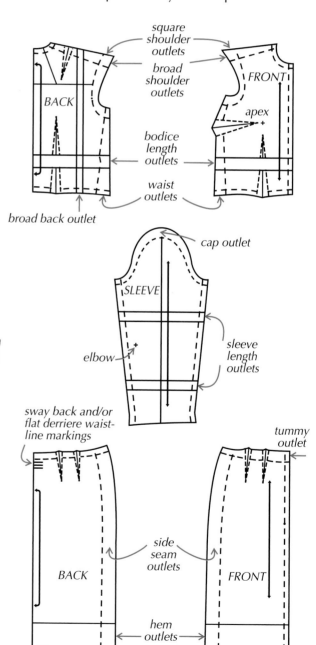

Pati and Susan also included five fronts in their fit pattern—one for every bra cup size A through DD. This is because fashion patterns are made for a B-cup. As a result, women with a DD-cup used to buy too large a pattern size. The McCall's fit pattern, which is available in nine sizes, allows you to actually try on a bodice in your proper bra cup size.

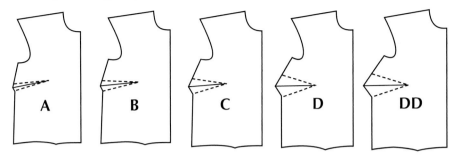

Using the Fit Pattern

After the fit pattern became available, Marta and Pati made up basic bodices in woven gingham fabric. Gingham has built-in grainline, making fit decisions easy. Since the pattern included fronts for five bra cup sizes, they sewed them in nine sizes, making a total of 45 bodices. Letting their students try them on was an easy way to find the right size and see necessary alterations.

At last! A method that worked!

Tissue-Fitting

To perfect the alterations, Pati and Marta "tissue-fitted" the same size pattern in which the student had been fitted in gingham. VOILA! They found a sure-fire, easy method. The altered pattern became the sewer's guide to her alterations...her personal road map.

Pati and Marta have been tissue fitting since their early teaching days, but with fashion patterns, not the basic dress pattern. They perfected tissue-fitting during the four-day fit workshops they have been teaching in Portland since 1989 and have been training teachers in their methods since 1990.

The Palmer/Pletsch pattern for McCall's makes fitting easy! Marta lets Denise try on the pre-sewn gingham shells. Marta puts her in a size 8 with a D-cup front.

Denise tries on unaltered tissue. The dart is too high and the pattern doesn't reach her center front. Always correct the dart position before deciding whether or not you need more bust fullness.

The dart is lowered (page 134) and the bodice fits perfectly.

NOTE: Chapter 9 shows the entire system on a real person, from determining the right size through fitting fashion. Read it first. Then YOU can do the same for yourself!

CHAPTER 2
A History of Pattern Sizing

One nagging question kept popping up while we were writing this book. How was sizing invented? Why is a size 10 a size 10? Does that number mean anything? Why aren't measurements used instead of arbitrary numbers?

We found a clue in a catalog from 1915. The caption to a "Misses' Dress" reads, "The pattern is cut in sizes 14, 16, 18, and 20 *years*." The caption for a design for a "Ladies' House-Dress" reads, "...cut in sizes from 34 to 44 inches **bust measurement**."

At that time "Misses'" referred to young women, probably unmarried. Sizes were by age. After the age of 20 years, a miss became a lady, and bust measurements were a more accurate way to determine size.

Misses' (years)									
Age	10	12	14	16	18				
Bust	28	30	32	34	36				
				34	36	38	40	42	
				Ladies' (bust size)					

Note that the bust measurements for sizes 16 and 18 and 34 and 36 overlap. What about ladies smaller than a 34" bustline? Did they have to buy the Misses' styles designed for young women? In the 1920s that may not have been a problem as fashion was pretty shapeless with no bust emphasis.

In a clothing catalog from 1915 designs Misses' (left) were more youthful-looking than the designs for Ladies' (right).

Misses' Dress, No. 6988.—The plain house closes in front, the open neck has a small, fancy collar, sleeves are full-length and plain with cuff. The skirt has a deep yoke and side-front closing; the lower portion has three gores. The pattern, No. 6988, is cut in sizes for 14, 16, 18 and 20 years. To make the dress in the medium size will require 3½ yards of 44-inch material, with ⅝ yard of 27-inch contrasting goods. Price of pattern, 10 cents.

Ladies' House - Dress, No. 7337. —The closing of this dress is placed at the left side of the front, and the edges of this and of the neck are trimmed with a bias band of contrasting material. The loose sleeves may be long or short. The skirt fits neatly at the top, and is also closed at the left side of the front. Wash-materials, cashmere, challis, and the like are used for these dresses, with braid or bias bands of material as trimming. The dress-pattern, No. 7337, is cut in sizes from 34 to 46 inches bust measure. Price of pattern, 10 cents.

In search of answers to some of our questions about where sizing came from, we flew to New York and met with Bruno Ferri, President and Owner, Wolf Form Company. As a young man, he started his career in the dress-form manufacturing business in the early 1930s. At that time, he told us, ages and bust measurements were no longer being used in ready-to-wear sizing.

Mr. Ferri showed us the actual 1930s ready-made measurements that had been hand-written in a book used by his company. He said, "At that time, size 16 (then a 34" bust) was the perfect body. She was sweet 16!" In the '30s and '40s a size 16 sewing pattern was also a 34" bust.

Then the ready-to-wear manufacturers began calling the same bust measurements by smaller size numbers. In 1967, pattern companies tried to become more similar to ready-to-wear and used as a guide the

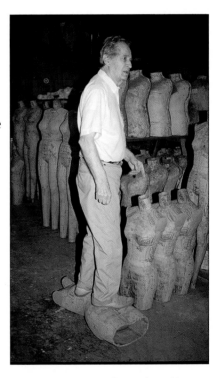

Bruno Ferri, President of Wolf Form Co., stands on a paper maché form to show how strong Wolf forms are.

measurements determined by a U.S. government Bureau of Standards study done in 1940. Up until 1972 patterns and ready-to-wear were indeed similarly sized.

Mr. Ferri then shared with us a chart of 1983 measurements that most manufacturers were using at that time. You guessed it! The 34" bust was now a size 10, no longer a size 16.

Today, ready-to-wear has changed even more. A size 10 is made for a person with a 37" to 38" bust. (See the Nordstrom chart on page 17.) If you are not yet thoroughly confused, read about Marta trying on size 12 ready-made jackets in a variety of price ranges and comparing them to a pattern size 12 (page 14). Actually, we concluded that they all fit similarly in one place—the shoulders!

Each manufacturer arbitrarily decides what its measurements will be. Enforced size standards in ready-to-wear have never existed.

Today, the Wolf Form Co. also makes the dress forms shown here for manufacturers targeting more mature figures. Marta was impressed to see one just like her with a spare tire, a full tummy, and a flat derriere!

The form below, shown in both a front and side view, has a 57" bust, a 50" waist, and a 63" hip.

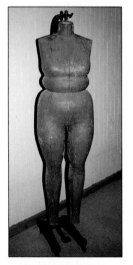

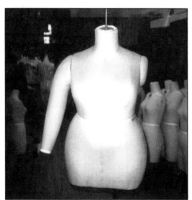

When did manufacturers stop using bust measurements for Ladies' sizes and substitute numbers? No one seems to have the answer. This change evolved over time and was not made by all manufacturers at once. There was no government directive or industry agreement. It just happened.

If vanity entered into the decision, the smaller Misses' size numbers were probably more palatable to most customers than the larger bust measurement numbers.

Old patterns give us some information. Between 1927 and 1931, we found the same patterns labeled as size 14 and size 36 Ladies' and Misses'. Eventually "Misses'" replaced "Ladies'" and size replaced bust measurement. Both were used during the transition.

the same Ladies' and Misses' *dress pattern, one a size 14, the other a size 36—both only 45¢*

Note that in the bottom left photo that more width is in the front of the form than in the back. Below are dress forms for all shapes, sizes and ages.

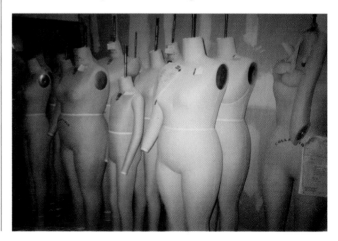

At one time we had only Misses' and Ladies' sizes. During the late '20s we began to see the first mention of Junior/Misses' and Misses'/Ladies'. "Junior" would replace "Misses'" eventually and "Misses'" would replace "Ladies'." Both were used during the transition. Today we have Girls', Misses' and Women's sizes.

This Butterick pattern from 1931 is sized by bust measurement.

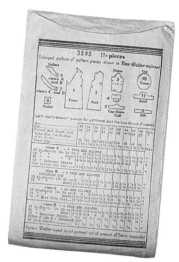

Today's size 12 was yesterday's size 16—two sizes smaller (see the two charts below). The 1940s' size 10 is a 2 today—four sizes smaller. Today, there is a 1" difference (grade) between the smaller sizes, 1½" between 10 and 12 and a 2" grade between the sizes larger than 12. In the '40s and earlier, a 2" grade was used between all sizes.

Let's Compare Some Old and New Measurement Charts

Current American Pattern Company Charts—Toddlers through Girls' size 14:
(Size is by age.)

Size	2	4	6	7	8	10	12	14
Chest	21	23	25	26	27	28½	30	32

Note that the 1940 Misses' chest measurements for sizes 12 to 14 are identical to the chest measurements of today's Girls' ages 12 and 14. This means that the evolution to using numbers for sizes originally came from age.

Bust sizes pattern companies used for Misses' in the '30s and '40s:
(Size was still a continuation of age—compare bust and chest measurements.)

Misses' size	10	12	14	16	18	20
Bust	28	30	32	34	36	38

Today's pattern company standard measurements:
(Same sizes allow larger bust measurements.)

Misses' size	4	6	8	10	12	14	16	18	20	22	24	26
Bust	29½	30½	31½	32½	34	36	38	40	42	44	46	48

Ready-to-Wear Today

Size Is Just a Number!

As ready-made clothing became more widely available, each manufacturer could do its own interpretation of a size because it was sold by a number rather than by bust measurement. To get customers, manufacturers invented "vanity sizing" (the more you pay, the smaller you can be). Today, the number no longer reflects the original **bust measurements** or **age** designations.

Marta sews with a pattern size 12. To find her correct size(s) in ready-made clothing, she went shopping. She tried on jackets at every price level. Amazingly, for best shoulder/upper chest fit, she wore a size 12 in all brands.

The ease in bust and hips varied a little among brands, even where styles were similar. The department company private label, Valerie Stevens, is cut with more ease, and Ralph Lauren traditionally cuts for small hips. (Maybe he doesn't want large-hipped people wearing his clothes! Or is he staying closer to the Bureau of Standards chart like the pattern companies?) What happened to vanity sizing? For hundreds of dollars in price difference, we want to be a smaller size!

Expensive clothes are often fashion forward. The current high-fashion trend is for a closer-to-the-body fit. Expensive clothes became more fitted in 1997 and the inexpensive didn't. This may be why all price levels fit about the same in 1997. A salesperson at Nordstrom said that in 1996 when DKNY did very fitted jackets, customers complained and didn't want to buy a larger size. In 1997 her jackets were roomier again.

Conclusion? Nothing is carved in stone, so be careful about making factual statements today that may not be factual tomorrow. FASHION IS CHANGE! Ready-to-wear fit is what each manufacturer wants it to be at any given time.

*This **unaltered** size 12 pattern fits Marta's hips like the Ralph Lauren jacket on the next page.*

McCall's

*Compare Marta Alto in the **altered** size 12 pattern at left with the size 12 ready-to-wear jackets to the right.*

Escada
$1,200

DKNY
$445

Patterns Today

Pattern Sizes Changed Four Times Before 1972

Fortunately for us who sew, American pattern companies, unlike ready-to-wear manufacturers, agree on the body measurements that are used for each size. Only fashion ease affects fit. However, these companies changed the standard body measurements four times before1972. Let's take size 16, for example, as shown in the chart at the right.

Year	1931*	1956	1967**	1972 (to current)
Size	16	16	16	16
Bust	34	36	38	38
Waist	28	28	29	30
Hip	37	38	40	40

* In this year, pattern envelopes often said "all our patterns are cut accurately for size and conform to the measurements recommended by the Bureau of Standards of the U.S. Department of Commerce."

**The year new sizing was adopted by American pattern companies to better reflect moderate-priced ready-to-wear and mail-order catalog sizing.

1940s 1954 1969 1968 1964 1930s 1970

Ralph Lauren
$425

Evan Picone
$186

Valerie Stevens
(department store)
$160

K-Mart
$39

Current Size Chart Used by American Pattern Companies for Misses' size range.

Size	4	6	8	10	12	14	16	18	20	22	24	26
Bust	29½	30½	31½	32½	34	36	38	40	42	44	46	48
Waist	22	23	24	25	26½	28	30	32	34	37	39	41.5
Hip	31½	32½	33½	34½	36	38	40	42	44	46	48	50

Other Pattern Company Improvements Between 1967 and 1972

In the 1970s, pattern companies agreed to some minor changes in shape:

◆ The bustline was lowered 5/8". This worked well for the mature figure, but also for softer bra styles—or no-bra youth.

◆ The back waist was lengthened 5/8" to accommodate the more rounded back that had become more characteristic.

◆ 1" was added to the waist measurement. We gave up the girdle!

Pattern Measurements Versus Ready-to-Wear

Today, the bust measurement that the Wolf Form Co. uses for most size 10 dress forms varies from 33" to 38". A pattern company size 10 is 32½." Pattern company measurements have remained the same since 1972 to avoid confusing customers who can't try on the design before buying it. Ease, however, changes with fashion.

ASTM and Sizing Studies

There is currently concern among ready-to-wear manufacturers, especially those doing mail-order, about the great variation in fit. ASTM (American Society for Testing and Materials) has a sizing committee of retailers, mail-order companies and ready-to-wear manufacturers.

ASTM was organized in 1898. It is a nonprofit association dedicated to creating voluntary product performance standards to assist American manufacturers. Anyone having an interest may join and may propose a standard or a change. There are 134 standard-writing committees that publish standards for paints, plastics, metals, textiles and more.

Marta and Pati joined the committee in 1995 as the only pattern industry representatives in some time. Their purpose was to learn how standards are developed and to be a voice in case new standards applied to patterns. How confusing it would be for sewers if all of a sudden body measurements were to change in patterns! Changes in ready-mades are fine because we can try on before we buy, but we can't try on patterns before we buy. The new sizing in the '60s was bad enough. We'd prefer not to go through that again.

The last study of body measurements of the U.S. adult female population was conducted in 1940. At that time, the study included only 1 percent of those 55 and older. Since many baby boomers turned 50 in 1996, a large percentage of women will fall into that category in the next 20 years. In the early '90s, the ASTM sizing committee, with the help of the United States Extension Service, conducted the first ever study of women over 50, led by Dr. Ellen Goldsberry of the University of Arizona. Over 6,000 women 55 and older were measured. The information gained will help manufacturers targeting this age group provide a better fit. We were pleased that the results of the study confirmed what we've learned from our fitting experience. See page 44, "Is Age a Size?"

It would be wonderful to do a study of women between 25 and 55 to see how people are shaped in America today. However, it would have to be privately funded and, may never happen.

Even with a new set of measurements, manufacturers would only be able to address the "averages" of the combined measurements from any study; they could not address each individual. Many do, however, target a certain shape. Pendleton just gave its dress form a slightly more forward shoulder and a little thicker waist to better target its customer. Sewing to fit is still the ideal way to achieve PERFECT FIT.

Mail-Order Ready-to-Wear

Today, mail-order is growing dramatically in the United States. Sears was the first, dating back to the mid-1800's, but has now dropped its mail-order catalog. Many other companies have entered into mail-order, including department stores.

We talked to Nicola Tamburino, Vice President of Tailoring Services at one very famous department store, Neiman Marcus. When customers don't have enough sizing information to order clothing accurately, mail-order businesses experience immeasurable losses from returns and associated mailing costs. Tamburino recommends additional labeling by ready-to-wear manufacturers. He feels we should not take away the creativity of manufacturers by dictating to them the measurements they should use for each size, but does suggest that labels should include the body dimensions for which the garment was constructed. Some mail-order companies do provide measurement charts.

We found the Nordstrom mail-order catalog interesting in that body measurements were given based on the department from which you ordered. For example, measurements for a size 10 were:

	Point of View	Town Square	Individualist and Studio 121
Bust	37	37	38½
Waist	28	28	29½
Hip	39	38	41

Where Did European Sizing Come From?

In Europe the circumference measurements are taken in centimeters. Originally, **"size"** was half the total circumference measurement in centimeters. If this were true, a size 14 (European 40) should measure 80cm in the bust, but today 80cm is a size 8. It looks as though the same thing happened in Europe as in America...vanity sizing! See page 27 for Burda's European size charts.

Shapes Change

The history of fashion is truly interesting. The bustline has been covered as well as exposed throughout history.

Skirt length has been everywhere from thigh-high to the floor. Even silhouette or shape has changed, often with the help of undergarments. Below are dress forms from three eras:

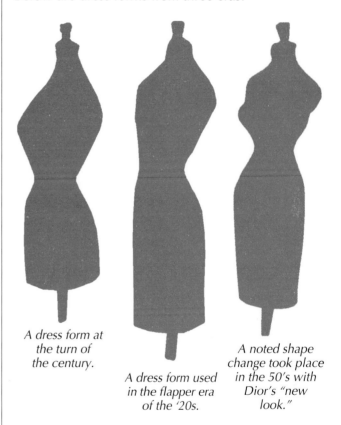

A dress form at the turn of the century.

A dress form used in the flapper era of the '20s.

A noted shape change took place in the 50's with Dior's "new look."

HISTORY NOTE: Patterns used as a guide for tailors appeared in the 16th century. The birth of the American pattern industry occurred in 1854 when Madame Demorest established her design company. In 1864, Ebenezer Butterick, a tailor, began marketing patterns in graded sizes. In 1872, James McCall became his chief competitor. A New York society magazine, Vogue, introduced patterns in 1899. Simplicity joined the ranks in 1927 by providing "three-in-one" patterns, appealing during the Depression. Simplicity also produced the F.W. Woolworth line of DuBarry patterns. Until 1921, when McCall's introduced the first printed pattern, there were no seamlines or construction symbols on pattern tissues.

Source: "Dreams on Paper: Home Sewing in America" was an exhibit at FIT (Fashion Institute of Technology) held during early 1997 in New York City.

Our Changing Shape

Imagine if you had lived through the centuries and had to fit some of the clothes sewn (by hand) during those times. In which era would you have most enjoyed fitting the styles of the day to your body? On this page you see clothing worn primarily by the wealthy who had dressmakers, dressers, and many servants to take care of them and their clothing. In fact, peasants could not have labored in these cumbersome styles.

1848-1870

Consulate First Empire
1800

Louis Philipe
1830-1848

Louis XVI Marie Antoinette
1780

Louis XIV Second Period
1666

crinoline with steel hoops

back-laced corset

corset

folding metal panniers

muslin bandeau

false lingerie undersleeve

back- and front-laced corset

Note how the underwear shaped the body to fit the styles of the day. Most of the time the foundation was designed to enhance the small waist and full bust of the female body. Only a couple of times were we allowed to breath freely. Then, in the 20th century, clothing became less voluminous, less fitted, and easier to move in. In the '70s, bras were burned and girdles tossed. How much will fashion repeat itself in the future? Well, the "body-shaper" and the Wonder Bra are our current version of foundations in this historical cycle.

1880-1890

1910-1920

1920-1930

1930-1942

Dior
1947

Dior
1954

*braided
wire
bustle*

*scalloped
and
flounced
petticoat*

*satin corset
worn over a
chemise*

*combination
brassiere
girdle and
drawers*

*seamless
elastic
foundation
garment*

*gartered
brassiere*

crinoline

CHAPTER 3

Fit Facts

There are a lot of fit myths out there. We cringe when we hear such adamant statements as "X pattern company fits better than all the others." The only way that could be true is if all bodies were identical. Marta and Pati have taught hands-on fit for over 25 years and have used patterns from all companies successfully.

Pati has also had the unique opportunity of working behind the scenes with pattern companies since 1975. That was the year Vogue/Butterick licensed her and Susan Pletsch as the first sewing experts to design fashion patterns. They started by creating new Vogue dress-fit and pant-fit patterns using their "outlet" concept. In 1980 McCall's allowed the pair to suggest fit tips and write entire guidesheets, including both sewing and fit information. Later Pati was allowed to add markings to the tissue that simplified fitting. See the new McCall's "Fit For Real People" patterns.

With their over 25 years of working closely with the industry, Marta and Pati can share these fit facts:

◆ Pattern companies design from a sloper or "staple," a tagboard master pattern WITHOUT seam allowances. They match standard body measurements, plus **minimum ease** of approximately 2½" in the bust, 1" in the waist, and 2" in the hip.

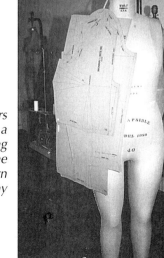

slopers hanging from a corresponding dressform at The McCall Pattern Company

◆ Because you can't try on a pattern to check fit before you buy it, pattern companies have standardized their sizing. The bust, waist, and hip measurements are the same for McCall's, Butterick, Vogue, and Simplicity patterns. Changes in body measurements are made only when these companies agree. See page 15 in Chapter 2, "A History of Sizing."

◆ All patterns, European and American, are more similar than different. Marta sewed the basic bodices shown in the photos on the opposite page. We tried them on the same model the same day. Even though European body measurements are slightly different, see how similarly they fit! See page 249 for actual tissue comparison.

The model's high right shoulder creates the same wrinkles above the bustline in all six bodices. Forget any minor differences in fit. They are SO minor, they are not worth mentioning.

◆ Once you have altered a basic pattern, you have a "body map" to altering the **most fitted** design you could ever sew! See Chapter 9, "Make a Body Map."

◆ The need for alterations depends on the pattern design. **Fitted patterns require more alterations than fuller designs.**

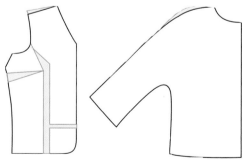

A fitted style may need full bust and square shoulder alterations.

An oversized style on the same person may only need the square shoulder alteration.

◆ Some alterations are necessary in nearly all designs. Round and sway back and forward shoulders are examples.

Living Proof that Pattern Brands Fit the Same

These bodices were sewn in the same fabric using the same size basic bodice patterns from six pattern companies. Their fit is more SIMILAR than DIFFERENT. We photographed them all on Catherine the same day, and the wrinkle pointing to her high right shoulder shows up in all the photos.

Vogue

Butterick

McCalls

Simplicity

Style

Burda

◆ **Pattern companies allow minimum ease for comfort and movement in garments sewn from woven fabrics, but there are no standards for design ease.** Even descriptions such as "loose fitting" give a **range** of ease. **Fashion is an art, not a science. It continually changes, so pattern design ease does too.**

Minimum Ease	Design Ease
Bust: 2	Up to the
Waist: 1"	designer
Hip: 1½"	

◆ Length of patterns is based on a height of 5'5"-5'6." However, don't assume you are short-waisted if you are 5'2"; all of your "shortness" may be in your legs. See Chapter 6, "Special Sizes."

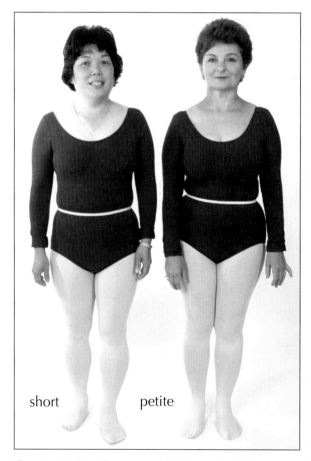

short   petite

Short vs Petite: *Sharon and Kathy are both about 5 feet tall. Sharon, on the left, is long in the body and short in the legs. She wears a Misses' size without shortening the waist length. Kathy is a "true petite." She is proportionately shorter throughout her body, both above and below the bust and waist as well as in her legs. She will need to shorten the waist length in a Misses' pattern.*

◆ **Pattern grading is based on an hourglass shape, regardless of size.** It is possible for any size to have an hourglass figure. After doing body graphs (Chapter 8, "Analyze Your Body") on dozens of people, we have found that most women are a variation of the hourglass. They may be slightly thicker in the middle or fuller in the hips, so they are not a "perfect" hourglass.

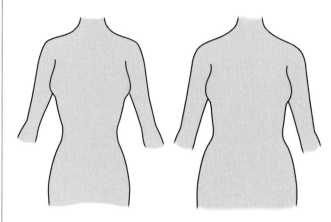

◆ **Pattern companies test patterns on a 5'5"-5'6," size 10 fit model** who must be exactly a size 10 according to the measurement chart.

◆ **The fit model must be youthful.** A mature figure may have a 34½" hip measurement, but more of it will be in the front and less in the back than on a 20-year-old.

Youthful Body   Mature Body

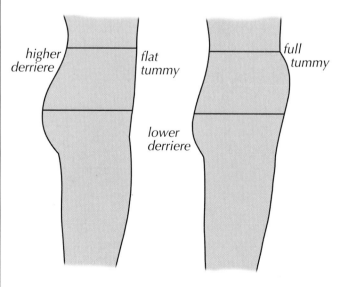

higher derriere   flat tummy   full tummy   lower derriere

The measurements are the same in the waist and the hip for both figures.

◆ **The more seams you have, the easier it is to alter.** This is especially true in fitted garments. You can adjust a seam exactly WHERE the adjustment is needed. For example:

Places to Adjust:

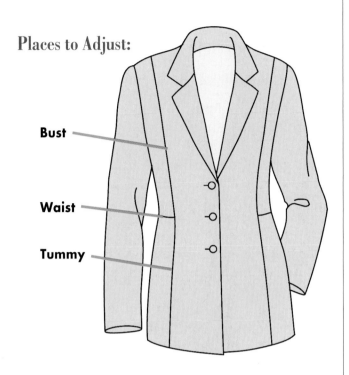

Bust

Waist

Tummy

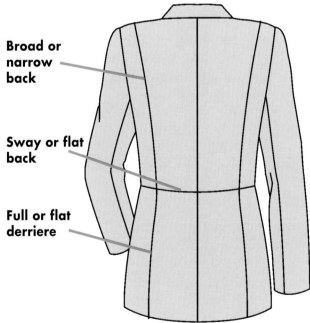

Broad or narrow back

Sway or flat back

Full or flat derriere

◆ **Patterns sold by small (8-10), medium (12-14) and large (16-18) are cut for the larger of the two sizes.** Keep this in mind when you are making your size decision.

◆ **Patterns are designed for a B-cup bra size.** If the fuller-busted figure shown below used her bust measurement to buy her size, she'd buy an 18. It would be huge in the shoulders and neckline. When she uses her high bust measurement (page 24), she determines that she is actually a size 10. After making a full bust adjustment to the size 10 pattern, the jacket fits perfectly.

size 18 jacket

size 10 jacket altered for full bust

Don't Let Ready-To-Wear Be Your Size Guide

◆ Ready-to-wear does not have to follow size standards. Why? Simply because you can TRY ON BEFORE YOU BUY! In fact, ready-to-wear manufacturers can call a garment any size they want. Read about how ready-mades differ from patterns, beginning on page 14.

◆ **Pattern companies still use the same sizing measurements today that were last revised in 1972.** Thank goodness! That way we always know which size to buy and which alterations to make. We simply tissue-fit to see if we like the "fashion ease" that has been added to a pattern. It's EASY! We thank the pattern companies for adhering to standards. See page 15.

Why can't ready-to-wear be like patterns and stay put? Some mail-order houses would like to see body measurements on the hang tags instead of, or along with, the meaningless size number. When sewing, you can go by body measurements and IGNORE SIZE once you've purchased your pattern!

CHAPTER 4
Buy the Right Size

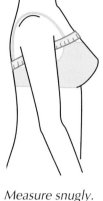

Fitting is easier if you start with the right size pattern, yet many people buy the wrong size. Patterns are made for the average B-cup bra size. If you are a DD and buy according to your bust measurement, your pattern will be too large in the neck and shoulder area. See the illustration on page 23.

We take only the absolutely NECESSARY measurements. For example, we don't measure back length because it generally tells us little. It may tell you that you are a Petite or Half-size, but you are better off learning how to alter a Misses' size pattern and having thousands of designs from which to choose. You don't have to settle for the more limited selection in special sizes.

The rest of this chapter will tell you how to arrive at your correct size(s). See page 27 for size chart comparisons so you can fill in this size chart.

My Sizes:

Top Size: _____

Bust Cup Size: _____

Bottom Size:

    Fitted Skirt: _____

    Full Skirt: _____

    Pant: _____

Rules for Measuring

◆ Measure over the underwear you plan to wear with your garment. The bra style you wear is important because your bust fullness and position can change with different bras.

◆ Measure, making sure your fingers are not under the tape. This is a snug, SKIN measurement.

NOTE: You may want to measure with and without panty hose to see if your measurements change.

Dresses and Tops

Measure the Bust

In the early 1970s, instead of measuring the bust to determine size, we started taking TWO measurements, the high bust and the full bust. If the full bust was 2" larger than the high bust, we used the high bust measurement as if it was the full bust measurement. But in our classes we were only using the high bust, because it worked! When we first wrote this book, we recommended taking both measurements, but now, seven years later, we are taking a bold step and suggesting you need to take only the high bust measurement to determine your size and get the proper fit in the neck and shoulder area. Yes, you will need to alter for a full bust, fuller hips, and possibly a broad back, but the pattern tissue and tissue-fitting will help you see which adjustments you need to make.

We've found historic precedence for our approach. In an 1873 publication for James McCall's Bazaar Glove-Fitting Patterns, the following instructions were given for measuring Ladies' patterns:

"Ladies' patterns...should be selected according to the bust measure. Pass a tape-measure around the bust just under the arms. Draw it one inch tighter than the dress is to fit. The number of inches then ascertained is the size of the bust."

Measure snugly. Place the tape above the bust in front and under the shoulder blades in back, where your bra normally sits.

If you are between sizes, go to the smaller size, because patterns have enough ease to cover you up to the next size.

Where did the term "bust" originate? The word was applied to head, shoulder, and chest sculptures in 1691. Perhaps James McCall was measuring the bottom edge of a sculpture bust, though eventually the word came to mean bosom.

To see if the size you have chosen is correct, try on the tissue of a basic bodice from a fit pattern in that size. If it fits perfectly across the upper chest, you probably have selected the right size. See page 77. If the pattern is too tight in the bustline, you are either full-busted or have a broad back or both.

Check the Back First!

If the center back on the tissue doesn't come to your center back, you have a broad back. Make that adjustment first. See page 118 for broad back adjustments.

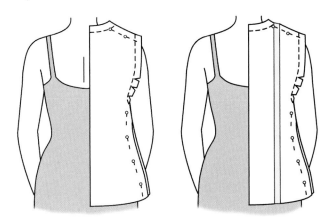

If the front tissue still doesn't come to your center front, you'll need to make a full bust adjustment. Measure the distance from pattern center front to yours so you will know how much to alter.

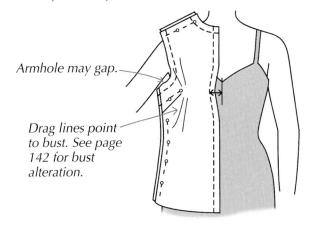

Armhole may gap.

Drag lines point to bust. See page 142 for bust alteration.

NEVER BUY A DRESS PATTERN BY YOUR HIP SIZE. If your hip measurement doesn't match the hip measurement for the size you have chosen by your bust or high bust measurement, you may need to take in or let out the side seams in the waist and hip areas.

See page 75 for how to tissue-fit a basic pattern.

Skirts

Measure waist and hip at the fullest part.

The fullest part of your hips may be above the crotch, about 7"-9" from your waist.

Or, it may be only about 3" from your waist.

Or, it may be below the crotch in the thigh area.

Measure snugly. If you are between sizes, go to the smaller size.

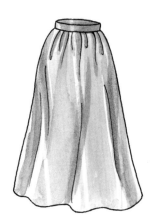

If your waist is small compared to your hips, buy straight skirts by your hip measurement and full skirts by your waist measurement. Full skirts will have enough width to cover your hips.

If your waist is similar in size to your hips, buy both straight and full skirts by your hip measurement. It's easy to alter the waist to fit (page 177). If you bought to fit your waist size, your skirt would be far too large in the hips.

If a fitted skirt is too small or large in the waist **or** high hip (tummy), adjust darts or side seams at the waist, *not* at the center front or the center back.

Waist Too Small:
Widen side seams or narrow or eliminate darts.

Waist Too Large:
Deepen side seams and/or darts.

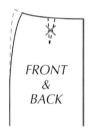 

FRONT & BACK   *FRONT & BACK*

NOTE: In our pant-fitting book we suggest that you buy pant patterns by the measurement at the fullest part of your hip **above the crotch**. You can then let inseams *and* side seams out below the crotch for full thighs.

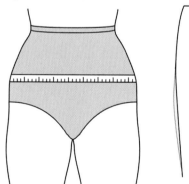 

But I'm Between Sizes

If you are between sizes, select the smaller size unless the garment is VERY fitted. Pattern companies generally add enough ease to cover you until you get to the next size. If in doubt, check the finished garment measurements, if they are printed on the back of the pattern envelope.

But My Top and Bottom are Different Sizes

Welcome to the club! Of the people who sew, 70 percent are one size on the top and another on the bottom. Multi-size patterns help with this. **You also have choices for patterns that include designs for both the top and the bottom:**

◆ Buy to fit your top and alter the bottom.

◆ Buy two patterns if necessary.

◆ Buy separates in the correct sizes for your top and bottom.

FIT Tip McCall's Palmer/Pletsch® patterns include alteration lines on the pattern tissue (pages 28 and 30) and fitting instructions in the guide sheets.

The Art of Compromise

It takes a bit of experimentation to find the easiest size to use. Marta measures size 16 in the full bust, because she has a broad back and has a C-cup bra size. Size 12 patterns with a broad back and C-cup alteration fit perfectly.

Pati is between sizes 12 and 14 on the top, but closer to a 14. In loosely fitting designs, she uses a size 12 pattern and in more fitted styles she prefers a size 14.

Small, Medium & Large Sizes

Patterns sold by small (8-10), medium (12-14) and large (16-18) are cut for the larger of the two sizes. Keep this in mind when you are making your size decision. Always check to see which sizes are actually in each range of small, medium, and large as they may vary from company to company.

American & European Size Charts Comparison

European pattern companies use slightly different body measurements for bust, waist and hip.

American Size (McCalls, Simplicity, Vogue/Butterick)

American pattern companies increase the bust measurement: 1″ in small sizes up to size 10; 1½″ between sizes 10 and 12; 2″ between sizes 12 and 14 and all larger sizes.

		6	8	10	12	14	16	18	20	22	24	26w	28w	30w	32w	34w
Bust	in.	30½	31½	32½	34	36	38	40	42	44	46	48	50	52	54	56
	cm	78	80	83	87	92	97	102	107	112	117	122	127	132	137	142
Waist	in.	23	24	25	26½	28	30	32	34	37	39	41½	44	46½	49	51½
	cm	58	61	64	67	71	76	81	87	94	99	105	112	118	124	130
Hip	in.	32½	33½	34½	36	38	40	42	44	46	48	50	52	54	56	58
	cm	83	85	88	92	97	102	107	112	117	122	127	132	137	142	147

European Size (Burda)

Burda increases the bust measurement by an even 4cm per size up to size 46. Sizes 46 to 60 increase by 6cm per size.

		32	34	36	38	40	42	44	46	48	50	52	54	56	58	60
Bust	in.	30	31½	33	34¾	36¼	37¾	39½	41	43½	45¾	48	50½	52¾	55¼	57½
	cm	76	80	84	88	92	96	100	104	110	116	122	128	134	140	146
Waist	in.	23	24½	26	27¾	29¼	30¾	32½	34	36¼	38¾	41	43½	45¾	48	50½
	cm	58	62	66	70	74	78	82	86	92	98	104	110	116	122	128
Hip	in.	32½	34¾	35½	37	38¾	40¼	41¾	43½	45¾	48	50½	52½	55¼	57½	60
	cm	82	86	90	94	98	102	106	110	116	122	128	134	140	146	152

NOTE: The numbers above are directly from the catalog charts. There can never be an exact comparison of centimeters and inches due to "rounding off." Also, Burda rounds to the nearest 1/4″ and Neue Mode to the nearest 1/8.″ The charts of Burda and Neue Mode differ, but very slightly. Their bust and waist measurements are the same in all sizes, but vary in the hip area.

All pattern company measurements are **similar** enough that once you find a figure difference in one, you will make that adjustment in all. If a Burda hip in one size is 1/2″ smaller, you'd just let out the hip 1/8″ at the side seams to make it equal to its American counterpart.

Burda differs from American companies as follows:

Bust:
Size 6 is ½″ smaller.
Size 8 is the same.
Sizes 10-14 are ¼″-¾″ larger.
Sizes 16-24 are ¼″-1″ smaller.
Size 26w is the same.
Sizes 28w-34w are ½″-1½″ larger.

Waist:
Size 6 is the same.
Sizes 8-18 are ½″-1¼″ larger.
Size 20 is the same.
Size 22-24 are ¼″-1″ smaller.
Sizes 26w-34w are ½″-1″ smaller.

Hip:
Size 6 is the same.
Sizes 8-16 are ¼″-1¼″ larger.
Sizes 18-22 are ¼″-½″ smaller.
Size 24 is the same.
Sizes 26w-34w are ½″-2″ larger.

Why are we making such a big deal about **differences?** Let's start talking **similarities** and **make fitting easier** for the sewer.

CHAPTER 5

But the Pattern Doesn't Come in My Size!

People who are tall or petite, large or small always ask, "Why do the pattern companies ignore us?" Basically, it's a matter of economics. The Misses' size range of 10-16 comprises most of the pattern sales.

Since it costs the major pattern companies $40,000 to create one design, they have to sell to the masses to warrant the cost of producing each of their patterns.

Pattern companies have tried to meet the needs of everyone by doing the following:

◆ Expanding the Misses' size range to 26.

◆ Making patterns multi-sized.

◆ Adding built-in fit adjustments to the tissue such as "petitable" shortening lines.

◆ All pattern companies include fit help in their basic fit patterns. McCall's Palmer/Pletsch patterns include fit tips, tuck lines and cut lines on most patterns for the following figure variations:

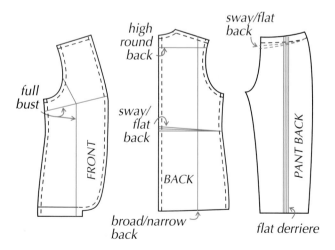

Reality Check

Let's LEARN TO TAKE CARE OF OURSELVES!
Pattern companies can give us the luxury of zillions of styles to sew. We can learn to use a size that is "close" to our size and easily make it fit! This is a very realistic approach and sewing will be a whole lot more fun! That is the goal of this book!

Grading a Pattern to Fit You

Pattern grading is tedious and complicated. In fact, **as the size gets larger, the amount of grade varies**. For example, the neck width doesn't increase as much as the hip width.

To give you a general idea of how patterns are graded, the following adjustments are made to increase a pattern by one size:

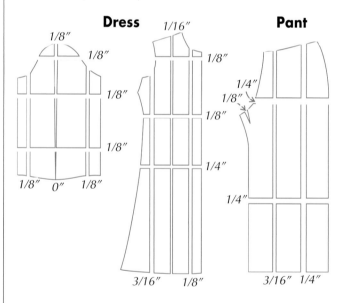

FIT Tip We have heard conflicting opinions about computer grading. Some say hand grading is better. However, pattern companies and ready-to-wear manufacturers who use computer grading said that computer grading is more consistently accurate and methods are continually improving. They also admit that when a design is complex, they may step in and do some hand grading in some sizes.

All Patterns Are "Petitable," "Tallable," and Can be Made Wider or Narrower!

When a pattern doesn't come in your size, be adventurous, but use the practical approach. To make the pattern your size and proportions, tuck or spread the tissue where you need it, which may be in the places shown below. Then try on the tissue to see if you have done it enough and in the right places:

If a pattern is too large, tuck as shown:

If a pattern is too small, cut and spread as shown:

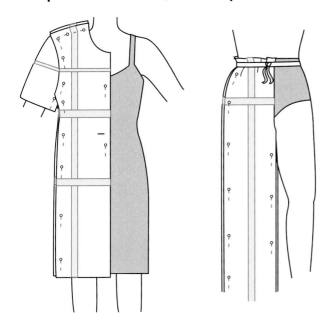

Be sure to tuck or spread the front and back pattern pieces the same amount so they will match when sewn together. In a dress, if you lengthen or shorten the upper chest area, adjust the sleeve cap the same amount. This is not grading-by-the-book, but works quite well in altering patterns.

For more on pant fitting, refer to our book *Pants for Real People*. See page 254.

Multi-size Patterns

Pattern companies are changing to primarily multi-size patterns. They waste less paper and give consumers more size choices. At first, they were confusing, but most pattern companies were responsive to consumer suggestions, and as people got used to them, there was less confusion.

We like multi-size patterns when only three or four sizes are included and when the size range overlaps. For example, sizes 8, 10, and 12 are in one package and sizes 10, 12, and 14 are in another. This way, if you are a 10 top and a 14 bottom, you can get that combination. If the size ranges didn't overlap and were 8, 10, 12 and 14, 16, 18, you would have to buy two patterns.

Connecting Lines
We like multi-size with connecting lines so you can cut-to-fit.

Overlaid
When patterns are simply overlaid, you don't have that advantage.

connecting lines   *overlaid*

Working with Multi-sized Patterns

Since most patterns are multi-sized today we find our students make mistakes in getting the pattern ready for fitting. Therefore, we have them prepare their multi-sized patterns for fitting using the following steps. Follow along and you will have better results.

STEP 1: Press the tissue with a dry iron set at the wool setting.

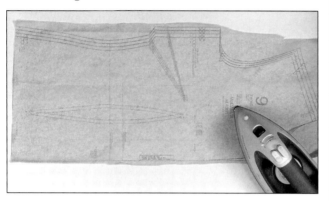

STEP 2: Mark the cutting lines for your size. If you are one size on the top and another on the bottom, gradually move from one size to another.

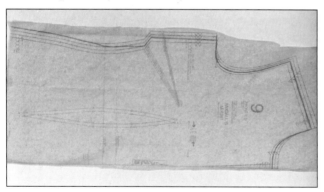

STEP 3:
Trim the tissue along your cutting lines. Then mark your stitching lines. Use a ruler or if your tape measure is 5/8" (1.5cm) wide, it becomes a handy seam width tool.

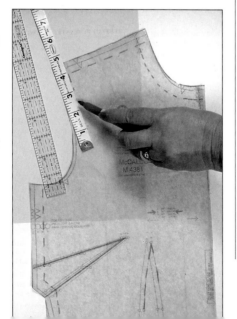

STEP 4: For fitted styles, tape the tissue's neckline and armhole just inside the stitching lines to prevent it from tearing when you are trying it on. Use ½" Scotch Magic Transparent Tape, the one in the green box. (It is sometimes easier to find ¾" tape, but ½" makes your pattern less stiff, so try to find it!) The tape won't melt if you press the tissue later, but for safety, press from the wrong side and NOT on top of the tape.

TIP: Get in the habit of taping all patterns from the right side and pressing from the wrong side. Be sure to use short lengths of tape around the corners, lapping ends about ½" as you go. (See pages 107-112 for more tips on preparing patterns.)

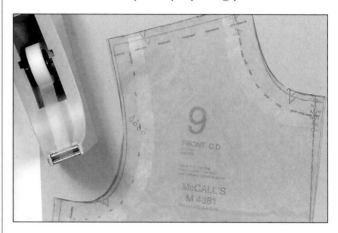

STEP 5: Clip all curved areas in the seam allowance to the seam line, but not through the tape. This allows for more accuracy when you try on the tissue. Then, gently tug on the tissue to make sure you have taped well. If it tears, add more tape. Remember, it is tissue. It can tear! But YOU have the tape!!! Get empowered!

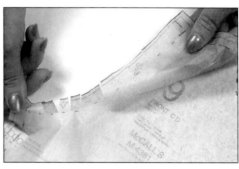

Now you are ready to try on the tissue and alter it. You can always add Perfect Pattern Paper tissue to the edges if you need more width in the hips or anywhere else. It is the same weight as the tissue, so it won't overpower your pattern. (See page 108.)

CHAPTER 6

Special Sizes

| Girls' | Young Jr./ Teen | Junior Petite | Junior | Miss Petite | Misses' | Half-size/ Women's Petite | Women's |

During this past century, the pattern companies have tried very hard to make patterns that fit you. They have developed many categories over the years, including some no longer available such as Young Junior, Junior Petite, Junior, Subteen, Teen, and Junior Miss. Today, even the Miss Petite and Half-size shown above are mentioned on some size charts but are rarely produced.

Why are several of these categories non-existent today? **SALES!** The only category with high sales is Misses'. With pattern companies facing financial challenges, they can't afford to create slow-selling, fringe-size patterns.

If you are a "special" size, how do you make the design you want to sew fit you? Some 12-year-olds are fully developed in the bust and others develop in their later teens. Don't worry! We will show you how even 12-year-olds can choose from the Girls' OR the Misses' size range and make a pattern fit.

See the tissue fitting and alteration chapters throughout this book for how to tissue-fit, with examples of REAL PEOPLE in each size category.

What Is a Miss Petite?

According to pattern company size charts, the Miss Petite figure is approximately 5'2", average in bust position, short-waisted and slightly larger in the waist than Misses'.

We like the term Petite. It has to do with height, so technically you can be a size 18 or 20 and be "petite."

Let's compare a size 14 Misses' to a 14 Miss Petite:

	14 Misses'	**14 Miss Petite**
Bust	36"	36"
Waist	28"	28"
Hip	38"	38"
Back Waist Length	16½"	15½"

Note that the differences are minor! However, what doesn't show in the chart is that true Petites are shorter proportionally in every part of their body than an average-height person.

This is where you would shorten a pattern if you were a true petite:

In fitting thousands of people, we have found that the majority of short people are NOT petite. They are short in the legs only. Some are even LONGER in the torso than a tall person (see page 22, "Fit Facts").

You can make ANY Misses' a Miss Petite by tissue-fitting. Try on the pattern and tuck where necessary. You can tuck above and below the waist and in the upper chest area with a matching tuck in the sleeve cap.

Armhole too deep: ### Tuck as shown:

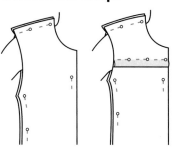

Tuck sleeve cap same amount.

Pant too long in crotch & length: ### Tuck as shown:

Skirts without details:

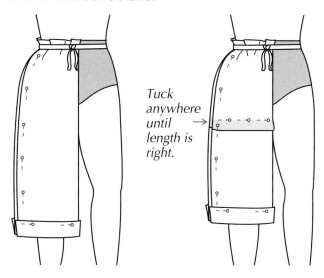

Tuck anywhere until length is right.

Skirts with details:

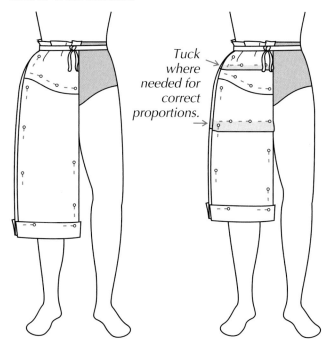

Tuck where needed for correct proportions.

What Is a Half-size?

If a Half-size meant we could be half the width we currently are, we'd want to be one! Honestly, we are not sure where the name came from. A lot of people associate Half-size with a short, stout grandmother.

A Half-size figure is approximately 5' 2", has a low, fuller (C-cup) bust, shorter waist, longer crotch, and thicker middle than a Misses' size.

Half-size was once very common in ready-to-wear and is now called a

Women's Petite. It has come and gone over the years. If it is unavailable as a pattern size, see below for how to alter a Misses pattern.

The size range for Half-sizes is 10½ to 24½. Here is a measurement comparison between a size 14 Misses' and 14½ Half-size or Women's Petite:

	Misses' 14	Half-size 14½
Bust	36″	37″
Waist	28″	31″
Hip	38″	39″
Back Waist Length	16½″	15½″

How Would You Turn a Misses' Size Into a Half-size or Women's Petite?

Top

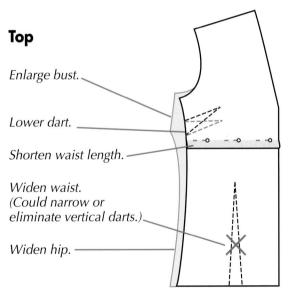

Enlarge bust.

Lower dart.

Shorten waist length.

Widen waist. (Could narrow or eliminate vertical darts.)

Widen hip.

Pant

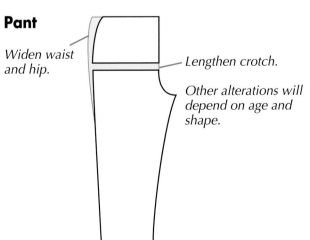

Widen waist and hip.

Lengthen crotch.

Other alterations will depend on age and shape.

What Is a Women's Size?

This person is an average height of 5'6″, has an average bust position and average waist length, and is more rounded in the back and thicker in the middle than a Misses'. She has a proportionally larger, more mature figure than the Misses' figure.

Here is a comparison of the only two sizes that overlap on the pattern-company charts:

	Misses' 20	Women's 38 (20W)
Bust	42″	42″
Waist	34″	35″
Hip	44″	44″
Back Waist Length	17¼″	17¼″

To Make a Misses' Size Into a Women's:

Widen the waist and/or eliminate the dart.

FIT Tip

In ready-to-wear, Women's sizes were labeled 48, 50, 52, etc. The trend now is to use 14W, 16W, 18W, 20W, etc. Also, 1X, 2X and 3X are like small, medium and large with 1X being 16/18W, 2X being 20/22W and 3X being 24/26W. The "W" sizes are roomier in the bust, waist, and hips than the same sizes in Misses'.

Comparing Girls' to Misses'

Over the years, we've been asked many times how to fit 12- to 14-year-olds. Pattern companies have tried to offer a range of patterns for this age group. They've been called Junior, Young Junior/Teen, etc. Today, pattern companies have given up. Why? At 12 years old, some girls are the height of a woman and well developed. Others are flat-chested at 14. This age range has no shape or height consistencies. Therefore, what height and width measurements are best? How shaped should the patterns be?

We will show you how easy it is to make either a Girls' or Misses' size fit the 12-14 age range.

Let's compare overlapping chest/bust sizes of Girls' and Misses':

Size	Misses' 10	Girls' 14
Bust/Chest	32½"	32"
Waist	25"	26½"
Hip	34½"	34"
Back Waist Length	16"	14¼"
Height	5'5"- 5'6"	5'1"

FIT Tip Remember that in the 1930s, a 32" bust was a size 14 Misses' as well as Girls'. Then Misses' sizes changed, but Girls' stayed the same chest measurement. (See Chapter 2, page 13.)

As you can see, all measurements are very close. Misses' height remains the same in all sizes, where Girls' get taller as the size increases. To alter a Misses' size to fit Girls', you will generally adjust width at the side seams, flatten the bustline unless the girl is developed, and shorten the waist and/or hem length depending on the girl's height.

Laurel
12 Years Old

Laurel, a junior high school honor student, shares her sewing experience.

Laurel's high bust measures 29½" and full bust/chest measures 30". She is closest to a size 12 Girls' or a size 6 Misses'. She could work with either size. She is 5'4" tall. A Girls' size 12 is based on 4'10½" tall. A Misses' size 6 is based on a height of 5'6."

In the following pages we've fit Laurel in many different sizes:

Size 12	Girls'	(Her best Girls' size.)
Size 6	Misses'	(Her best Misses' size.)
Size 8	Misses'	(The smallest sizes available in two of the chosen designs.)
Size 10	Misses'	

Girls' Dress Size 12 For tissue-fitting how-tos see pages 50, 75 and 107.

Before

The waist marking on the tissue is 1″ above her waistline.

After

The bodice was lengthened so the waist is correctly positioned. The sleeve is slipped into place for a quick check and looks fine in width and length.

waist marking

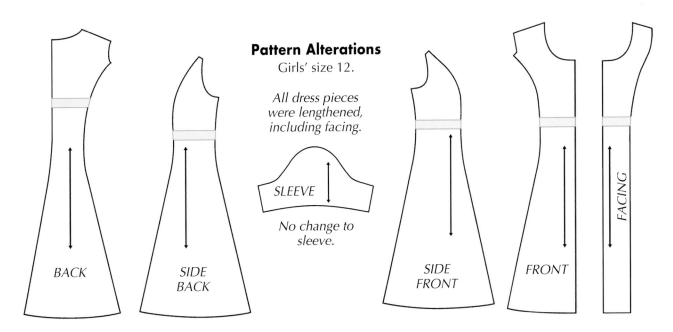

Pattern Alterations

Girls' size 12.

All dress pieces were lengthened, including facing.

SLEEVE

No change to sleeve.

BACK

SIDE BACK

SIDE FRONT

FRONT

FACING

Misses' Dress Size 6

Before

The tissue is loose in the bust/chest area.

After

To remove the bust/chest fullness, the side panel was taken in in the bust curve area and the front piece was shortened (page 154).

Close-up of bust/chest fullness:

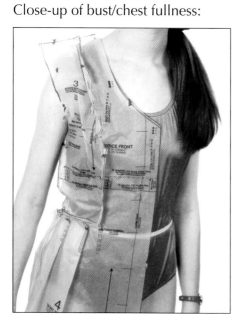

Pattern Alterations

bust curve taken in

SIDE FRONT

FRONT

1/4" tuck

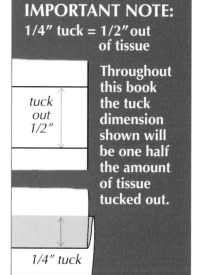

IMPORTANT NOTE:
1/4" tuck = 1/2" out of tissue

tuck out 1/2"

Throughout this book the tuck dimension shown will be one half the amount of tissue tucked out.

1/4" tuck

Misses' Vest Size 8

Often a pattern is not made in a size smaller than a Misses' 8 or 10. Don't worry. You can make it fit!

Before

The waist length is a little long and the vest is too big around.

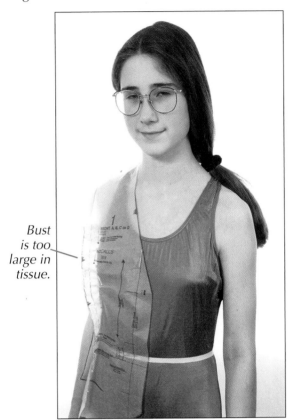

Bust is too large in tissue.

After

We tucked Laurel's pattern vertically where she needed it narrower to make the width fit her. It took two different size tucks in the front and side front to get the bust fullness in the right place. One tuck in the back was enough for perfect back fit. We also shortened the waist length.

Pattern Alterations
Misses' size 8, altered to Junior Petite size 6.

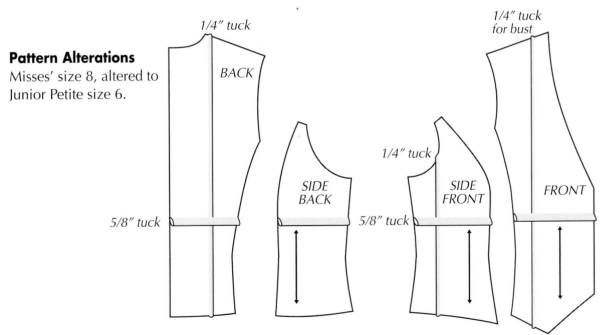

1/4" tuck

BACK

5/8" tuck

SIDE BACK

1/4" tuck

5/8" tuck

SIDE FRONT

1/4" tuck for bust

FRONT

Misses' Dress Size 10

This pattern was not available in a size smaller than a Misses' size 10.

Before

Only the bodice requires adjustment because the skirt is full. The top is too long in the waist and too big around.

After

We made a horizontal tuck to bring the waistline marking up to the bottom of the elastic. It was not necessary to flatten the bust because this dress wasn't very shaped in the bustline.

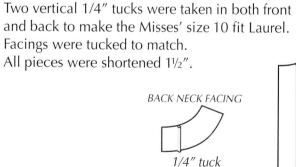

waist marking

Pattern Alterations

Two vertical 1/4" tucks were taken in both front and back to make the Misses' size 10 fit Laurel. Facings were tucked to match.
All pieces were shortened 1½".

After making these tucks it was necessary to add tissue and redraw ("true") the front neckline to smooth out the cutting lines. See page 113. We raised the front neckline at the same time.

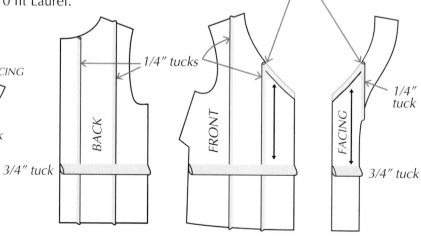

BACK NECK FACING

1/4" tuck

1/4" tucks

3/4" tuck

BACK

FRONT

FACING

1/4" tuck

3/4" tuck

First Fabric Fitting

This is the time to see if the fabric fits differently than the tissue. When you sew a dress, especially one with a full skirt, the mere weight of the fabric can lengthen the dress or make darts too low.

Laurel felt the dress was too low at the underarm to wear sleeveless. Also, she felt the low waist seamline was too low proportionally for her.

Adjustment in Fabric

We pinned the shoulder seam deeper so it would be better as a sleeveless dress. This also brought the low waist seam up to a position she liked better on her figure.

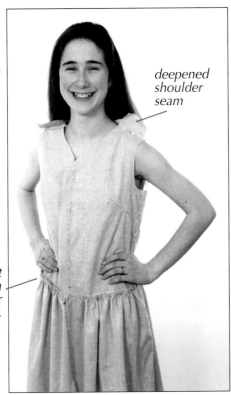

deepened shoulder seam

The waist is now in a better position.

Finished Dress

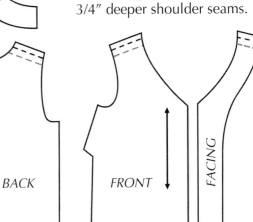

BACK NECK FACING

Pattern Alterations

After fitting in fabric we sewed 3/4″ deeper shoulder seams.

BACK *FRONT* *FACING*

Brittany

13 Years Old

Brittany, an avid swimmer, measures 33″ in the high bust (Misses' size 10) and 35½″ in the full bust (Misses' size 12). Since there is more than 2″ difference between bust and high bust, we will fit her in a Misses' size 10.

The Front Before

The tissue center front doesn't come to Brittany's center front. She is fuller busted than the pattern standard of a B cup.

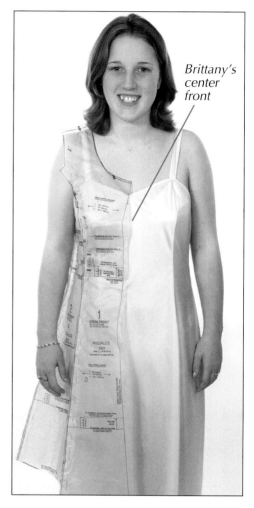

Brittany's center front

The Back Before

The back looks good, but there is a gap in the neck. She has a slightly **rounded back**, not uncommon for a swimmer's figure (see page 122).

Close-up of back neck:

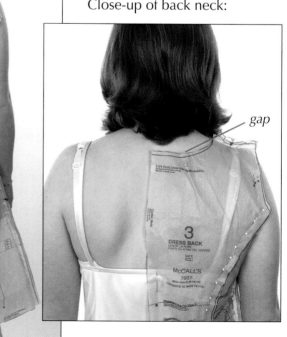

gap

The Front After

We added 3/8″ to the side front at the bust and lengthened the front so the seams would be the same length. (New haircut too!)

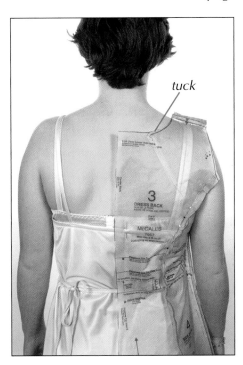

The Back After

To eliminate the gap, we pinned out the fullness with a dart-shaped tuck, tapering to nothing at the seam. The wrinkles at the waist from the tissue being shaped in to the body won't be there in fabric. She also has **forward shoulders** (page 162).

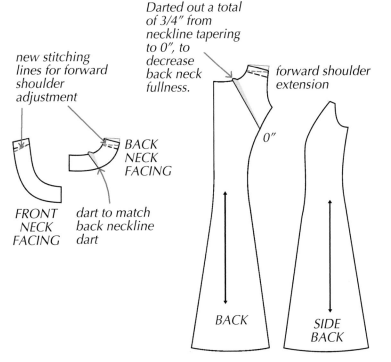

tuck

Pattern Alterations Misses' size 10.

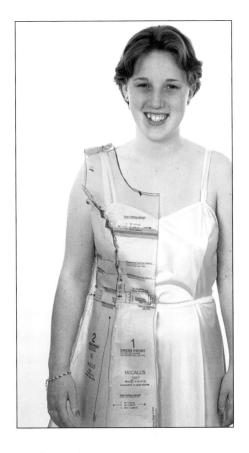

3/8″ added to bust

forward shoulder adjustment

1/4″ added for extra length over bust to match side front.

SIDE FRONT

FRONT

new stitching lines for forward shoulder adjustment

FRONT NECK FACING

dart to match back neckline dart

BACK NECK FACING

Darted out a total of 3/4″ from neckline tapering to 0″, to decrease back neck fullness.

forward shoulder extension

0″

BACK

SIDE BACK

Pin-Fitting the Fabric

We notice Brittany has a **low right shoulder**. Since the left side looks good, we pinned the right shoulder seam deeper. We didn't see this difference in tissue because we only fitted half of her body.

The Front

The Back

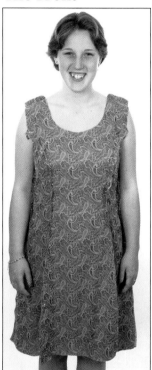
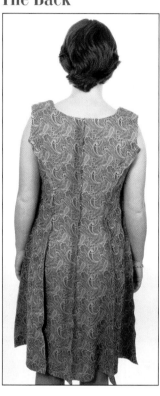

Marta feels Brittany's dress would be more a flattering shape if the princess seams were taken in at the waistline in the front.

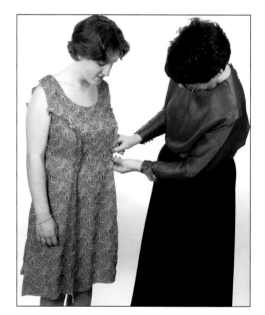

The Sleeve

Now Brittany slips on the sleeve to check the length. We pinned it at the underarm so it would be in the correct position. Then we added a few pins in the cap to hold it up.

Brittany's Finished Dress

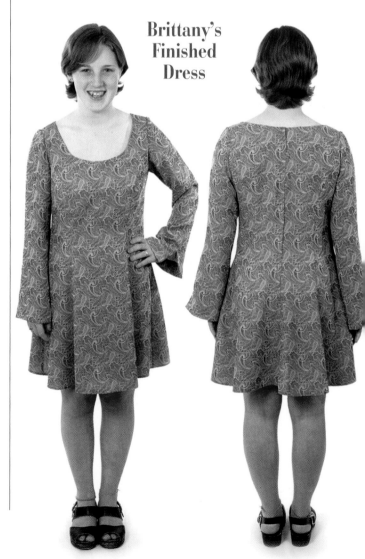

Tissue-Fitting a Skirt Is Easy

The Front Before

Tie elastic around the waist. We slipped the front and back skirt pieces under the elastic so the bottom of the elastic rests on the stitching line, and the center front and back are at her centers. Then we pinned the side seam to fit her shape. The dart on the pattern was too deep and puckered. We made it half the depth.

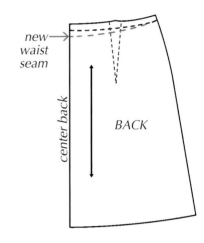

Pattern Alteration

Since fitting adjustments are minimal and can be done in the fabric, it is not necessary to make these changes in the tissue before cutting. The swayback adjustment can be made by simply pulling the waist up on the back.

new waist seam

center back

BACK

dart too deep

bottom of elastic on seamline

center front lines up

The Back Before

The back swings toward the side due to a **swayback**.

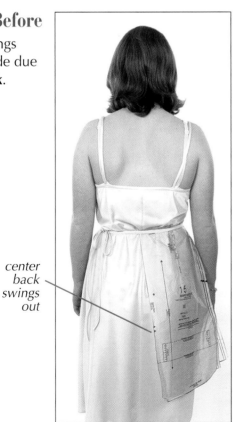

center back swings out

The Back After

We pulled up the skirt at the center back waist until the center back seam was straight.

pulled up center back

side seams pinned to her shape

Is Age a Size?

Our bodies do change with age, but everyone changes differently. That is why it would be difficult to come up with a "mature" size that would fit everyone.

We have fitted over 100,000 people. The changes shown here seem to occur commonly with maturity:

◆ The waist thickens because the pads between the vertebrae flatten. This means we get shorter as well.

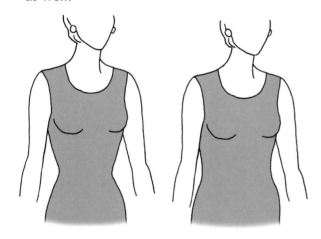

◆ Shoulders move forward from doing close work, causing the upper back to become more rounded.

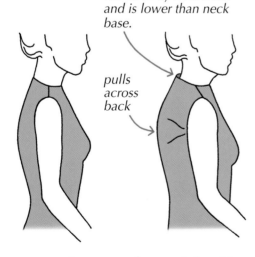

Garment back neck stands away from neck and is lower than neck base.

pulls across back

normal shoulder position   **forward shoulder and slightly rounded back**

◆ Carrying books, babies, groceries, or a golf bag on one side of the body may result in a low shoulder and hip on that side.

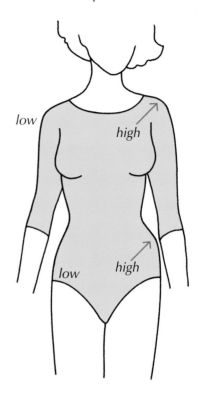

low   *high*

low   *high*

◆ Sometimes the high hip and high shoulder are on opposite sides.

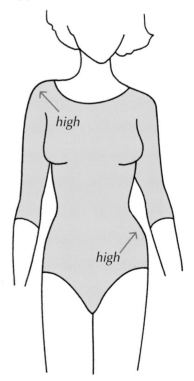

high

high

◆ Basic bone structure and body types are inherited. Often as you mature, you become the shape of your parents. The following are common changes as we age:

- Shoulders move forward.

- Back becomes more rounded.

- The body shortens because the pads between the vertebrae get thinner.

- Bustline drops.

- Bustline often gets fuller.

- Waist thickens. May also rise in front and drop in back.

- Tummy gets fuller.

- Derriere gets flatter as fullness drops.

- Hips often get smaller unless there is major weight gain.

The good news is that if your clothes fit, you will look great!

Palmer/Pletsch patterns for McCall's address these issues with alteration lines printed on the tissue. Some fit help is in every guidesheet. See pages 28-30 for examples of how the pattern tissues are marked.

For more on "Maturity" see page 58.

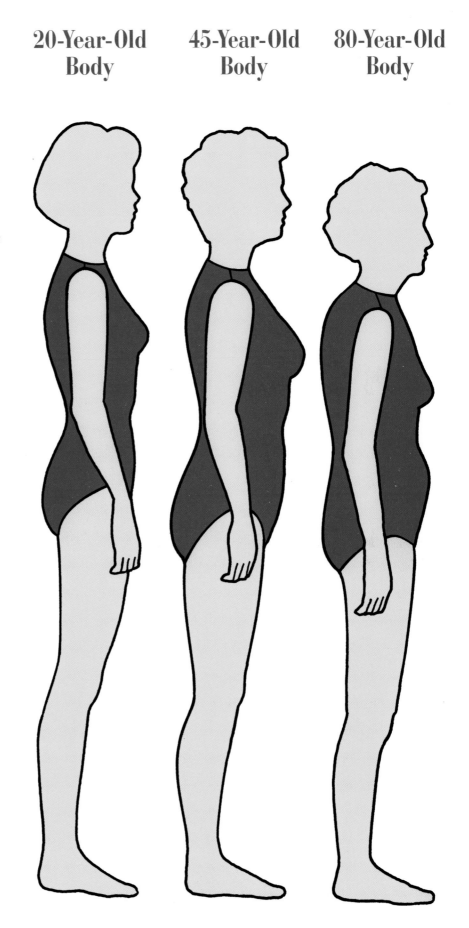

20-Year-Old Body   45-Year-Old Body   80-Year-Old Body

*Fashion comes in
a myriad of styles ranging
from close-fitting
to very loose.*

CHAPTER 7

What About Ease?

What Is Ease?

Ease is the difference between body measurements and garment measurements. Some people like tight clothes and others like loose-fitting clothes. The amount of ease you find comfortable is personal preference. It varies with size, age and lifestyle.

Minimum Ease

This is the amount of fullness pattern companies allow for wearing comfort (or wiggle room) in a fitted garment made from a woven fabric. It is the amount found in the basic fit dress patterns offered by the pattern companies (see page 53). Their **minimum** ease for a fitted garment is as follows:

Bust: 2"-3"   Hip: 1½"-3"
Waist: 1"-1½"   Upper Arm: 1½"

Design Ease

This is the amount of fullness added to a garment in addition to minimum ease to achieve the fashion silhouette intended by the designer.

Body Measurements + Minimum Ease + Design Ease = The Fashion Silhouette

Fabrics Have Ease

More give:	Less give:
loose weaves	tight weaves
knits	wovens and nonwovens
natural fiber fabrics	synthetic fiber fabrics
thin fabrics	heavy fabrics
bias grain	straight grain
	permanent press finishes

During our research for this book, we compared tissue-fit to fabric fit. In nearly every case, the fabric ended up bigger than the tissue. Bias would be an exception. It gets significantly narrower as it hangs.

To see if the weight of a full length dress would affect fit in any way, Pati sewed the same dress in two fabrics—a grey wool jersey (knit) and a red wool crepe (woven).

The wool jersey got thinner in the middle than the tissue.

The wool crepe actually seemed a little bigger than the tissue.

We feel that generally if you fit the tissue snugly for a fitted design, the garment will fit with adequate ease. If in doubt, cut 1" "in-case" side seam allowances "in case" you need more room.

No Ease

Some patterns have little or no ease. It may be due to the style, such as fitted jeans, or because the design requires a stretch fabric. A swimsuit has **minus ease**. If it didn't "stretch to fit," you might lose your suit in the pool!

Fashion Changes Design Ease

Armholes can be large and deep or close and tight. Shoulders can be broad, cut in, squared with shoulder pads, or natural. Pants can be full through the hips or fitted. Darts come and go depending on the latest fashion silhouette.

Design Ease Changes Over the Decades

The following are shown in the same size, but sewn in different years:

Early 1980s

high armholes, thin shoulder pads, minimal design ease

Late 1980s

wider shoulders, thicker shoulder pads, deeper armholes, more ease for a roomier fit

Late 1990s

thinner shoulder pads, more fitted torso and sleeves, higher armholes, but not as high as 1980

Early 1980s

high armholes, less ease

Late 1980s

oversized

Late 1990s

more fitted again

Designer Tip

Since we started writing this book in 1996, designer fashion has become closer to the body, with narrower sleeves and more fitted waists.

Shoulder pads have gotten thinner again and super-short skirts have returned once more.

With the return of closer-fitting clothing has come the return of the foundation—now called the body shaper—and push-up bras such as The Wonder Bra®.

Photos courtesy of The McCall Pattern Company.

The Pinch Test

To find out how much ease you prefer in the hip area of garments, try on various styles of jackets, blouses, straight skirts and pants in your wardrobe and **pinch** them. Pull all the fullness to one side at the fullest part of your hip. If you can take a 1"-deep pinch of fabric, you have a total of 2" ease, since you are pinching double thickness.

The Tape Measure Test

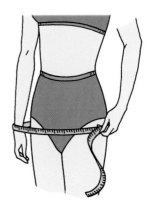

Wrap yourself in a tape measure and then loosen it gradually. You will see that 4" ease is probably less than you thought when you consider the entire body circumference.

The Clothes in Your Closet Test

Get to know yourself. You must have jackets, dresses, blouses, skirts and pants in your wardrobe that are comfortable. If you don't, spend some time in a store's fitting room. Try clothes on. How do they feel? Which fit is most comfortable?

Measure the bust, waist and hip areas of the most comfortable clothes to see how big they are. Next, subtract your body measurements to determine the amount of ease in that garment. Try on ready-made garments as new fashion trends appear to check ease and determine what feels best to you.

That's what we do, and we nearly always end up thanking the store with a purchase! If we buy nothing else, we can always thank them with a panty hose purchase!

Fill out this handy chart.

Item	Garment Bust	– My Bust	= Bust Ease*	Garment Hip	– My Hip	= Hip Ease

If a garment is 48" and your bust is 40", the ease is 8".

Now look for similar-style patterns or alter patterns to give you the amount of ease you like in the bust and hips. You will find finished garment measurements on some pattern envelopes and on most pattern tissue to use as a guide.

The Tissue-Fitting Test

Tissue-fitting prevents sewing disasters! It helps you determine the ease in the design and it also helps you visualize the silhouette on **your** body.

Pin the unaltered pattern to your center front and back—to your underwear, that is! If tissue-fitting a jacket, try it on over a blouse. Insert a shoulder pad if you plan to use one.

Are the proportions good? Is there too much fullness? Not enough?

Check the following:

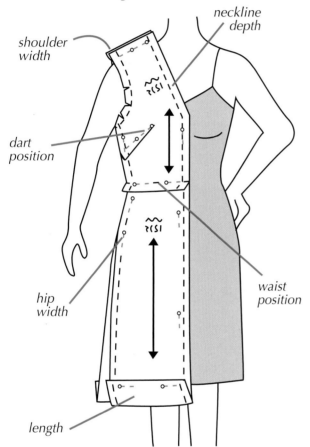

Then pin the sleeve at the underarm and check it:

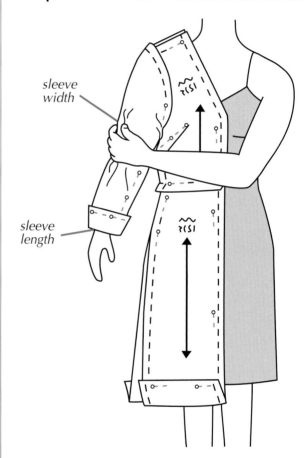

NOTE: Be sure to wear the same undergarments you plan to wear with the finished dress. On a full-busted woman, the bust level can change up to 3" (or more) depending on bra style.

See page 112 for how to prepare the pattern for tissue-fitting.

See Chapter 10, "Tissue-Fit & Fit-As-You-Sew," for how to tissue-fit fashion patterns.

Too Much Ease in a Design? Buy a Smaller Size.

Too much ease can overwhelm small and even large-size people with too much fabric. When the designer intends a fashion to be very full, it is OK for you to buy it a size or two smaller. Let the finished garment measurement chart help you make your decision.

small person in a jacket designed to be oversized   *same person in a smaller size*

The ease in a jacket will be partially taken up by the interfacing, lining, and other clothing you wear under it. Heavier jacket fabrics will use up more ease than lighter ones.

The ease in the bustline of a top or in the hip-line of a full pant may seem like a lot, but in soft fabrics, you won't notice it. If you are short or a very small or large size, it could, however, be overwhelming.

large person in her usual pattern size with all of the ease the designer intended   *large person in a pattern two sizes smaller with less ease than intended*

Bra Cup Size Is Another Factor

If you buy a pattern by high bust measurement because you are larger than a B-cup bra size, you may not have to do a full bust adjustment (page 141).

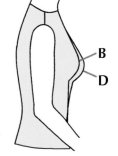

As long as the garment is large enough, you can choose to have less ease than the designer intended, say 6" instead of 10". You may prefer that amount if you don't want to add even more fabric fullness to your already full bustline and there are no unflattering drag lines in the fabric.

The bottom line is that **ease is personal preference**. Get to know what you like best!!

What Is "Normal Ease?"

Pattern companies give you finished garment measurements to help you pick the right size based on the ease you like. However, if you don't know what you like, even after the "tests" we've suggested, then learn what average or "normal" ease is in these basic styles:

	Slim Skirt	Classic Trousers	Full Trousers	Very Full Pant	Fitted Dress	Roomy Blouse	Blazer	Oversized Jacket
Bust:					3-5″	8-12″	8-10″	11-15″
Waist:	1″	1-2″	1-2″	1-2″	2-3″			
Hip:	2-3″	5″	8″	10-15″		4-8″	5-8″	8-15″

How to Use the Pattern for Fit Clues

There is a lot of information on the pattern envelope.

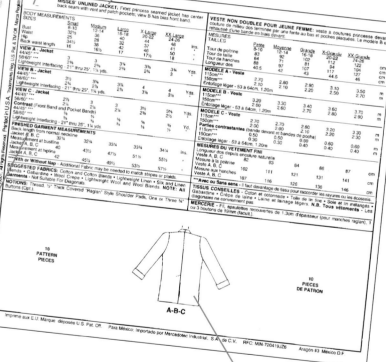

The fashion sketch—This is usually accurate. The artist draws what he or she sees, looking at the garment on a dress form.

Body measurements—These are found on the back of the envelope or on the flap.

The garment description—This gives you design details such as "dropped shoulders" or "blouson."

The photograph—It gives you a clue to fit, but it depends on the size of the model. A loose-fitting cardigan could look like a very loose-fitting cardigan if the model is extra thin!

Finished garment measurements— What a great tool! Pattern companies have always given finished lengths and hemline fullness on the back of the envelope.

Today, most pattern companies are also printing the finished measurements of the hip and bust on the pattern tissue. Look for the circle symbol paired with a number:

40" (102cm)

Some pattern companies also print finished garment measurements on the back of the pattern envelope. This tells you about fit before you buy the pattern. If the ease is more than you want, you can choose to buy a smaller size.

The line art—Line art is fairly accurate for the same reasons the fashion sketch on the front is accurate. The main purpose of line drawings is to show the seamlines and other details in the design more clearly.

How Finished Garment Measurements Work

This pattern shows two different skirts. Use the finished measurements to tell you about design and fit:

BODY MEASUREMENTS

Size	14
Hip	38"

FINISHED GARMENT MEASUREMENTS

Straight skirt

Hip	41"
Bottom width	39"
Length	24"

Full skirt

Hip	45"
Bottom width	76"
Length	30"

NOTE: To determine ease, subtract the body's hip measurement from the pattern hip measurement. Here the straight skirt has 3" of ease and the full skirt 7" of ease.

Finished garment measurements, though a wonderful tool, will not help you if you don't know how much ease you like in different garment styles. See "What Is Normal Ease?" on page 51.

close-fitting   *loose-fitting*   *fitted*

NOTE: These pattern company fit descriptions for dresses are based on bust fit, not on waist or hip fit.

FYI—Basic Fit Bodice Comparisons

Marta measured the tissues for all the basic dress-fit patterns in size 10. As you can see in the chart, there are differences, but they are really insignificant.

Burda varies more, but remember, Burda uses slightly different body measurements. What this really shows is that each company has a different minimum ease standard.

	Ease	McCalls	Simplicity	Vogue & Butterick	Burda
Bust:	2" to 3"	35½"	35½" all three based on a 32½" bust	35½"	35" based on 33" bust
Waist:	1" to 1½"	26"	26½" all three based on a 25" waist	26"	27¼" based on 26" waist
Hip:	1½" to 3"	36¾"	37" all three based on a 34" hip	36¾"	37" based on a 35½" hip

See pages 249-251 for actual bodice tissue comparison and page 21 to see actual bodices sewn, and on the same person.

Pattern Envelope Fit Description*

The description may say loose-fitting or fitted so you have a fit clue.
The fit description for tops and dresses is based only on the bust fit, not on the waist or hip fit.

Dresses, Shirts, Tops, Vests, Blouses

	Close Fitting	Fitted	Semi-Fitted	Loose Fitting	Very Loose Fitting
TOTAL EASE IN BUST:	0 - 2 7/8"	3" - 4"	4 1/8" - 5"	5 1/8" - 8"	Over 8"

Lined or Unlined Jackets

	Close Fitting	Fitted	Semi-Fitted	Loose Fitting	Very Loose Fitting
TOTAL EASE IN BUST: (hips can be different)	no close-fitting jacket styles	3 3/4" - 4 1/4"	4 3/8" - 5 3/4"	5 7/8" - 10"	Over 10"

* Vogue uses these descriptions for ease in fit. Amounts may vary from company to company.

	Close Fitting	Fitted	Semi-Fitted	Loose Fitting	Very Loose Fitting
TOTAL EASE IN BUST: (hips can be different)		5 1/4″ - 6 3/4″	6 7/8″ - 8″	8 1/8″ - 12″	Over 12″

Lined or Unlined Coats

no close-fitting coat styles

	Close Fitting	Fitted	Semi-Fitted	Loose Fitting	Very Loose Fitting
TOTAL EASE IN HIP:	0 - 1 7/8″	2″ - 3″	3 1/8″ - 4″	4 1/8″ - 10″	Over 10″

Skirts

CHAPTER 8

Analyze Your Body

Fit is more than buying the right size. You must also learn about your shape and body proportions. So "get honest." For an unbiased look at your body, place a paper bag over your head and stand in front of a full-length mirror. DO cut eye holes in the bag!

Speaking of full-length mirrors, do you own one?
___ If yes, you get 5 points.
___ If it is in your sewing area, you get 10 points.

Is There Such a Thing as a Perfect Body?

If there is, she doesn't come to our classes. We have been fitting for over 25 years and have yet to see someone make no adjustments. People are uniquely different from the so-called "standard."

In the past the ideal shape was more pear-shaped than today's ideal. This painting of Odalisque showed the ideal female figure. She was never slim-hipped. If you were, you weren't beautiful—you were too poor to have much to eat.

Today, we all dream of being tall and slim. Edith Head, designer for many beautiful movie stars, once said that women are too hard on themselves and should play up the positives and stop worrying about what they consider their flaws.

Odalisque, Jean-Auguste Dominique Ingres

Why Are People's Bodies So Different?

Genetics

You are born with a certain skeleton. It has its own shape and proportions. Your bones may be large, medium, or small. Your shoulder bones may be more square or sloping than "average." You may be longer or shorter in the waist than "average." When you fit a pattern, you are fitting your skeleton plus your "fluff."

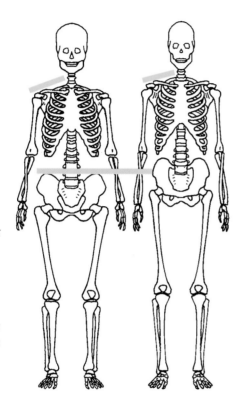

Note the differences in two skeletons of the same height. For example, look at the differences in the shape of the rib cage, the slope of the shoulders and the shape and width of the pelvis.

Maturity

With maturity things just seem to fall. Blame it on gravity! We started fitting in our 20s and saw how people changed as they matured. It was a rude awakening. In spite of all of this, we have determined that **40 isn't fatal**. Nor is 50, 60, 70, etc. If you think your body has gone downhill, remember, it is balanced by your intelligence, insight and compassion, all of which have gone uphill. (See "Is Age a Size?" on page 44 for more details on what happens as you age.)

Young   Mature

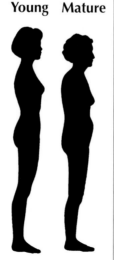

Posture Affects Fit

Encourage your children to stand up straight and to pull their shoulders back. We are seeing more 13-year-olds with rounded backs and forward shoulders than ever before. They are the computer generation and posture is reflecting it. Poor posture becomes permanent. It causes hems that sag or hike up, jackets that won't stay on the shoulders, and collars that stick out at the back neck. Stand up straight, put weight evenly on both feet, don't cross your legs, and don't carry book bags or grocery bags or heavy purses on one shoulder, or babies on one hip. You'll look smarter, younger and thinner and have a healthier back!

Weight Distribution and Shape

You will differ from the hourglass figure if you carry more or less weight in any area. Causes can include genetics and age, but shape is also affected by how physically active you are and what type of exercises you do. Also, for many, shape changes after pregnancy.

Two people who weigh the same can be shaped differently.

Body Proportions

Proportion is the length of the different body sections in relationship to each other. Three people standing in a row may all be the same size and height, but vary in waist and leg length.

Proportioned patterns are not necessarily the answer for a tall or short person. **Find out where you are tall or short** and learn how to lengthen or shorten a regular pattern in the right places. Most short people have average waist length and crotch length. Their shortness is in their legs.

"But we're all 5'4" and wear a size 12!"

The Pattern Company Nightmare

All of the women below sew with a size 10... in the shoulders. Look at the differences in bust-line, height, waist length, shoulder slope, posture and silhouette or shape. Imagine the nightmare of pattern companies trying to design patterns to fit all of these figures.

It would be IMPOSSIBLE to come up with a **perfect pattern** to fit each of these shapes, let alone the myriad other body shapes in the sewing population. Therefore, pattern companies stick to a standard. Once you know your standard alterations, you can sew any design from any company.

Don't Under-estimate the Power of Illusion

Though bodies come in many shapes, color and line are powerful tools to create the illusion of a different shape. In the photo below you see an example of a rectangular body shape camouflaged by color and the lines of a princess seam to give the illusion of an hourglass shape.

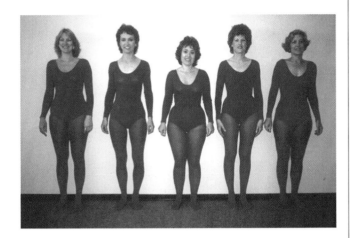

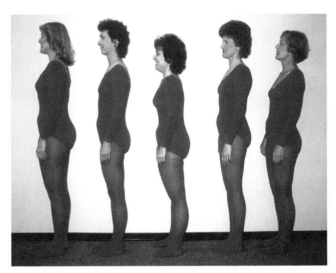

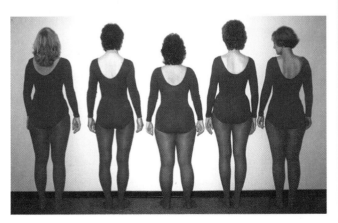

*For more information on selecting your best clothing styles and on creating illusions, see our book **Looking Good** by Nancy Nix-Rice. It's the best wardrobe-planning book on the market!*

59

There are five common categories of shape. Most people are one of the following:

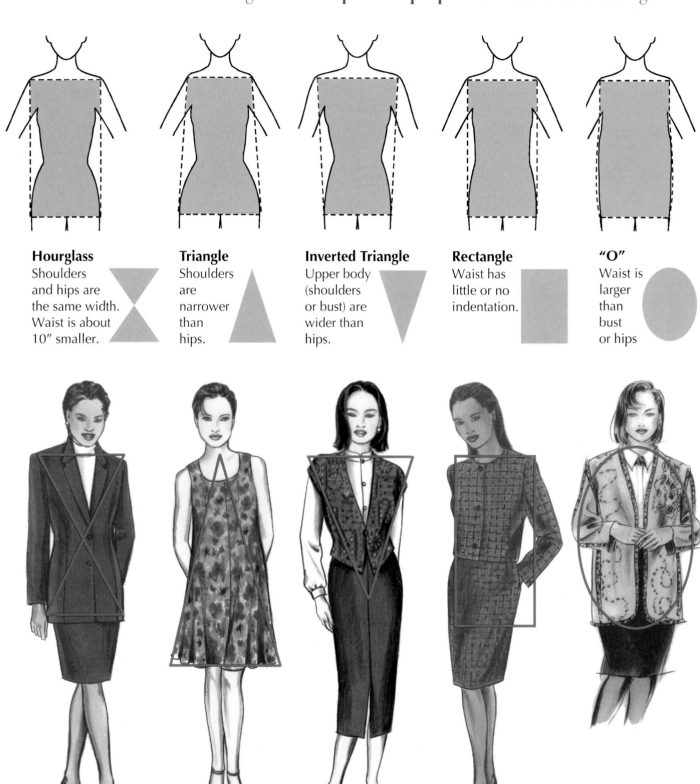

Hourglass
Shoulders and hips are the same width. Waist is about 10" smaller.

Triangle
Shoulders are narrower than hips.

Inverted Triangle
Upper body (shoulders or bust) are wider than hips.

Rectangle
Waist has little or no indentation.

"O"
Waist is larger than bust or hips

Sewing clothing that is similar to your shape requires the least amount of fitting. Of course, if you are a rectangle and choose an hourglass design, you'll now know that you will have to let out the waistline to achieve a good fit.

Use These Tools to Analyze Your Body

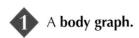 **1** A **body graph.**

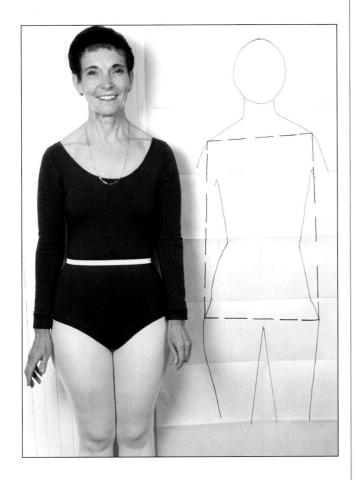

 2 An **altered fitted basic dress** made from a pattern company's basic pattern (Chapter 9).

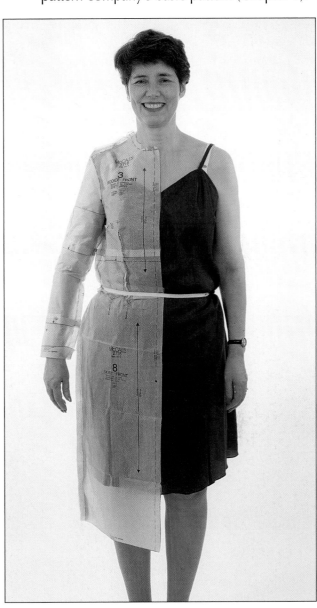

How Does a Body Graph Help?

You will learn about your proportions and shape. If you are short, where are you short? Did you know your shoulders or hips are uneven? What is your shape?

Turn to the next page to learn how to make your own body graph.

Make a Body Graph

A "body graph" is a quick, fun and simple way to identify your shape and proportions regardless of your height. We have tested and fine-tuned the steps of making a body graph with students in our workshops.

A body graph is easiest to do in groups of three-to-four—one being graphed, one holding a ruler, and one marking while another stands back to make sure the pencil is perpendicular to the wall.

Preparation

1. Cut newsprint or butcher paper wider and taller than you are. (Tape two widths together if the paper is too narrow.) Fold it in half lengthwise and crease. Mark the foldline using a pen and yardstick.

Quick Tip

Use the gridded tissue called Pati Palmer's Perfect Pattern Paper for McCall's.

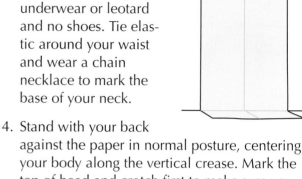

2. Tape the paper to a wall. Cut or crease the paper even with an uncarpeted floor.

3. Wear nonbinding underwear or leotard and no shoes. Tie elastic around your waist and wear a chain necklace to mark the base of your neck.

4. Stand with your back against the paper in normal posture, centering your body along the vertical crease. Mark the top of head and crotch first to make sure you are centered on the fold. Look straight ahead. DO NOT LOOK UP OR DOWN!

5. Have a friend plot the points shown in the illustration below, using a new, long pencil, and a nonflexing yardstick. Have her keep the yardstick close to your body, holding the opposite end so the entire yardstick is perpendicular to the wall. Then have her mark the paper at the edge of the yardstick that is next to your body.

← crease

Top of head (not top of hair). Mark on center line of paper.

Bottom of head. (Turn head sideways, mouth closed and head straight—not tilted up or down. Mark just under chin.)

Underarm. (Raise arm to find spot. Lower arm to mark spot.)

Hip (where leg is joined to hip bone).

Base of neck (where necklace sits). Mark both sides. (Marks may not be at the same level.)

Shoulder (in the middle of pivot bone or at the top of a well-fitting, smooth, set-in sleeve cap).

Waist. (Mark the bottom of the elastic on both sides. The marks may not be at the same level.)

Fullest area below the waist (not always the "hip").

Crotch. (This allows you to measure hips from center on both sides to see if hip is fuller on one side. Be sure mark is on center line of paper.)

Knee (where it creases in back).

Step ①

Top of head: Make sure your head is centered on the fold and the ruler is perpendicular to the wall, firmly on top of your head, not hair. Mark the top of the head.

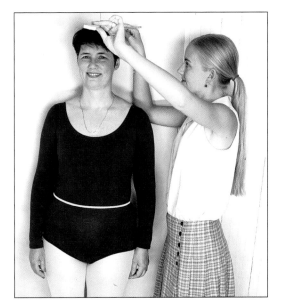

From the side view you can easily see if the ruler is perpendicular to the wall.

Step ②

Crotch: Mark the crotch to make sure your entire body is centered on the foldline. Put the ruler up close to body.

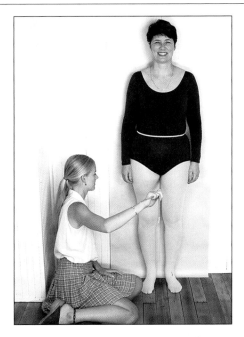

Step away and mark. Not only does this marking ensure you are centered on the foldline, it also allows you to measure each half of your body to see if your hip is fuller on one side than on the other.

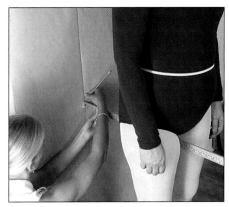

Step ③

Bottom of head: Turn head sideways, mouth closed and head straight—not up or down. Mark just under chin. This determines head size in proportion to the rest of your body.

Step 4

Base of neck: Mark base of neck on both sides where necklace sits. Marks may not be at the same level, depending on the curvature of your neck and slope of each shoulder.

Step 5

Shoulders: Mark the point on the top of the shoulder where the arm pivots (the top of a fitted, set-in sleeve cap).

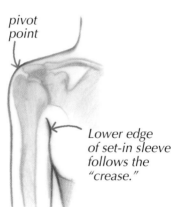

pivot point

Lower edge of set-in sleeve follows the "crease."

Step 6

Underarm: Raise arm to find the spot. Lower arm to mark the spot using a ruler and pencil, or pencil alone if you can keep it perpendicular to the wall.

Using just pencil to mark.

As an alternative, use a pencil with a wide ruler that will rest on the wall and be perfectly perpendicular. (We found the ruler shown in this photo to be too flexible for some of the other measurements.)

Step

Waist: Mark the bottom of the elastic on both sides.

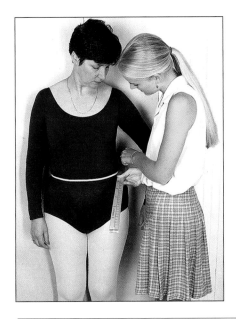

Step

Hip: Mark where leg is joined to hip bone—where you crease when you raise your leg to the side. It is not necessarily the fullest part below your waist.

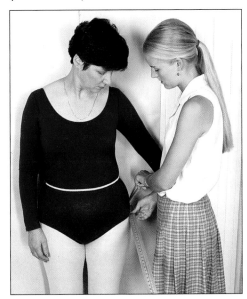

Step

Fullest hip: This could be any area below your waist such as your high hip, hip, or thighs.

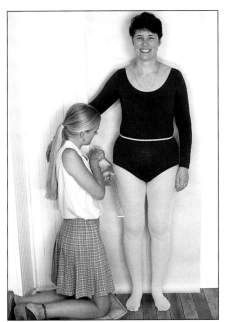

Step

Knee: Mark where knee creases in the back when you bend it.

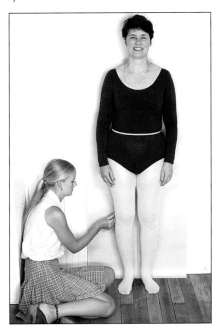

Step

Have a friend trace around your silhouette, connecting the dots to create your shape. Start at the neck. For accuracy the pencil must be perpendicular to the wall. Hold it with two hands. This helps you double-check the accuracy of your dots. If any marks appear to be off, check and remark if necessary.

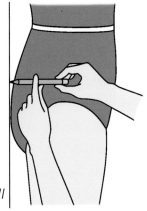

wall

Step

Step away. With paper still taped to wall, fold it in half, matching the bottom of your feet with the top of your head. Fold it in half again and then again, creasing it into eight equal sections.

NOTE: The average figure is eight heads tall. The "ideally" proportioned body is divided as shown in the illustration on page 67.

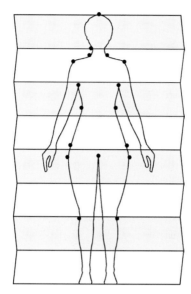

Step

Draw a straight line from the base of the neck in both directions to above the shoulder dots, parallel to the nearest foldline. If dots are uneven, use the highest dot.

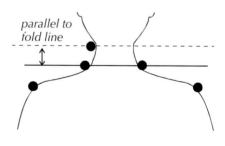

Step

Draw a dotted line box that connects your shoulder dots to the fullest hip area dots.

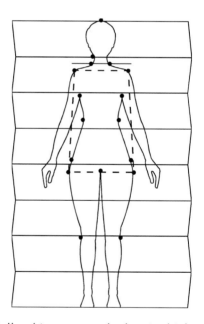

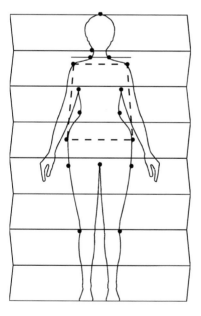

Fullest hip area may be low in thigh area...or it may be just below the waist.

Step

Now analyze your body, comparing your shape to the "ideal" proportions on the next page. Then fill out the Body Graph Worksheet on page 69. (If you prefer, make a photocopy of page 69.)

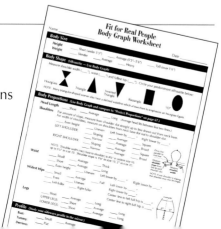

Now Compare Yourself to "Perfect" Proportions*

Although no one is perfect,
you have to start somewhere to have a point of comparison.

"Ideal" Proportions

Width from neck base dot out to shoulder dot is 4¾" for a size 10, up to 5¼" for size 20. See note below.

Shoulders **slope** 1⅝" from neck base if you are a size 10, up to 2" for a size 20.*

Underarm is halfway between top of head and hip.

Waist is halfway between underarm and hip.

Hip where leg is joined divides body in half.

Hips are 1" narrower than shoulders for garments to fall freely over hips.

Knee is halfway between hip and feet.

Soles of feet.

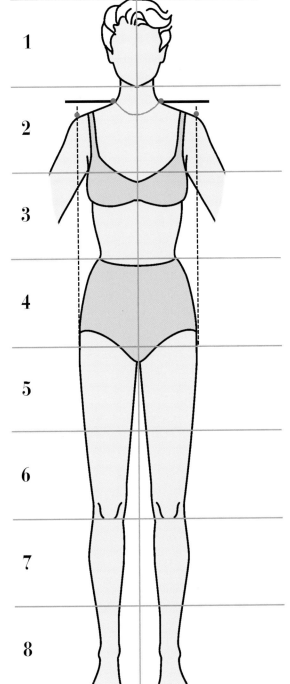

Possible Variations

If your shoulders slope 1/2" more or less than the ideal, you are sloping or square.

NOTE: If your shoulders are uneven, the one that slopes more will measure longer. This doesn't necessarily mean it is broader.

If your waist is more than 1" above or below the ideal, you are short- or long-waisted for your height.

If your leg length is more than 1" longer or shorter than half your body length, you are long- or short-legged.

*Measurements are based on pattern company basic patterns (page 53).

Marta's Body Graph and Body Graph Worksheet

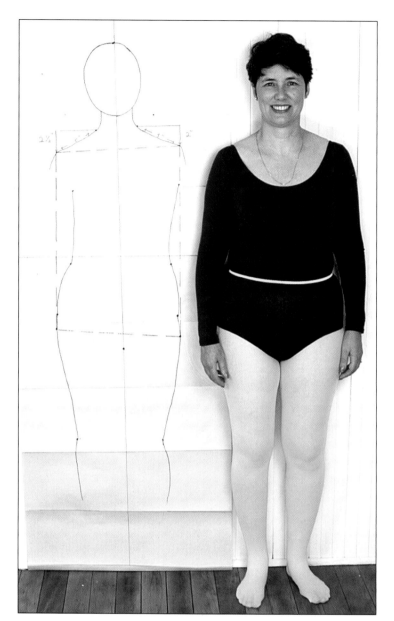

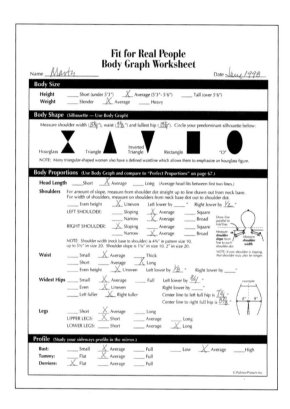

Fit for Real People
Body Graph Worksheet

Name: Marta   Date: June 1998

Body Size

Height: ___ Short (under 5'3") _X_ Average (5'3"- 5'6") ___ Tall (over 5'6")
Weight: ___ Slender _X_ Average ___ Heavy

Body Shape (Silhouette — Use Body Graph)

Measure shoulder width (15¼"), waist (9⅛") and fullest hip (11¼"). Circle your predominant silhouette below:

Hourglass   Triangle   Inverted Triangle   Rectangle   "O"

NOTE: Many triangular-shaped women also have a defined waistline which allows them to emphasize an hourglass figure.

Body Proportions (Use Body Graph and compare to "Perfect Proportions" on page 67.)

Head Length: ___ Short _X_ Average ___ Long (Average head fits between first two lines.)

Shoulders: For amount of slope, measure from shoulder dot straight up to line drawn out from neck base. For width of shoulders, measure on shoulders from neck base dot out to shoulder dot.
  ___ Even height _X_ Uneven Left lower by ___ Right lower by ½"
  LEFT SHOULDER: ___ Sloping _X_ Average ___ Square
                 ___ Narrow _X_ Average ___ Broad
  RIGHT SHOULDER: _X_ Sloping ___ Average ___ Square
                  ___ Narrow _X_ Average ___ Broad
  NOTE: Shoulder width (neck base to shoulder) is 4¾" in pattern size 10, up to 5½" in size 20. Shoulder slope is 1⅛" in size 10, 2" in size 20.

Waist: ___ Small _X_ Average ___ Thick
       ___ Short ___ Average _X_ Long
       ___ Even height _X_ Uneven Left lower by ⅛" Right lower by ___

Widest Hips: ___ Small _X_ Average ___ Full Left lower by ¾"
             ___ Even _X_ Uneven Right lower by ___
             ___ Left fuller _X_ Right fuller Center line to left full hip is 7¼"
                                                Center line to right full hip is 6⅛"

Legs: ___ Short _X_ Average ___ Long
      UPPER LEGS: _X_ Short ___ Average ___ Long
      LOWER LEGS: ___ Short ___ Average _X_ Long

Profile (Study your sideways profile in the mirror.)

Bust: ___ Small _X_ Average ___ Full ___ Low _X_ Average ___ High
Tummy: ___ Flat _X_ Average ___ Full
Derriere: _X_ Flat ___ Average ___ Full

© Palmer/Pletsch Inc.

◆ Marta has a 2" shoulder drop on her left shoulder, which is slightly sloping for a size 12. Her right shoulder drops 2½" meaning it is slightly sloping. Marta uses an extra shoulder pad on her right side to balance her shoulders. In a sleeveless dress, she sews the right shoulder 1/2" deeper at the armhole edge.

◆ Marta is slightly long-waisted. Her waist is about 1/2" below the waist fold. Since she is the average height of 5'6", she will need to lengthen the bodice waist on patterns.

◆ Marta is long-legged because her hip dots are above the hip fold. Her lower legs are long as her knee is above the knee fold. This will affect flattering skirt lengths.

◆ The box around Marta's torso connecting the shoulders to the widest hip area is about the same width top and bottom, making her fairly hourglass in shape. Her right hip is fuller than the left and higher as well.

Body Graph Worksheet

Fill out the worksheet on the next page to discover your figure challenges as well as ASSETS. It is equally important to enhance your assets as it is to camouflage your liabilities. See our book, **Looking Good**, for clothing ideas to help you look your best.

Fit for Real People
Body Graph Worksheet

Name _____   Date _____

Body Size

Height   _____ Short (under 5′3″)   _____ Average (5′3″- 5′6″)   _____ Tall (over 5′6″)

Weight   _____ Slender   _____ Average   _____ Heavy

Body Shape (Silhouette — Use Body Graph)

Measure shoulder width (____″), waist (____″) and fullest hip (____″). Circle your predominant silhouette below:

Hourglass   Triangle   Inverted Triangle   Rectangle   "O"

NOTE: Many triangular-shaped women also have a defined waistline which allows them to emphasize an hourglass figure.

Body Proportions (Use Body Graph and compare to "Perfect Proportions" on page 67.)

Head Length   _____ Short   _____ Average   _____ Long   (Average head fits between first two lines.)

Shoulders   For amount of slope, measure from shoulder dot straight up to line drawn out from neck base.
For width of shoulders, measure on shoulders from neck base dot out to shoulder dot.

_____ Even height   _____ Uneven   Left lower by _____ ″   Right lower by _____″

LEFT SHOULDER: _____ Sloping   _____ Average   _____ Square
                              _____ Narrow   _____ Average   _____ Broad

RIGHT SHOULDER: _____ Sloping   _____ Average   _____ Square
                               _____ Narrow   _____ Average   _____ Broad

Draw line parallel to fold line.

Measure shoulder slope from line to each shoulder dot.

Measure shoulder width.

NOTE: Shoulder width (neck base to shoulder) is 4¾″ in pattern size 10, up to 5½″ in size 20. Shoulder slope is 1⅝″ in size 10, 2″ in size 20.

NOTE: *If one shoulder is sloping, that shoulder may also be longer.*

Waist   _____ Small   _____ Average   _____ Thick

_____ Short   _____ Average   _____ Long

_____ Even height   _____ Uneven   Left lower by _____ ″   Right lower by _____″

Widest Hips   _____ Small   _____ Average   _____ Full   Left lower by _____ ″

_____ Even   _____ Uneven   Right lower by _____ ″

_____ Left fuller   _____ Right fuller   Center line to left full hip is _____″

Center line to right full hip is _____″

example: 8″ | 9″

Legs   _____ Short   _____ Average   _____ Long

UPPER LEGS: _____ Short   _____ Average   _____ Long

LOWER LEGS: _____ Short   _____ Average   _____ Long

Profile (Study your sideways profile in the mirror.)

Bust: _____ Small   _____ Average   _____ Full   _____ Low   _____ Average   _____ High

Tummy: _____ Flat   _____ Average   _____ Full

Derriere: _____ Flat   _____ Average   _____ Full

Examples of Variations from "Perfect" Proportions...

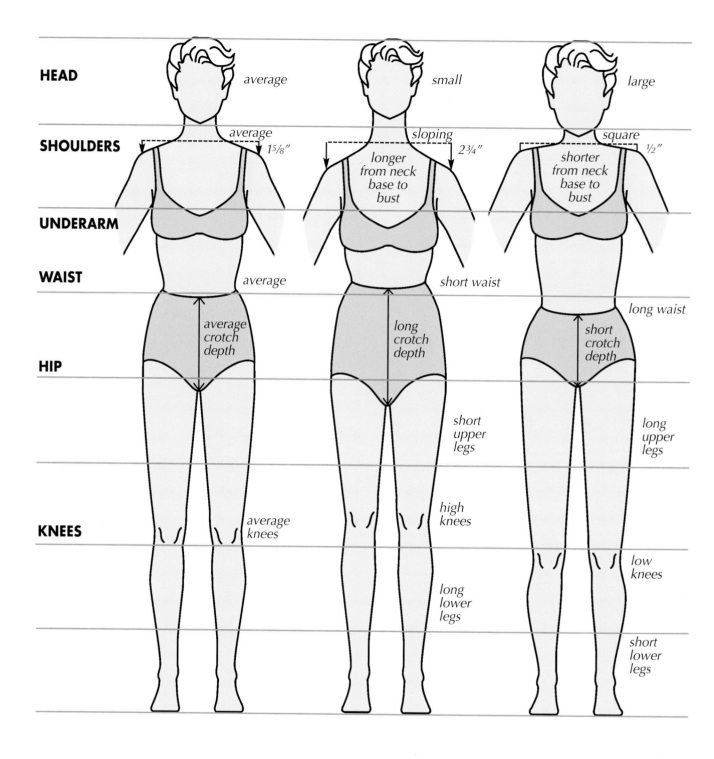

HEAD

average

small

large

SHOULDERS

average 1⅝"

sloping 2¾"

square ½"

longer from neck base to bust

shorter from neck base to bust

UNDERARM

WAIST

average

short waist

long waist

average crotch depth

long crotch depth

short crotch depth

HIP

short upper legs

long upper legs

KNEES

average knees

high knees

low knees

long lower legs

short lower legs

and What They Mean

Head size
Finding out if your head is small, medium or large can help you determine the best haircut to maximize or minimize head size for better proportions. Also, does your neck appear long or short? This can help you determine standup collar height.

Shoulders
If your shoulders slope, use shoulder pads to bring them to normal position. Shoulder pad camisoles are nice to use. When shoulder pads are needed, use thinner ones if shoulders are square, thicker ones if shoulders are sloping. Use two different thicknesses to balance uneven shoulders.

Upper chest length
If you are long from neckbase to underarm, you may need to lengthen patterns above the bust. A true petite would be short in this area and would have to shorten patterns in this area instead.

Underarm to waist
The distance from underarm to waist determines belt width. If you have a long distance, you can wear wide belts. If short, narrow waistbands or faced waistlines or dropped-waist dresses are usually best. The bust generally falls below your underarm. If your bust is full and low, narrow waistbands and belts may look better.

Crotch depth
The distance between waist and crotch helps determine the crotch adjustment on a pant pattern. If you are short, but long in the crotch for your height, you may not need any crotch adjustment. If you are long in the crotch, your legs may be short in proportion to your height. If you are short waisted and have a long crotch depth, your legs may be average length for your height. The easiest way to tell whether or not you are long or short in the crotch is to tissue-fit a pant pattern. Try a McCall's Palmer/Pletsch pant pattern, complete with tissue-fitting instructions.

Hip
This is the joint where legs and hip meet. The crotch is below this point. The hip joint in a person of average proportions divides the body in half. If your midpoint is low, your legs are short. If it is high, your legs are long in proportion to your height. This doesn't mean you are long or short in the crotch, however. That is a relationship between the waist and crotch.

Knees
If your back-of-knee crease is above the line, you are long in your lower legs. If your knee crease is below the line, you are short in the lower legs. Find your best short, long and just-below-the-knee skirt lengths (page 183). Measure along your side from your waist to hem.

Real People and their Body Graphs

During a recent workshop, we did a body graph on each student. We drew around each person as she stood against paper taped to the wall. To our surprise, most students looked somewhat hourglass in shape. However, to be a true hourglass, you not only need a waist indentation, but your hips and shoulders must be equal in width.

Lila

Lila has slightly wider hips than shoulders so is triangular. Her chin is above the head size crease so she has a small head in proportion to her body. You can see that her right shoulder is lower than the left, but both are sloping. Her right hip is higher and fuller than the left, making her waist shorter on that side. Most of her body is "ideally" proportioned. Her body sections fall right at the folds of the paper.

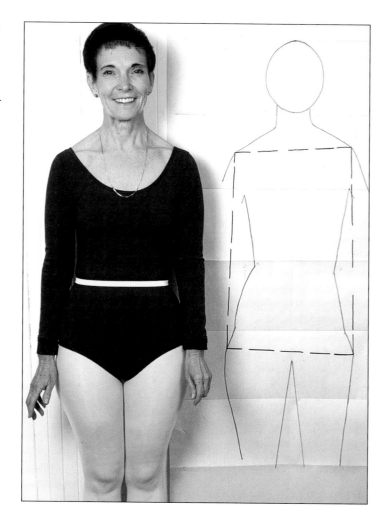

Back Waist Length Is Not Necessarily a Guide to Size

Lila and Kathy are close to the same height. Their waists appear to be about the same length, yet...

◆ Lila's back waist length actually measures 17½" and Kathy's 16¼". Why is this??? Lila's upper back is more rounded and her head sits forward on her body.

◆ Kathy's front waist length is 1" **longer** than Lila's because she is fuller busted.

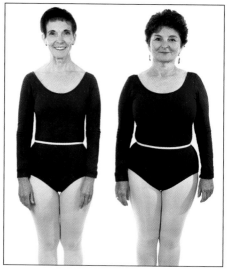
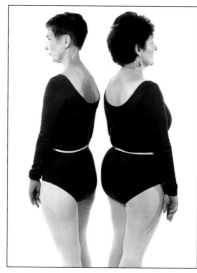

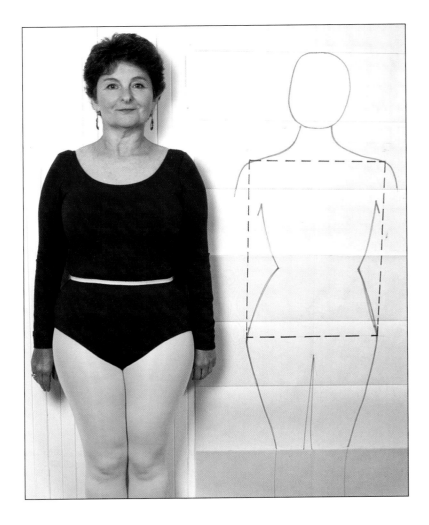

Kathy

Kathy is almost hourglass, but since her shoulders are wider than her hips AND she is full busted, she is an inverted triangle. She has a large head for her height. Her right hip is slightly higher and fuller. She is long waisted in proportion to her 5' height, but not for patterns made for the height of 5'6".

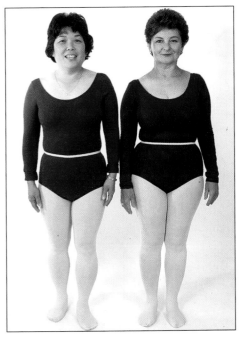

Sharon & Kathy

Sharon on the left is "short" and Kathy on the right is "petite." Sharon is simply short in the legs, while Kathy is short throughout her body, not just in her legs. A true petite is shorter proportionately between head and bust, bust and waist, waist and hip, and in the upper and lower portion of her legs. This person can shop in petite departments.

CHAPTER 9

Make a Body Map

Make a basic pattern for a fitted dress. Alter it to fit you and VOILA! You have your **"body map"** to successful fitting. You will know where you are different from a pattern company's sloper.

A basic dress is VERY FITTED with minimum ease. It has darts, a waistline, set-in sleeves and a straight skirt. If you make it up, it will feel quite fitted, especially if you have been wearing over-sized fashions.

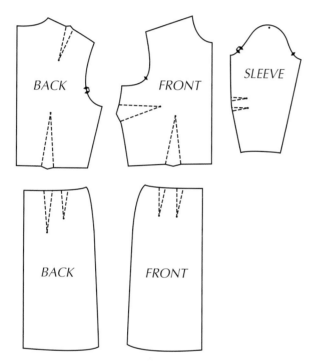

Most pattern companies offer a fit pattern drafted from the "sloper" (also called a master pattern, block, or staple) from which they create all their designs. After altering your basic, you will know the **maximum** number of changes you will have to make on the most fitted design you will ever sew.

The GOOD NEWS is, the fuller the design, the fewer alterations you have to make. Out of 10 changes made to the basic fit dress, you may need to make only three on a fashion pattern.

How do you know which alterations will be necessary in any pattern? **Try on the tissue.** Once you are aware of your body variations, tissue fitting will quickly show you which alterations are necessary.

Which Basic Pattern to Use?

When you sew a basic to make your "body map," you can use any company's basic fit pattern. American pattern companies use one set of body measurements and their basic fit patterns are more similar than different.

We made up the basic bodice from each pattern company and photographed them on the same person on the same day, so you can see how they compare. See page 21 for more information.

See how similar they really are? If you are long-waisted in one, you will be in all.

Make an "Adjustable" Basic Pattern

After you have selected a basic pattern to fit you, make life easier by adding larger seam allowances and outlets as shown in the following places:

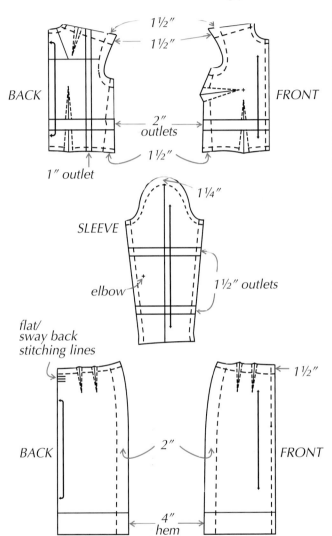

BACK   FRONT
1½"
1½"
2" outlets
1½"
1" outlet

SLEEVE
1¼"
elbow
1½" outlets

flat/ sway back stitching lines

BACK   FRONT
1½"
2"
4" hem

An alternative is to purchase a pattern with outlets. Most pattern companies have outlets built into their basic dress pattern and also provide separate fronts for each bra cup size. Use the front that is your cup size. If you are unsure of what you are, start with the B-cup front.

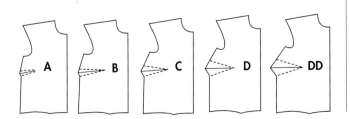

A   B   C   D   DD

Prepare for Tissue-Fitting

Trim around the basic pattern tissue for the bodice front and back, sleeve, and skirt front and back. Trim OUTSIDE of the black line. Press the tissue with a dry iron set on wool setting.

For more on tissue preparation, see page 112.

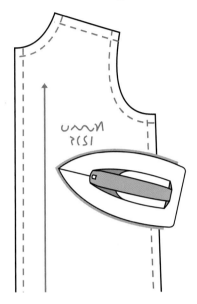

Reinforce the Pattern

1. Tape the bodice armholes and neckline with Scotch® Magic Transparent Tape® (the cloudy one) INSIDE the stitching lines. Lap ends of short pieces of tape around curves.

2. Snip seam allowance to BUT NOT THROUGH the seamline in curved areas.

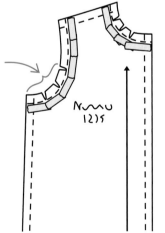

NOTE: McCall's #2718 is excellent to use because it has stitching lines marked on the tissue. It is a special-order pattern available through fabric stores that carry McCall's patterns.

3. If you are using a basic pattern with built-in outlets, or have added them to your pattern, close the outlets for waist length and broad back by bringing the solid lines together. Pin in place.

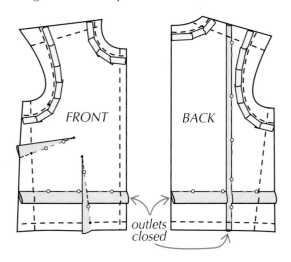

4. With pattern tissues wrong sides together, pin darts, shoulders, and underarm seams along stitching lines. Place pins on seamlines PARALLEL to the edge and pointing away from neck and underarm. Do not put pins within the seam allowances. Point vertical pins down so they won't fall out of the tissue during fitting.

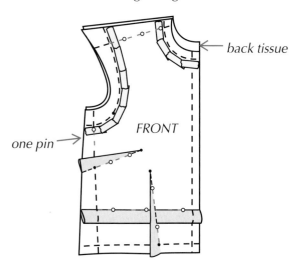

If you know you will need to let out the waist, you can pin the back to the front with only **one pin** placed just below the armhole.

MEASUREMENT CHART			
Size	12	14	16
Bust	34″	36″	38″

Here's How it Works On a Real Person

Select the Right Size

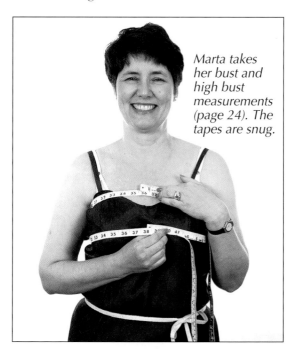

Marta takes her bust and high bust measurements (page 24). The tapes are snug.

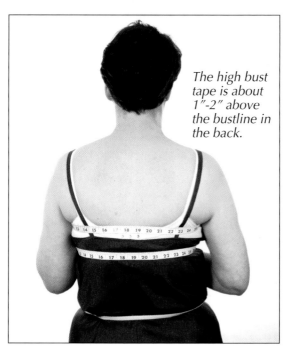

The high bust tape is about 1″-2″ above the bustline in the back.

Marta's high bust is 35½″ (size 12) and her full bust is 38″ (size 16). Since the bust is 2½″ larger, she selects a size 12. (See Chapter 4, "Buy the Right Size," page 24.)

Marta tries on a 16 bodice (full bust size) to illustrate that it would be too large for her. The area across the chest from center front to where the sleeve would be set in is too wide.

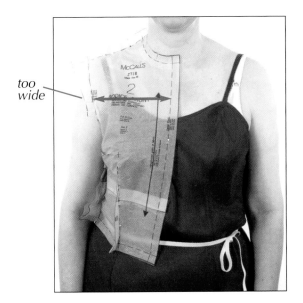

too wide

It's best to use the size that fits best at arrow (in the illustration below). If you look at the shoulders instead of the mid-chest area, you can be thrown off if the shoulders are narrow or broad.

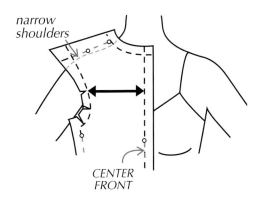

narrow shoulders

CENTER FRONT

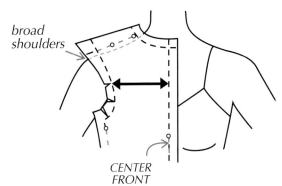

broad shoulders

CENTER FRONT

Try On the Unaltered Tissue

Marta tries on an unaltered size 12 tissue. It comes to her center front in the chest, but not at the bust. This indicates she either has a full bust or a broad back or both.

(We are using a pattern with outlets and larger seam allowances. If yours doesn't have these, you can add them. See page 75.)

Fit Yourself by Following this Order

1 ▶ Back

Start with the back. Why? If you adjust back width, it affects front width (and total circumference). The pattern center back reaches Marta's center back in the neck area, but not at the shoulder blades. Marta has a **broad back**, but not broad shoulders.

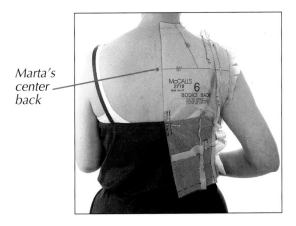

Marta's center back

We have let out the broad back outlet tuck 1/2". (See Chapter 14 for back alteration tips.) The waist is still tight and will be adjusted later.

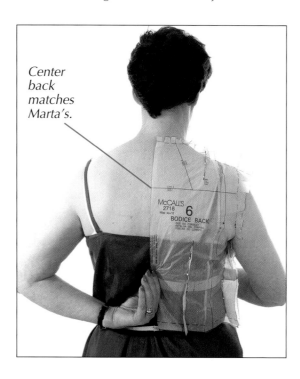

Center back matches Marta's.

② Bra Cup Size

Even after making the broad back alteration, Marta couldn't quite get the pattern to match her center front.

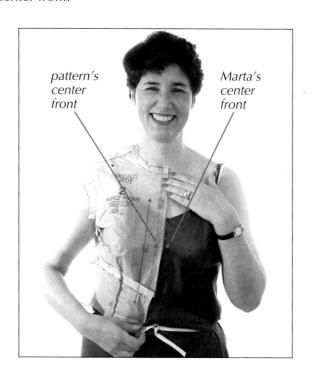

pattern's center front

Marta's center front

Here she tries on the C-cup front instead. Now the front comes to her center front, but the waist is still too small. The "+" marking the bust point doesn't seem in the right place, but don't remark it yet. Get the width and length right first.

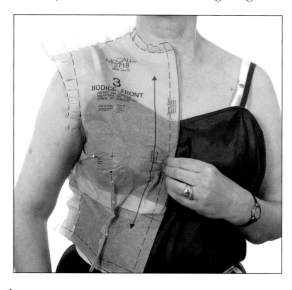

③ Width Around Middle

Let out sides and possibly the vertical darts until center front is in the correct position. Don't worry about waist length yet unless you are really long- or short-waisted. If you are, you may have to adjust before letting out the width and fine tune it later.

NOTE: Although the neckline is too high in front, it will drop into position when other adjustments are made.

➍ High Round Back

Marta is wearing a chain necklace to help establish her neckline. The neckline seam is usually at the top of the neck bone. Marta's seam doesn't reach the chain, meaning she has a **high round back** (page 122). Clothing often pulls toward the back off her shoulders. This is also why the neckline in the front was too high. It can't drop into place until after this alteration is made.

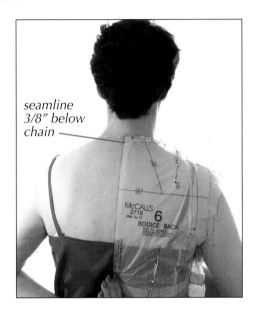

seamline
3/8" below
chain —

Marta tries on the tissue after altering. Now her back neckline is at the base of her neck in the back and the shoulder seam comes forward at the neck enough to correct the neckline at center front.

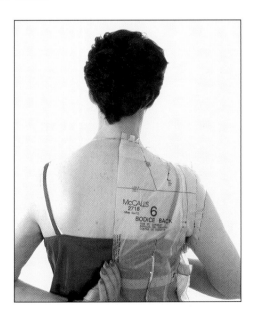

NOTE: A **very round back** is rare. You probably already know if you have this body shape. The alteration is shown on page 124.

➎ Waist Length

Marta is a little **long waisted**. She let out the waist length tuck 5/8" until the waist seamline at the center front was at the bottom edge of the elastic.

Since her **right hip** is **higher** than her left, we have marked in red the stitching line for the right side. The original seamline will be for her left side. When we fit the skirt, we will need to **raise** the skirt waist seamline on the right side.

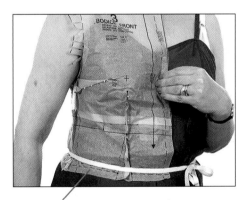

Mark new waist seam in front.

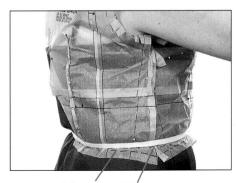

Also mark back and sides.

6 Shoulders

Check for square, sloping, broad, narrow and forward shoulders.

Marta has **forward shoulders** (page 162). This is very common today, caused by doing close work over a desk or sewing machine. The arm rotates forward at the point where it pivots at the shoulder. This often is found in conjunction with a **high round back**.

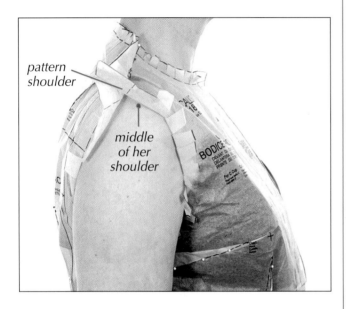

To adjust the shoulder seam so it sits at the middle of her shoulder, we pivoted the seam forward by letting out the back shoulder seam and taking in the front shoulder seam (page 162).

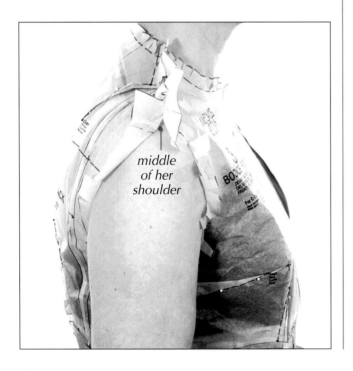

Forward Shoulder Pattern Alteration

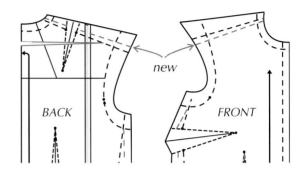

7 Darts

Marta's darts fit well. We will fine-tune them later after we make the bodice in gingham, because dart position often shifts in fabric.

8 Now Tissue-Fit Sleeve for Width and Length

Tape underarm of sleeve as shown and clip curves.

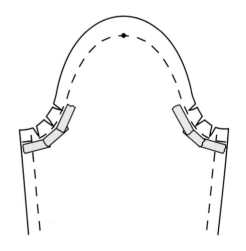

Pin sleeve outlets and underarm seams together. Put on altered bodice tissue. Carefully slip on the sleeve tissue and line up the **underarm seams** of bodice and sleeve. DO NOT line up the top of the sleeve with the shoulder.

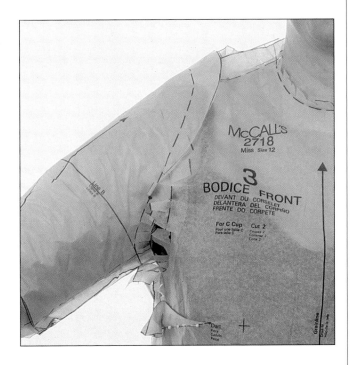

The elbow "**+**" is at Marta's elbow, where it should be. Marta is pinching 1/2". You should be able to pinch a minimum of 1/2" of tissue at the fullest part of the arm for a total of 1" ease. You may prefer a little more ease in an actual garment.

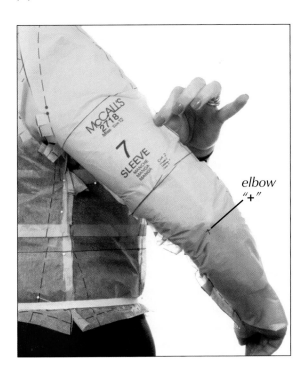

elbow "+"

The sleeve length is fine, just below wrist bone.

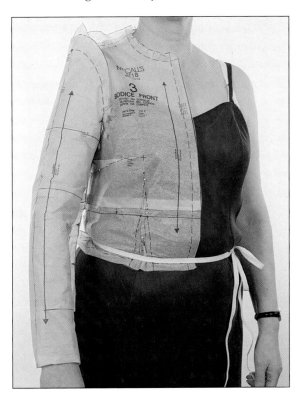

Now Tissue-Fit the Skirt

Slip the skirt front and back under the elastic with center fronts and backs matched to yours. This is a quick way to see if you need more width.

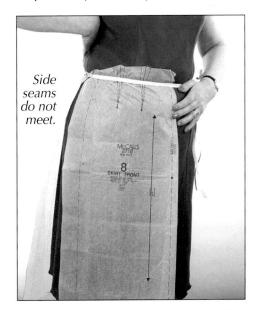

Side seams do not meet.

It is not unusual for hips to be two to four sizes larger than the bodice size. Marta will need to add tissue to the side seam allowances before we can pin it to her shape, since it's easy to see there's not enough tissue at the side seams of her pattern.

Tissue has been added to the sides. The tissue droops below the darts. This is very common if you have a **full tummy**, because your fullness is near the center and you are **hollow** on both sides of the tummy.

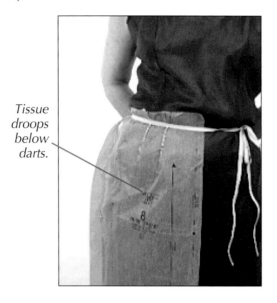

Tissue droops below darts.

We pulled up on the tissue above the darts to eliminate the droop. We also eliminated the darts. If you have a full tummy, generally avoid front darts. Turn the fullness into gathers, ease, or tucks instead. Marta will ease some of the dart fullness into her waistband instead. We also pulled the center front down to allow for more length over the full tummy.

We have pinned the side seam to fit Marta's curve. Since she has a **full**, rounded **high hip**, we let out more in that area than in the waist and normal hip area.

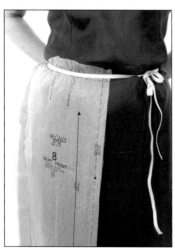

Look at the side seam. It is not perpendicular to the floor. It swings forward and the skirt is longer in the back than in the front.

At the center back, the skirt is not hanging straight. The back tissue is also too full across Marta's **flat derriere**.

Straighten the center back and level the hem by pulling the tissue up at the center back under the elastic.

Remove the fullness from the back with a tuck the full length of the back. Marta does not need the dart closest to the center because she does not curve there, so we tucked right through the dart and eliminated it.

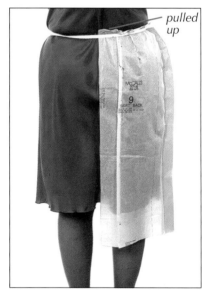

pulled up

We've pulled the pattern down slightly over the "pillow" on her side back, because the fullness caused a need for more length.

She will ease the waist to her waistband above this fuller area.

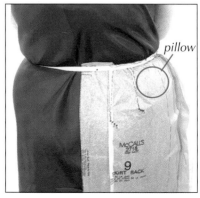

pillow

Because we pulled the tissue up at the center back, the side seam is now straight as well.

Mark the waistline of the skirt below the elastic.

Now Marta knows what she'd need to do to a skirt pattern in a coordinates pattern that fits her top. On page 101 she fits a pattern that she bought using her hip size.

Marta's Body Map

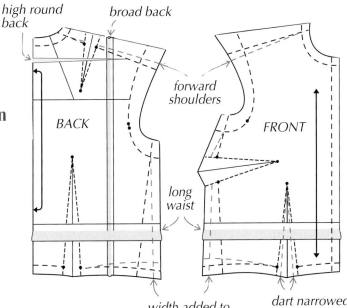

Mark Final Stitching Lines on Pattern

Remove the bodice and skirt. Unpin the pattern and press from the wrong side so you won't touch the tape with the iron.

Mark your new stitching lines with a colored marker so you can see them easily.

Trim seam allowances to an even 5/8″ from the stitching lines. Now you are ready to test your pattern in fabric!

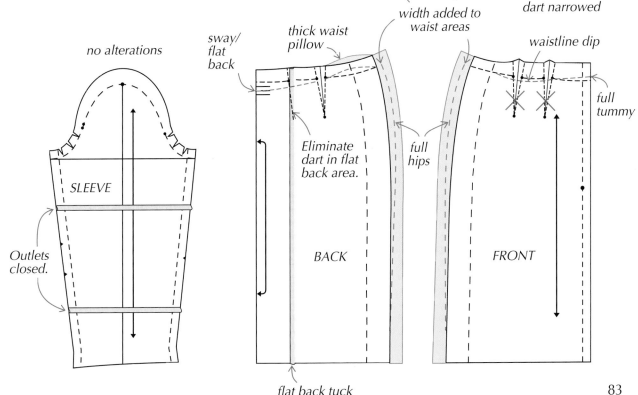

If You Are Full-Busted

If you are full-busted but used a pattern with fronts for various cup sizes, practice altering the B-cup front now. See Chapter 17, "Bust," page 141. It is easy and you'll need to know how to do this in fashion patterns.

Marta altered a B-cup front to fit her C-cup front. Only in very fitted garments will Marta need to do this alteration. If you are a DD, you will need to alter almost every fashion pattern.

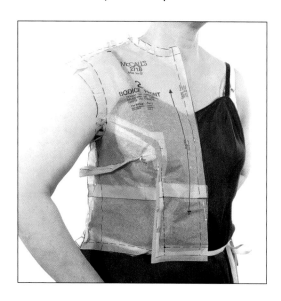

If you are full-busted, it is also very helpful to learn how to turn darts into tucks, gathers and seams as shown on pages 136 and 137.

Test the Altered Pattern in Fabric

You have just fitted the **right** side of your body. Now you need to see if the left side of your body is bigger or smaller than the right.

Fit the Bodice

Fit the Skirt

Gingham Makes It Easy

Quarter-inch gingham is available from Dan River and is carried by most stores.

◆ The built-in grainline makes fitting easier.

◆ The checks make altering easy. After you've adjusted the gingham, just count the checks and you'll know the size of the adjustment you'll need to make on the pattern.

◆ Gingham is lightweight and soft enough to imitate knits. It also acts like a woven fabric because it is one.

Cut and Sew

Step

Straighten gingham before cutting. Fold the fabric lengthwise, matching selvages.

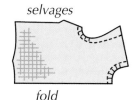
selvages
fold

If ends are not even, straighten the fabric by grasping one short end and the opposite edge. Pull diagonally across the fabric until the ends are even when the fabric is folded lengthwise.

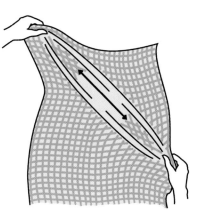

Step

Lay out the fabric. Using a "T"-square or a sheet of paper, check to see that checks are square. The horizontal checks should run along one edge and the vertical along another.

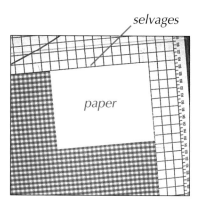
selvages
paper

Step 3

Place your altered pattern on the gingham with grainlines running along lengthwise checks. Cut. Mark darts and seamlines using a tracing wheel and tracing paper.

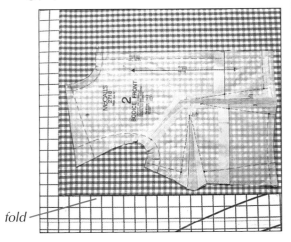

fold

Step 4

Staystitch the bodice front and back on neck and armhole seamlines. Clip curves to stitching.

Staystitch the front and back skirt waistline seam.

Step 5

Machine baste the darts in the bodice and the skirt.

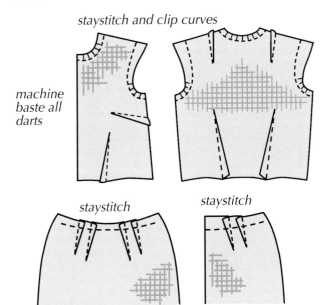

staystitch and clip curves

machine baste all darts

staystitch   *staystitch*

Pin shoulders and side seams with wrong sides together so seams are sticking out from your body. Pin along the seamline where you would sew.

Try On the Gingham Bodice

Does the back look good? It seems to be wide enough for Marta now. As is always necessary in a **broad back** alteration, Marta eased the widened back shoulder seam into the front.

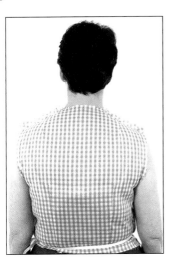

The front fits in the chest and bust areas. The darts are pointing to the bust. The waist is wide enough and the waistline seamline is at her waist.

The shoulders need a little tweaking because her **right shoulder** is **lower** than her left. You can see the drooping wrinkles on the right side where her shoulder slopes.

droop wrinkles

We've pinned a deeper right shoulder seam. The waist seam allowance will be deeper on the right bodice because Marta's **right hip** is **higher**.

Try On the Gingham Sleeve

If you question the sleeve fit, sew it in gingham and slip it on now. Marta's sleeve fit well in the tissue, so we didn't bother to cut it out. We don't feel it is worth your time to **sew** the sleeve into this bodice. Every fashion sleeve is drafted differently to achieve the look intended. The cap height, width, and ease will vary and each style will have to be "tweaked" when you fit-as-you-sew. Also, every fabric will set into the armhole differently.

Try On the Gingham Skirt

We needed to fine-tune the side seams and the waistline. Marta's **right hip** is **higher** and **fuller**. We tissue-fitted the right side, so it is fine, but we also needed to pin a deeper seam on her flatter left side.

Since the left side is less rounded, it didn't need as much vertical length. We pulled up at the waist until the skirt was smooth.

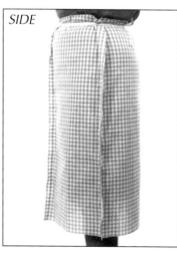

FRONT

SIDE

We eliminated her front darts and will turn them into ease or soft gathers depending on the fabric. If you have a **full tummy**, it is almost impossible to keep front darts from puckering at the points. Ease at the waist is the best alternative.

The side seam hangs straight and the hem is level because, in the tissue, we shortened the center back for her **flat derriere** by lowering the back waistline seam.

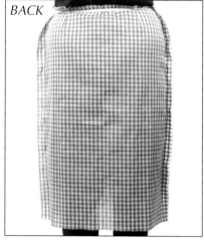

BACK

We moved the back darts out toward the curves at the side seams where Marta is fuller. We also shortened them. They will be sewn as convex curved darts (page 135).

Also notice that we pulled the skirt down over her fullness close to the right side seam. That area needed even more vertical length than we added in tissue.

Fine-tune the length. Use this skirt to determine your most flattering above or below the knee length for a classic straight skirt (see page 183).

After tweaking, we marked her new waist seamline just below the elastic.

For Uneven Hips, Mark Seamlines in Different Colors

Marta will remove the skirt and mark where pins are on the left and right sides. She will then transfer the final stitching lines to her pattern by placing the pattern on the gingham and marking her left side and right side stitching lines in different colors.

She will make side seam allowances an even width from the green line (her largest side) and pin-fit her smaller side while fitting as she sews.

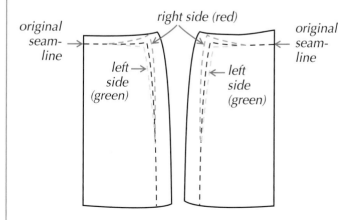

original seamline · right side (red) · original seamline · left side (green) · left side (green)

See page 88 for basic pattern alteration worksheet.

What Do You Do with Your Body Map?

❶ Get to Know It

You have altered the basic dress to fit you. It is the most fitted design you will ever sew.

❷ Don't Trace It

If you trace it onto pattern tracing paper, you won't be able to see the original stitching lines showing how your body varies from a fitted pattern. It's not worth the time unless you plan to design from it.

❸ Hang It

Put it up in your sewing room to remind you how you vary from a fitted pattern.

pattern pinned to folding, fabric-covered foam-core screen

❹ Look at It

When you are analyzing a new fashion pattern, look at your basic to remind you of your alterations. Which ones would most likely be needed in the new design?

NOW, let's have fun and see how this body map will help you fit fashion patterns. Read on!!

Keys to Good Fit in the Most Fitted Styles

First, What Is Good Fit?

Do you know what good fit is? A trip to the mall will prove most people don't. Once you wear clothing that fits, you won't settle for less. The following example is for a fitted basic dress. Fashion changes these standards. Armholes can be larger, shoulders can be broader and more square, and the waist can be higher or lower. However, train your eye by learning how to achieve GREAT FIT on the most fitted of garments.

Shoulder seam - Seam at center of shoulder.

Shoulder width - Armhole seamline is where arm pivots (page 64).

Center front and center back - These meet your center front and back.

Sleeve - At the fullest part of the upper arm, you should have 1½" ease. The sleeve should hang smoothly. The sleeve hem should be just below your wrist bone and the elbow dart or ease should be at your elbow. You can easily see if your upper or lower arm is shorter or longer.

Armhole - Fits smoothly. If the armhole gaps in front, it means your bust is fuller than the pattern; if the armhole gaps in the back, it means you have a rounded back.

Bust - Darts point to bust, but end 1" from the bust point for a B-cup (less for an A-cup and more for a D-cup).

Waist - It should be at waist with a little bit of ease for raising arms.

Grainline - It hangs perpendicular to floor at center back and center front.

Side seams - Centered so seamline is inconspicuous from front and back, with front and back width of skirt similar from side view. Seams should hang straight and perpendicular to the floor. If they are not, you may have a full tummy, flat derriere or slanted waistline, front to back.

Hem - Should be parallel to floor, all the way around.

My Own Body Map Worksheet

Name _____   **Date** _____

Size _____

Cup Size _____

Handy Checklist for Altering Your Basic

Determine Size:

____   Measure high bust and bust and determine size. See page 24.

____   Write size and bra cup size in space at top of this worksheet.

Get Basic Pattern Ready for Tissue-Fitting:

____   Trim around bodice back, front, and sleeve, and skirt front and back.

____   Tape armhole and neckline inside seamline, NOT in seam allowance. Use Scotch® Magic Transparent Tape® to reinforce tissue. Use short pieces around corners and lap ends of tape 1/2″.

____   Snip neck and armhole curves to seamlines, but not through tape.

____   Pin outlets, darts and seams WRONG SIDES TOGETHER with all outlets, darts and seams sticking out. Vertical pins should point DOWN so they don't fall out while fitting.

Tissue-Fit the Bodice First, Then Sleeve, Then Skirt:

____   Tie 1/4″ elastic around your waist. Follow steps in this chapter.

____   Take off tissue to make alterations. Try on again.

____   Take off and mark all new stitching lines. Make all seam allowances an even 5/8″.

TIP: Don't use removable tape to reinforce neck and armholes. It doesn't stick as well as regular tape.

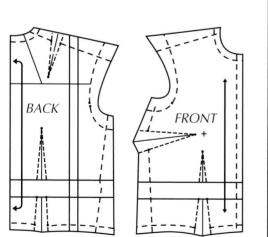
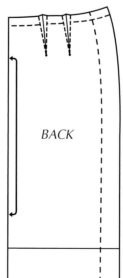
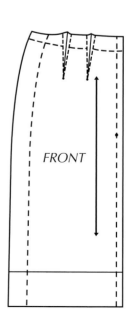
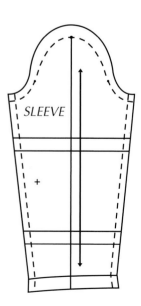

CHAPTER 10

Tissue-Fit & Fit-As-You-Sew

First, Tissue-Fit...

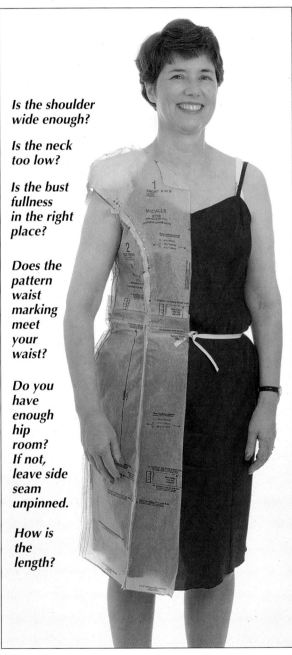

Is the shoulder wide enough?

Is the neck too low?

Is the bust fullness in the right place?

Does the pattern waist marking meet your waist?

Do you have enough hip room? If not, leave side seam unpinned.

How is the length?

Do you need a thicker shoulder pad on one side?

Are the seams pinned to your shape?

If the fabric is heavy, it may cause the bust curve to hang too low.

What length is best?

...then, Fit-As-You-Sew

To make adjusting easier, pin fabric wrong sides together so seams are sticking out. After fitting, mark pin positions and re-pin right sides together.

Why Tissue-Fit?

Tissue-fitting prevents sewing disasters! It helps you determine the amount of ease in the design and visualize the silhouette on your body. Are the proportions good? Is there too much fullness? Would gathers be better than darts?

We have found that if the design doesn't look good in tissue, it won't look any better in a $100-per-yard silk fabric!

Always try on the unaltered tissue FIRST! Then you can see which alterations are needed. Remember, you may not need all the alterations made on your very fitted basic pattern. Follow our tissue preparation instructions on page 112. Pin seamlines wrong sides together with seam allowances sticking out so you can easily make adjustments. Make sure your center front and back match the pattern's. Slip in a shoulder pad if it is required. Fit the sleeve after the bodice is altered to fit.

It's OK to fit close to the body. If you are in doubt, use 1" seam allowances. We have found that **the design generally grows in fabric**. We can confidently say, if your tissue is large enough to go around you, the garment will generally be a little looser. See page 47 for exceptions to this rule.

The Next Step— Fit-As-You-Sew

Trying on the garment after cutting and before sewing, will save you time in the long run. Why can't you just cut and sew from the altered tissue? Fabric has drape, ease, and bias give that tissue doesn't have. Also consider the following:

- **Every fabric fits differently.** Fine-tune by fitting-as-you-sew. For example, in a long dress of a medium-to-heavy weight fabric, bust darts may become too low. The weight of the fabric drags them down.

- **Cutting error.** It is so easy to make cutting errors. Variances of 1/16" can add up.

- **Weight fluctuation.** If you gain or lose a few pounds between cutting and sewing you can fine-tune while fitting-as-you-sew.

- **Sewing error.** If you sew a **trouser-style** pant or skirt, you have four tucks, two darts and two side seams. If you sew each one 1/8" deeper, it would make a total difference of 2". We suggest 2" side seam **allowances** in the waist/high hip area to compensate for errors.

- **Use the art of camouflage.** Pin-fit fabric to your shape, so it "glides" over your lumps and bumps, rather than clinging to them.

Now, Marta Sews a Shirtdress

Our philosophy is to take small steps when you are learning something new. After you make your fitted gingham "body-map," try tissue-fitting **loose-fitting fashion first**. A shirtdress is ideal and we can all use a classic, good-fitting shirtdress! This style requires little tissue preparation other than trimming and pressing.

Follow along with Marta on the next few pages to see the tissue-fitting sequence she followed.

As you gain confidence, try more fitted and more complicated patterns.

For hand-holding help, refer to "Real People," page 186, "Fit Decisions," page 219, "Make It Flattering," page 231, and "Designing and Redesigning," page 245.

Marta's shirtdress is part of the Palmer/Pletsch Fit pattern, McCalls #2718.

The Back Before

Look at the *unaltered* back. The dress doesn't come to Marta's center back across the shoulder blade area. Remember, she has a **broad back**.

The neck seamline isn't coming up to the base of her neck. She has a **high round back**. See page 124 for high round back alteration in a yoke.

The Back After

We have broadened the back, high rounded the yoke, and taken a tuck across the tissue at the center back, tapering to nothing at the side seam. With the tuck, the hem is even and the side seam is straight. See page 128 for how-tos. The extra back width forms a deeper pleat below the yoke.

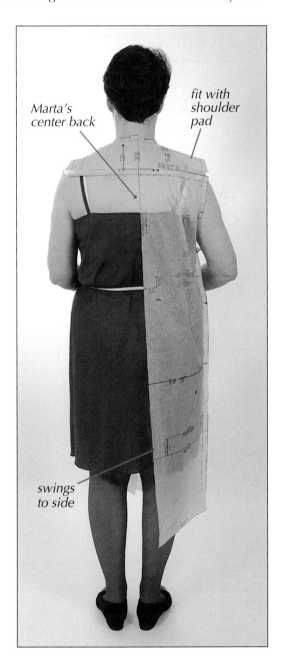

Marta's center back

fit with shoulder pad

swings to side

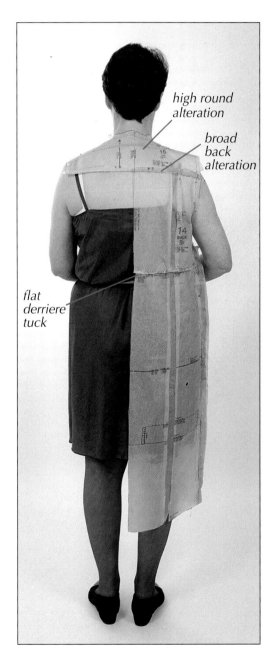

high round alteration

broad back alteration

flat derriere tuck

The center back swings to the side away from her center back. Marta is fairly **flat in the derriere** and doesn't need the length allowed in the pattern to fit over a average, fuller derriere curve.

NOTE: By taking care of back alterations first, it will be easier to fit the front more accurately.

The Front Before

The waist marking is 1/2" above Marta's waist, about the same as in the basic bodice. However, this is a straight dress, so it isn't necessary to lengthen the waistline to match her body proportions. It won't make a difference in the finished dress.

There isn't quite enough ease in the hip area, but the pattern appears to fit well otherwise.

The Front After

Tissue has been added to the front and back side seams, to allow for more ease through the hips. The side seams have then been pinned to fit Marta.

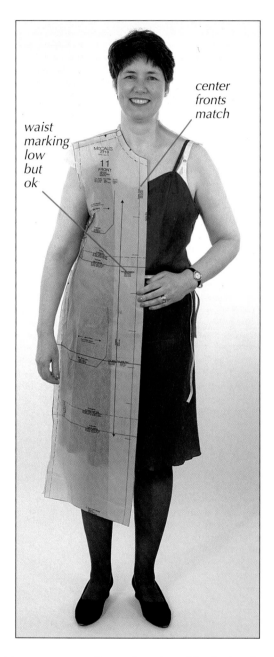

waist marking low but ok

center fronts match

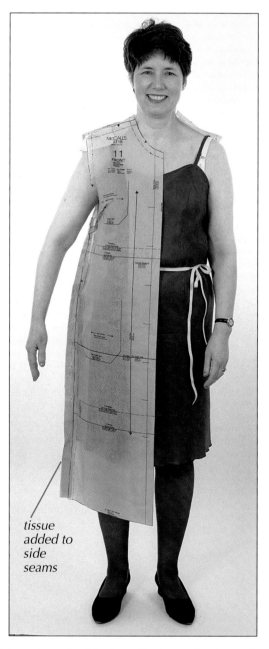

tissue added to side seams

Marta wears a C-cup bra, but this design has plenty of design ease through the bustline so she doesn't need a pattern alteration. If she were a D, she would need to alter the front.

Marta has decided to eliminate the bust dart in this loose dress. See page 146 to learn how to "smoosh" the dart.

The Sleeve

Marta tries on the sleeve to check the width. There is no need to pin the cap to the shoulder, but the underarm seams of the sleeve and dress must match.

Marta pinches 1½" (a total of 3" of ease since there are two layers of tissue in the pinch). This is adequate ease so no sleeve adjustment is necessary.

A Typical Shirt Sleeve Drape

Marta matches the sleeve dot to the shoulder marking on the yoke to see if she likes the look. The "drag lines" you see in the pattern tissue are typical in a shirt sleeve because shirt sleeves have flat caps.

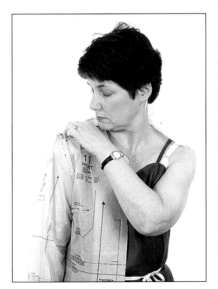

A Shirtdress with Style Makes a Statement

Marta prefers a broader shouldered look to de-emphasize her fuller hips. She has squared and widened the shoulders and added height to the sleeve cap so it fits the larger armhole. Pati squared the shoulder even more on her shirtdress from the same pattern (page 234).

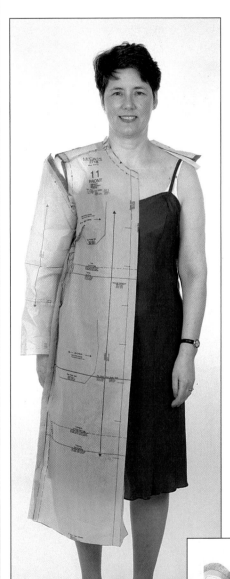

Marta checks the sleeve length without the cuff. If it hits just below the wrist bone, a 2"cuff will create the perfect amount of drape for ease during wear. If the pattern has, or you prefer, wider cuffs, it's best to fit the sleeve with the cuff attached.

Close-up of shoulder:

Now, Fit-As-You-Sew

Marta chose a lightweight wool gabardine for the shirtdress. For the fitting, she pinned the seams in the dress and sleeves with the wrong sides together (just like tissue fitting). Pinning this way makes Marta appear larger than she really is since the seam allowances stick out at her sides. Be aware of this when you pin-fit!

Marta uses one shoulder pad on the left and two on the right to balance her uneven shoulders.

She pins the sleeve in to check length.

Shoulders fit well.

The hips are too full for wool gabardine. She is going to take in 1/2" on each side from the hip to the hem.

After you make all your fine-tuning adjustments, mark new seamlines. Spread open the seam allowances and mark at the pins on the WRONG SIDE of the garment using tailor's chalk or a water-soluble marking pen.

Unpin the seams. Repin them with right sides together and sew along the marked seamlines.

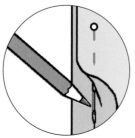

The Finished, Belted Shirtdress

Back width is good.

Shoulders look balanced.

Hem is level.

Side seam is perpendicular to floor.

Quick Tip Marta added elastic to the waist to control fullness. Tie 1/4″ elastic around the waist, adjust ease and mark. Sew a casing on the wrong side of the fabric and insert elastic. The belt will cover the stitching.

Marta Fits a Vest

Fit a vest over what you plan to wear with it.

The Back Before

The center back is not at Marta's center back in her shoulder blade area. The neck seam is a little low. The pattern is also too tight in the hip area and is longer at the center back. Gee—the same adjustments that were needed on her basic bodice AND on her shirtdress!

Marta's center back

swings to side

The Back After

We did a **broad back** alteration, raised the neck seam (**high round adjustment**), added to the side seams for hip width, and took a tuck at center back to nothing at the side seam. The back looks great!

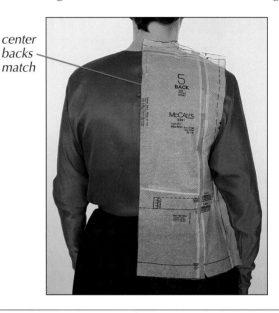

center backs match

The Front Before

There is a gap in the armhole and the center front on the tissue doesn't meet Marta's center front, even after widening the back. She needs to add a dart. The vest is tight in the hip area as well.

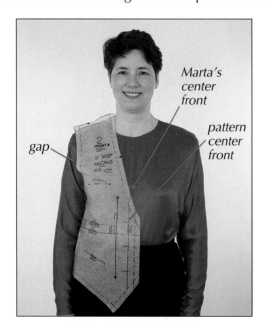

Marta's center front

pattern center front

gap

The Front After

We did a **bust enlargement** (page 142), which added a horizontal bustline dart as well as front waist and hip width. We added additional hip width to the side front and back and did a **forward shoulder** adjustment so the seam is positioned at the center of her shoulder.

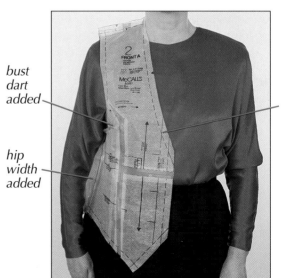

bust dart added

hip width added

center fronts match

Pattern Alterations Front and Back

First do full bust alteration.

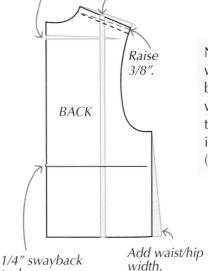

Lower 3/8".

FRONT

Add waist/hip width.

Widen 5/8".

FACING

5/8"

Add the same 5/8" to front facing.

3/8" high round alteration

1/2" in width added for Marta's usual broad back alteration. (See note.)

Raise 3/8".

BACK

1/4" swayback tuck

Add waist/hip width.

> NOTE: A broad back alteration widens the shoulder seam on the back pattern piece. The excess will be eased into the front when the seam is sewn. No adjustment is made on the front pattern piece. (See page 118.)

Eliminating the Dart to Sew a Creative Vest

Marta wants to sew a creative vest. A pattern without darts is easier to embellish. First we transferred the horizontal dart to a vertical dart. Then we removed the width of the vertical dart at the side seam. See dart manipulation, page 136. A very large-busted person may not be able to do this. In that case, a solution would be to transfer the dart to the shoulder, an easier place over which to add creative embellishment.

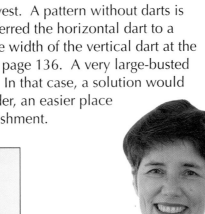

FRONT

Transfer underarm dart to vertical dart.

Then take width off side seam instead of sewing vertical dart.

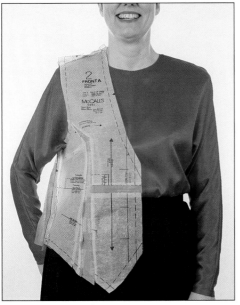

The Finished Vest

Marta Fits a Fitted Jacket

Let's see if the same alterations that were made in the vest are needed in a jacket. Always fit a jacket over a skirt and a blouse (including blouse shoulder pads if desired) similar to the ones you plan to wear with it. Insert the correct jacket shoulder pads.

The Back Before

The neck seam should be a little higher. The back is too narrow in the shoulder blade area. The center back swings to the side and is longer than at the side seam. Again—the same adjustments she needed on previous garments!

The Back After

The neck was raised 3/8" for Marta's **high round back**. The back was spread 1/2" for her **broad back**. This adds hip room as well. We took a horizontal tuck across both back pieces, tapering to nothing at the side seam for her **flatter derriere**.

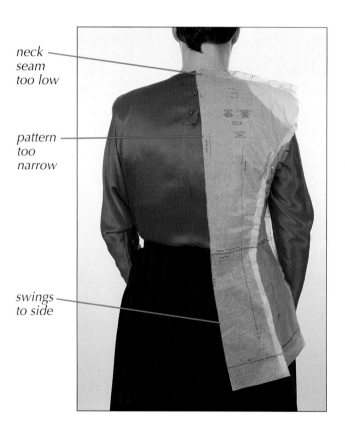

neck seam too low

pattern too narrow

swings to side

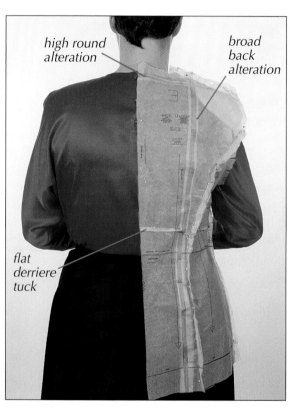

high round alteration

broad back alteration

flat derriere tuck

The Shoulder Before

The seam is not centered on Marta's shoulder. It also is too far back at the neck, but the neck seam will move forward after the **high round back** alteration is made.

too far back

By raising the back neck with the **high round** alteration, the neck seam is now in place, but her shoulder seam still needs to be moved forward.

high round alteration

seam correct at neck

shoulder seam still back too far

The Front Before

The center front marking on the tissue is 3/8″ from Marta's center front (at pin). There isn't enough room through the hipline.

center fronts don't match

The Front After

We let out the side front over the bust and continued to the hem to give tummy room. Then we let out the side seams, tapering from armhole to hem until the jacket fit Marta's hips.

center fronts match

The Shoulder After

We have repositioned the shoulder seam, deepening it on the front and letting out the back, tapering to the normal seamline at the neck.

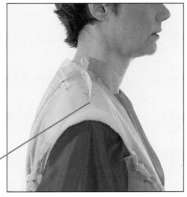

shoulder seam moved forward

The Sleeve

During the first fitting, before altering the jacket, Marta tried on the sleeve tissue with the hem pinned up. She matched the underarm seams and checked length and width. It was fine.

Pattern Alterations

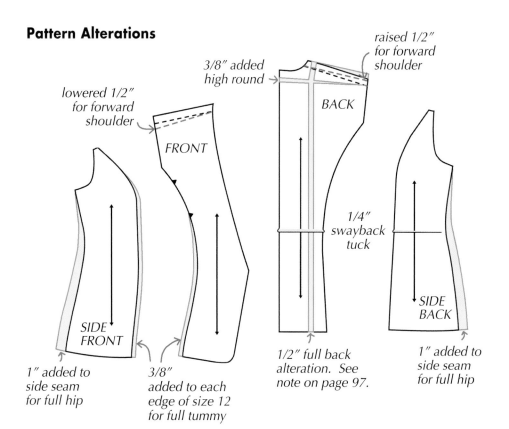

lowered 1/2"
for forward
shoulder

3/8" added
high round →

raised 1/2"
for forward
shoulder

FRONT

BACK

SIDE
FRONT

1/4"
swayback
tuck

SIDE
BACK

1" added to
side seam
for full hip

3/8"
added to each
edge of size 12
for full tummy

1/2" full back
alteration. See
note on page 97.

1" added to
side seam
for full hip

NOTE: It was not necessary to lengthen the front bust seam to match the new side front bust seam because the pattern front had ease in the bust area (between notches). Therefore we simply lessened that ease. See page 148-154 for more information on princess alterations.

Pin-Fitting in Fabric

The front fits well.

There are pulls across the **high hip** area due to fullness (pillows) below the back waist. The right back is fuller than the left.

We let the side back and side seams out until the wrinkles disappeared.

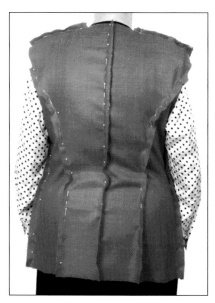

seams let out

Pin-Fit the Sleeve

Pin-baste the sleeves into the armholes (page 241). Then check the following:

1. Is the sleeve hanging straight without wrinkles?

2. Do you like where the armhole seam is on your body? Would you like to move the cap in or out to narrow or widen through the shoulders?

3. Is the length right? Note Marta's right arm falls lower due to her lower right shoulder. Since she added a shoulder pad to the right side, she would normally need to lengthen the right sleeve, but in this jacket we need to shorten the left instead.

Now she's ready to sew in the sleeves.

Before Marta finishes her jacket, she will make the skirt that goes with it. A photo of the finished jacket is on page 104.

Marta Fits a Straight Skirt

Buy the pattern by your fullest hip measurement then make it fit using one of the following options:

Option 1: Measure Your Body

Take body measurements and compare them to your skirt pattern measured in the same places. Measure waist.

Measure tummy about 3″ below waist.

Measure hip at fullest part and the distance from waist to hip.

Measure pattern in the same places as above and make sure you have 1″ ease at the waist, 1″ ease at the tummy, and 2″ ease at the hip. Then, since this is MINIMUM ease, cut a straight skirt with 1″ side seam allowances. We call these "in-case" seam allowances since they are larger, "in case" you need them.

Option 2: Simply Try On the Tissue

Tuck the front and back tissue under your elastic so the **bottom** of the elastic touches the waist seamline marked on the pattern. The center front and back should line up with yours.

After Marta looks at the front, back and sides, she sees the need for exactly the same alterations done on her basic skirt except she bought this skirt by her hip size, so she doesn't need to add tissue to the side seams.

The Front Before

Her **full right hip** is hiking the skirt up so the center front swings away toward the side. The dart points to a hollow area and puckers below her **full tummy**.

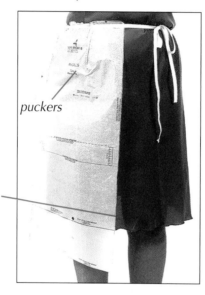

puckers

swings to side

The Front After

She unpinned the dart and will ease this area into the waistband. She pulled up on the waist in the dart area until the puckers disappeared. She also pulled the skirt down a little at the side for her full hip.

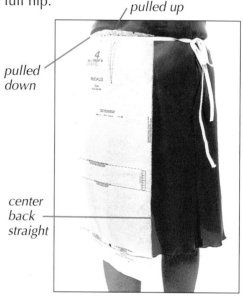

pulled up

pulled down

center back straight

The Back Before

The center back swings to the side because Marta has a **flat derriere** and because of the **full right hip**.

swings to side

The Back After

Marta pulled up at center back and down over the full right hip until the back hung straight. The tuck removes width for her flat derriere. She had to let the side seams out a little bit.

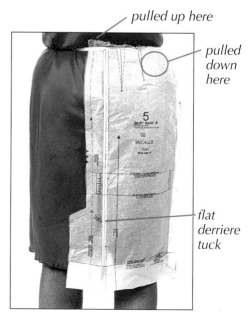

pulled up here

pulled down here

flat derriere tuck

The Side Before

The side seam swings forward at the hem and the back is slightly longer than the front. The side seam needs to come back a little.

The Side After

The side seam is in the middle of her leg and the hem is level. Never level a hem at the bottom unless the skirt is bias. Level at the waist.

Pattern Alterations Front and Back

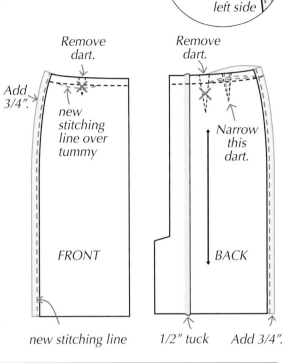

raised back for "fluff"

new right side

new left side

swings forward

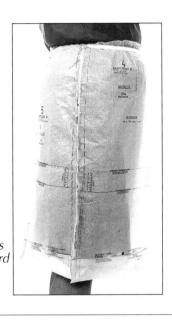

Remove dart.

Add 3/4".

new stitching line over tummy

FRONT

new stitching line

Remove dart.

Narrow this dart.

BACK

1/2" tuck

Add 3/4".

Marta Tries on the Skirt

Marta sewed the zipper into the center back before fitting. Elastic at the waist holds the skirt in place.

The Front

Marta cut the skirt to fit her fuller right side, then pinned the left side seam deeper to fit her smaller side.

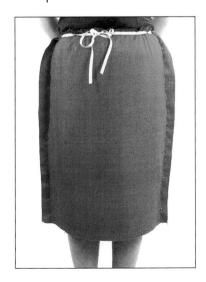

The Back

She's pinned narrow darts on the outside so she can move them if they are not in the correct place.

The Side

The side seam is straight and the hem level.

The seam allowance flips forward but the seam itself is straight.

The waistband is pinned on and the hem pinned up. Marta wants to sew both side seams 1/8" deeper for a closer fit.

She puts a pin where she will taper back to the normal seam.

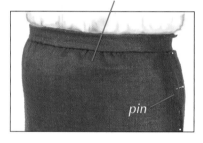

The waistband has been lowered on the left side to eliminate the bubble you see above. Voila! A beautifully fitted skirt!

Marta Models Her Finished Suit

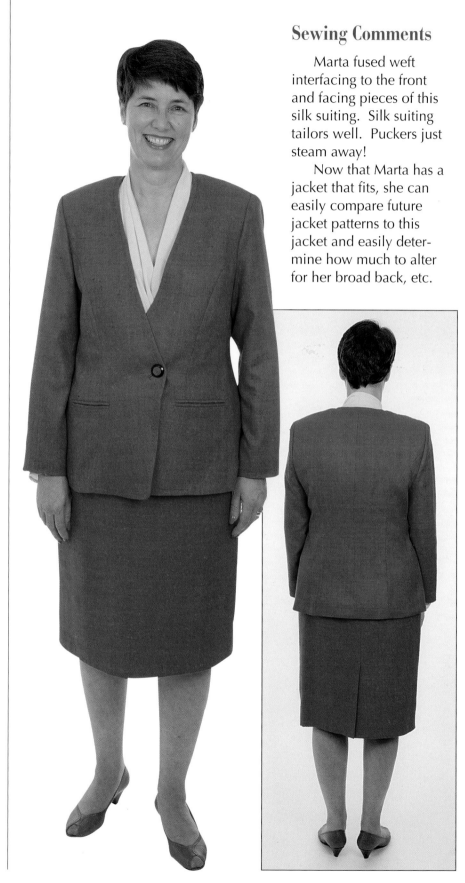

Sewing Comments

Marta fused weft interfacing to the front and facing pieces of this silk suiting. Silk suiting tailors well. Puckers just steam away!

Now that Marta has a jacket that fits, she can easily compare future jacket patterns to this jacket and easily determine how much to alter for her broad back, etc.

Your Fashion Fitting and Sewing Checklist

Tissue-Fitting

___ Trim around main pattern pieces such as front, back, yoke and sleeve.

___ Pin pattern pieces with **wrong sides together**.

___ Use shoulder pads if required.

___ Fit, alter, refit, finalize alterations.

___ If pattern has a sleeve, pin sleeve to garment at underarm. Fit, alter, refit, then finalize alterations.

NOTE: If a shirt sleeve seamline hits just below wrist bone without the cuff, it will be just right with a 2″ cuff.

Cutting and Marking

___ Cut out fashion fabric.

___ Transfer pattern markings by snipping, chalk marking, tracing with a wheel, tailor basting or using a water-soluble pen to mark where you've pin-marked.

Some Sewing Is Always Necessary Before Fitting

___ Staystitch if fabric is extremely ravelly or stretchy or is to be handled a lot.

___ Apply zipper in center front or back, since fitting is done at the side seams. (Side zippers are more difficult because side seams are usually curved.)

___ Machine-baste darts right sides together or pin-baste them on the outside.

Fit-As-You-Sew

___ Pin-baste main sections with **wrong sides together** and try on. Use shoulder pads if required. Adjust width, length and darts. See page 244.

___ After permanently sewing main seams, baste in sleeve and try on.

___ Stitch in sleeves.

___ Try on again to mark sleeve and bottom hems.

Fit Principles Summarized

Also see page 114, "The Ten Steps to Perfect Fit."

1. **The bigger the bump, the more length and width it needs and the deeper the darts must be.**

2. **Wrinkles point to the problem.**

3. **Hems should be parallel to the floor all the way around.**

4. **Leveling is done from where the garment hangs on the body, such as at the shoulder or the waist.**

5. **Pin to fit YOUR shape at the side seams.**

6. **Use the "T" principle. Crosswise grainline at bust and hips should be parallel to the floor and lengthwise grainline should be perpendicular to the floor (except in bias-cut garments).**

NOTE: Some people like to "preserve" a pattern by fusing an interfacing to it. We don't do that because it is no longer transparent (for plaids) and it makes some marking methods more difficult (page 238).

Permission is granted to photocopy this page for personal or teaching use only.

CHAPTER 11

Two Ways to Alter Patterns

All alteration methods fall into two categories:

 Cut into the tissue by...

altering where it is needed and filling in with tissue,

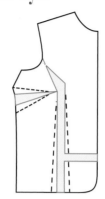

OR

moving seam allowances and filling in with tissue.

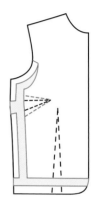

 Add to outside edges by...

adding tissue AND tissue fitting,

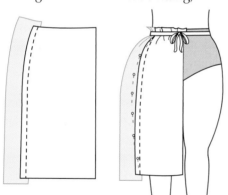

OR

if you know the amount, alter as you cut using pivot OR slide.

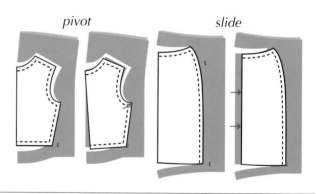

pivot　　　*slide*

We don't use any one method exclusively. We decide which is the easiest for us and the pattern style. For example, each of the following accomplish the same end result. Which would be easiest for you?

Three ways to add height to the sleeve cap:

Slide or add tissue to outside edge.

Slash and spread.

Move seam allowance.

Now that we are exclusively tissue-fitting, we let our students do what is easiest and most visual. See "Real People," Chapter 21, for what they have chosen. Also, whenever you cut into tissue, do it with extreme neatness and accuracy. See our tips in Chapter 12.

Professional Alteration Tips and Tools

Accuracy, Accuracy, Accuracy

As teachers doing hands-on classes, we've seen it all. But the one thing that impresses us most is the need to be accurate. Otherwise, mistakes multiply. Here is how to avoid them.

Get the Pattern Ready

 Trim Around the Tissue Just OUTSIDE the Black Line

(Read about "the cutting line" on page 114.)

Trim around the tissue first to improve your accuracy when cutting fabric. It keeps the tissue from moving during the cutting process. Also, if using a multi-sized pattern, pre-trimming on the correct cutting lines helps prevent mistakes.

Quick Tips for Trimming Patterns

◆ If using paper scissors, don't use small ones. Use scissors with long blades.

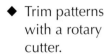

◆ Trim patterns with a rotary cutter.

❷ Press the Tissue

Do not tissue-fit or cut using wrinkled tissue!! Press it with a DRY IRON set at the wool setting. A "warm" iron isn't hot enough.

Steam and water drips spoil the pattern tissue. Empty water from the iron if dripping is a problem.

❸ Fit the Tissue

The first fitting is to see what alterations you will need.

❹ Unpin the Tissue and Press Again

Recently, a student tried to do a bust alteration with the front and back still pinned together. It's simply impossible. So, after your first tissue-fitting, **unpin**, then press your tissue.

Collect Your Tools

1 Work on a Gridded Cardboard Surface

You need a large work surface. No part of your tissue should hang off the surface while altering. The surface must be pinnable. Cardboard is the easiest surface on which to work.

Buy a gridded folding cardboard cutting board or a gridded cardboard cutting table. The grid makes altering easier.

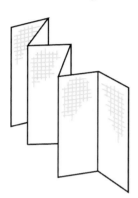

To protect the board when marking tissue patterns with marking pens, place plain newsprint or scrap paper under the pattern. In our classes we have students use a lead pencil only. They can later mark *final* alterations with a colored pen.

2 Pattern Alteration Tissue

As long as you are "*tissue*-fitting," alter with *tissue*! Heavy paper or non-woven fabrics overpower the lightweight tissue.

You can find brightly-colored tissue in a gift-wrap department or in an art supply store, or try Perfect Pattern Paper from McCall's, developed by Pati Palmer at the suggestion of her students. It's the same weight tissue used in McCall's patterns so it is not overpowering. Since it's white, you can tell it from the pattern tissue. It has a handy 1/8", 1/4", 1/2" and 1" grid printed on it, making alterations easy and accurate.

Perfect Pattern Paper Uses

◆ Add the same amount to several pattern pieces, following the grid.

Perfect Pattern Paper

108

◆ If a pattern is printed on paper too heavy to tissue-fit, trace pieces onto Perfect Pattern Paper.

Sandra tissue-fits a Kwik Sew pattern traced onto Perfect Pattern Paper.

◆ Make a body graph (page 62). The grid makes body variations such as one low shoulder very obvious and eliminates measuring during your body analysis (page 69).

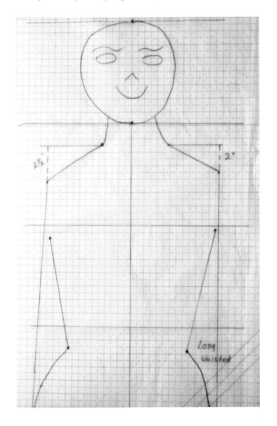

PRO Tip Start a new habit. Alter with pattern pieces RIGHT SIDE up. Put alteration tissue UNDER the pattern. Tape pattern to alteration tissue from the RIGHT SIDE of the pattern. **Always put tape on the right side of the tissue only.** Then always press the WRONG side of the tissue only, so the iron won't directly touch the tape. Make this a habit! Neatness and consistency will prove to be your friends.

See page 111 for more tape tips.

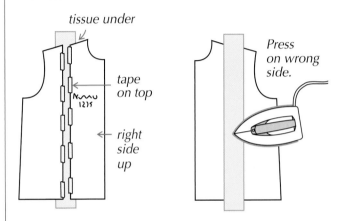

tissue under

tape on top

right side up

Press on wrong side.

3 Rulers

These two great plastic rulers both have 1/8" and 1" grids. One is 2" wide and the other is 6" wide. The wider one can be used as a "square." Perfect Pattern Paper also acts as a ruler.

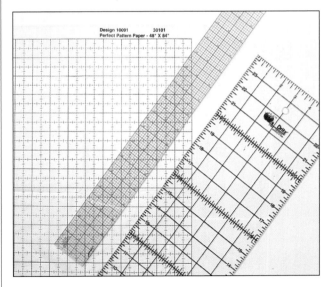

If you do a lot of altering, you may also want a yard- or meter-stick for extending lines the full length of a pattern. Or, use Perfect Pattern Paper instead.

French Curves

How is a French curve used? In designing, it is used to create curved shapes. In sewing, it is used to alter a curved shape.

For example:

Broad Shoulders:

Match curve to the pattern's armhole.

Pivot out when redrawing armhole.

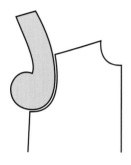

Square Shoulders:

Redraw shoulder seams, then match the curve to the pattern's underarm.

Slide up for redrawing the underarm.

French curves often don't match a curve on your pattern exactly. The solution? Use the built-in French curves on your pattern.

Cut all areas that aren't changed, then pivot or slide the tissue, making your changes.

For example, to get this result for a square shoulder alteration, follow the steps in the next column.

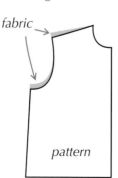

fabric

pattern

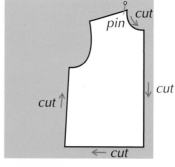

1. Cut through the fabric around the bodice except at the armhole and shoulder.

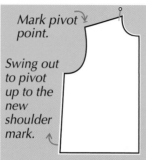

Mark pivot point.

Swing out to pivot up to the new shoulder mark.

2. Mark new shoulder line. Pivot pattern to move the shoulder cutting line up to the mark.

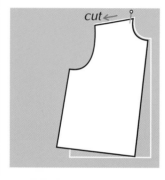

3. Cut the new shoulder.

Slide up to here.

4. Pivot pattern piece back to original position, then slide underarm up the same amount.

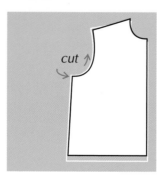

cut

5. Finish cutting the side seam. Cut the new armhole.

See **Mother Pletsch's Painless Sewing** for more practical uses of pivot and slide.

5 Tape

Do not use
clear cellophane
tape! Use Scotch® Magic® Transparent Tape®,
the translucent one. It won't scrunch the tissue or
buckle under the iron as easily as clear tape does.
Or, try surgical tape which also won't buckle under
an iron (available from Nancy's Notions as Sewer's
Fix-it Tape).

Removable tape is excellent for testing an
alteration. It easily lifts off without tearing the
tissue. However, it doesn't stick very well, so you
won't want to use it in areas where there is stress
or for final alterations.

If you need to remove regular
tape, slit the tape at the lapping
point and gently tear it.

pull up

slit tape

 Quick Tip Free up one hand by putting your
tape in a weighted tape dispenser.
You can buy one for about $3.00 at some
office supply stores. However, we prefer the
heavier ones.

6 Pencil

We used to use a red, plastic-tip pen to mark
alterations on the pattern, but it penetrates the
tissue and makes a mess of your cutting board.
We now recommend using a pencil.

7 Pins

Invest in 1⅜" extra fine (.5mm) glass head
(won't melt) pins. Dritz, Collins, and Clotilde offer
wonderful, quality pins.

*Use 1⅜" (.5mm)
extra fine, glass
head pins.*

*Don't use quilting
pins. They can be
painful in tissue-fitting.
They also make a big
hole in the tissue and
fall out easily.*

These pins are made from steel so you can use
your magnetic pin cushion to pick them up.

8 Mirrors

For accurate tissue-fitting you shouldn't twist
or bend to see your alterations. If you have a
three-way mirror, great, but it's not necessary. All
you need is a full-length mirror and a hand-held
rear-view mirror.

It is interesting to watch some people trying to
use a rear-view, hand-held mirror. They put it
everywhere except over their shoulders trying to
see the back. One even held it behind her, facing
the full length mirror. Therefore, silly as it sounds,
in our classes we give a mirror lesson!

Prepare for Tissue-Fitting

To find out which alterations are necessary, you need to **try on the unaltered tissue first!**

1. Press tissue with a dry iron set at the wool setting.

2. In fitted garments, strengthen the tissue by taping the neckline and armhole curves, just inside the seamline.

   With tissue right side up, tape neckline and armhole. Lap short pieces of tape 1/2" around the curves.

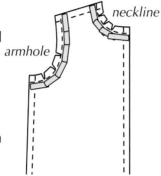

3. In curved areas, clip through the seam allowance up to, but not through the tape.

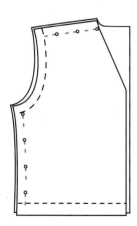

4. Tug lightly on tissue to see if it is taped securely.

See page 148 for how-tos on preparing princess-style patterns.

Pin Tissues Together

Point pins down. (They won't fall out!)

No pins in waistline seams (OUCH!).

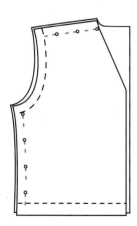
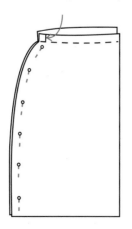

Don't pin the bodice to the skirt if your pattern has a waistline seam. Fit each separately.

Be Accurate!

Pin, Pin, Pin

Are we starting to sound like grade school teachers? Trust us. We've seen too many pattern messes!

When you pin into a pattern, point pins toward the center of the pattern so your pattern can't move.

Wrong - *tissue can move*

Right - *tissue can't move*

1. Place alteration tissue **under** the area to be altered. Anchor the parts of the pattern that won't be moved when making the desired alteration.

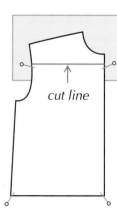

cut line

2. Anchor the alteration tissue.

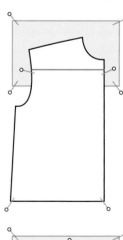

3. Alter and anchor the parts you have moved.

4. **Now**, tape in place and trim away excess tissue.

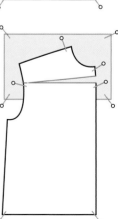

Do not tape as you go. Tape **only** after all pieces are pinned and lying totally flat.

112

More Alteration Tips

Alter Up to Stitching Line Only

If you cut to the edge of the pattern, the seamline will change in length.

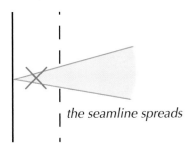

the seamline spreads

Instead, cut UP TO the seamline.

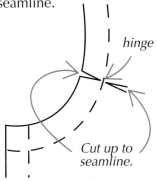

hinge

Cut up to seamline.

The seamline is then the same size after altering.

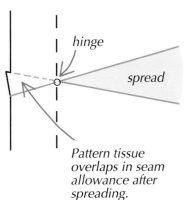

hinge

spread

Pattern tissue overlaps in seam allowance after spreading.

True the Lines

When you make a tuck across a pattern and the edges are not parallel, you will need to "true" the lines.

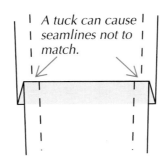

A tuck can cause seamlines not to match.

As a general rule, mark the midpoint between the two lines. Then draw from one stitching line to the next through the midpoint. Do this for the cutting line as well.

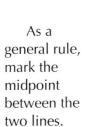

midpoint

OR in some cases, connect the two ends when redrawing the seamline and the cutting line for the same results.

new cutting line

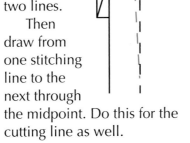

new seamline

To true princess bust seamlines, see page 149.

Blend Lines

For example, if you are adding to side seams, GRADUALLY blend the new cutting line into the old.
Don't do it too abruptly.

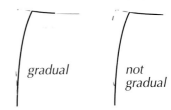

gradual   *not gradual*

Press Tissue After Tissue-Fitting

Do not use wrinkled tissue to cut out a garment! Remember to press tissue from the wrong side and avoid tape as much as possible.

Mark Final Seamlines

Mark the waist seamline at the bottom edge of the elastic while tissue is on your body. Use a red plastic-tip pen.

original seamline

Remove the pattern and mark pin positions in the rest of the seams. Use a red plastic-tip pen, which will penetrate both layers of tissue at the same time.
Front and back side seams must be identically marked. Always mark them pinned together with cut edges matching! You can also trim to even seam allowances at this time.

The Cutting Line

Should you cut inside or outside the black cutting line?

 On most patterns, from the stitching line to the black cutting line is 5/8". The width of the cutting line is 1/32"- 1/16", depending on the pattern brand.

Sewing machine companies commonly mark metric measurements on the throat plates and pattern companies use inches for seam allowance widths. The 5/8" seam allowance is slightly more than 1.5cm.

To make things even more complicated, each machine is different. Pati's machine has a left and a center needle position, but the markings are for the left position.

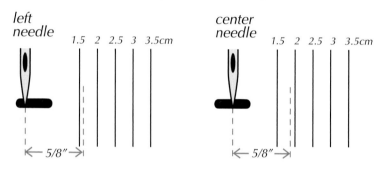

The answer? Cut where you want to but be consistent. If you like seeing the black line, fine. (We do!) Place a wide piece of masking tape on the bed of your machine. Put your trimmed pattern on your machine and lower the needle into the stitching line. Mark a line on masking tape at the pattern edge. Now you can sew exactly on the stitching line.

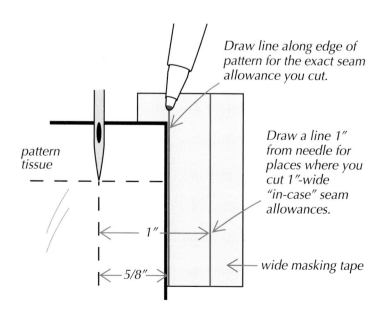

Draw line along edge of pattern for the exact seam allowance you cut.

pattern tissue

Draw a line 1" from needle for places where you cut 1"-wide "in-case" seam allowances.

wide masking tape

The Ten Steps to Perfect Fit

1. **Trim and press the tissue.**

2. **Tape neck and armhole if close fitting.**

3. **Pin tissue WRONG SIDES together for fitting.**

4. **Try on and determine alterations.**

5. **Unpin, press, and alter, using pencil, ruler, pins, tape, and alteration tissue.**

6. **Pin together again.**

7. **Try on. Check fit using two mirrors (full-length and hand-held).**

8. **Unpin, press and mark any additional alterations.**

9. **Pin tissue to your fabric.**

10. **Cut out the pieces.**

Remember these steps. Make a copy and tape it to your cutting table. Go slow. Have fun. Be accurate. You'll be well rewarded.

CHAPTER 13

Length & Width

Tissue-fitting shows you instantly if a change is needed in length or width. In a bodice, after you make sure the back width is fine, get the waist length right and then work on bust, waist and hip widths. In a skirt, we generally adjust the width, then find the best hem length.

LENGTH

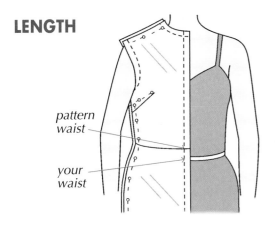

pattern waist

your waist

WIDTH

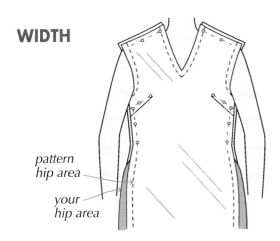

pattern hip area

your hip area

Lengthen and Shorten Tips

◆ If you did a body graph (page 62), you gained insight about your proportions, but, remember, the patterns are designed for a height of 5'5"-5'6". If you are 5'2" and very long-waisted in proportion to your height, the pattern waist length may be fine. It won't be, however, if your waist length is proportionately average or less than average for your height.

◆ The larger the size, the longer the waist length will be. Marta used to sew with a size 8 and needed to lengthen the waist about an inch. She now sews with a 12 and only needs to lengthen it 1/2".

◆ Make the same lengthening or shortening changes in all places that match horizontally. If you shorten the armhole, for example, you must do it to the front and the back, and to the sleeve.

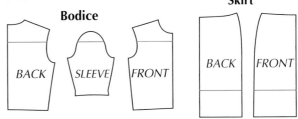

Bodice

BACK   SLEEVE   FRONT

Skirt

BACK   FRONT

◆ To avoid altering the sleeve cap height on flatter, shirtsleeve styles, tuck or spread the sleeve *vertically* to fit the front and back armholes.

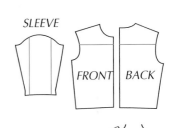

SLEEVE

FRONT   BACK

◆ If pockets are in the wrong place, mark the new position on the tissue (or move them, page 238).

new pocket marks

◆ Add length to straight-cut garments at the bottom edge unless there is a detail like a vent.

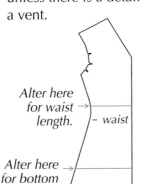

Alter here for waist length.

– waist

Alter here for bottom length.

◆ Alter shaped garments exactly where you need more or less length.

115

◆ Many people who are tall or short are average in body length. It's just their leg length that varies. For example:

Short Person   **True Petite Person**

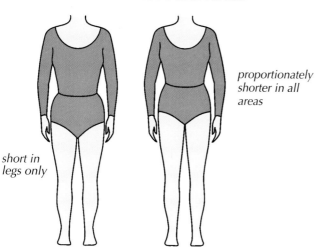

short in legs only

proportionately shorter in all areas

◆ Use the slide method to change length on an A-line pattern piece. Cut all the edges except the hem.

Then slide the pattern to the length you want and finish cutting across the bottom edge.

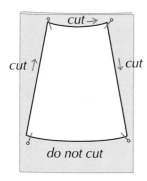

cut →
cut ↑
↓ cut
do not cut

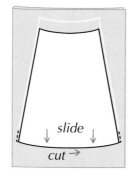

↓ slide ↓
cut →

◆ When you lengthen or shorten a diagonal line you will need to true the seam. See page 113.

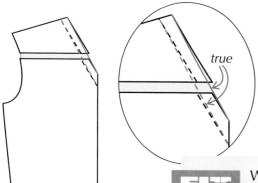

true

Width Tips

◆ Add the **same** amount to the side seams of the front and back pattern pieces.

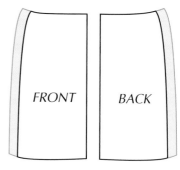

FRONT   BACK

See Chapter 20 for more on fitting skirts.

◆ Change width only where you need it in fitted shapes **or** add the same amount from the fullest point to the hem.

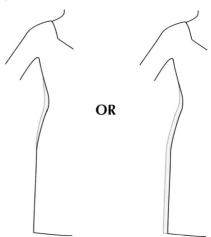

OR

◆ Where there are many seams, you can add a little to each rather than all to one seam for a more balanced fit.

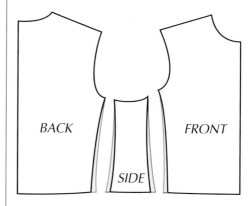

BACK   FRONT

SIDE

See "Real People," Chapter 21, for more examples of length and width changes.

FIT Tip   When pin-fitting, pin the same curves in the side seams of your garment that you have in your body. If you don't have any curves then you'll need to straighten the side seams.

CHAPTER 14

The Back

Broad Back—Three Clues

1 One clue to a broad back is tightness in the front of the upper sleeves when you **reach forward**. This is because there isn't enough ease in back for reaching room.

2 Another clue is the position of the back armhole seam.

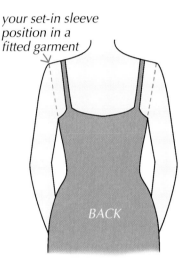

your set-in sleeve position in a fitted garment

BACK

Try on the bodice tissue of the basic pattern and pull the center back to match yours. Fold back the armhole seam allowance. Does the folded edge of the pattern reach your armhole seam position? (You will need a helper to check this.)

seam allowance turned back on basic fit bodice

center back

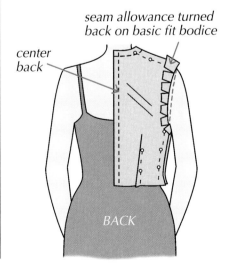

BACK

3 Another clue is wrinkles.

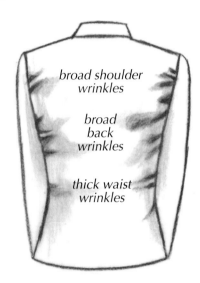

broad shoulder wrinkles

broad back wrinkles

thick waist wrinkles

Don't confuse broad shoulders with broad back (page 162).

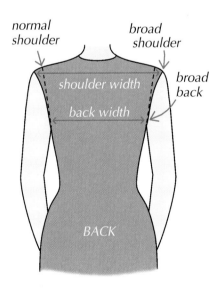

normal shoulder   *broad shoulder*

shoulder width   *broad back*

back width

BACK

Broad Back—Three Alteration Methods

Method 1

If you are only very slightly broad through the back:
Redraw the armhole so you get a little more width. You can widen the center of the back armhole about 1/4" on each side, gaining 1/2" across the back.

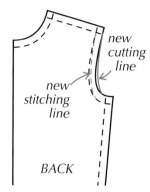

new cutting line

new stitching line

BACK

Method 2

If you are quite broad, cut and spread the entire back:
This is what we usually do as most of our students are also a bit rounded in the shoulders and thicker in the waist. We normally spread 1/4"-3/4".

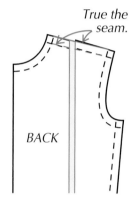

True the seam.

BACK

Method 3

If you are broad only in the upper back:
Cut and spread as shown in the illustration.

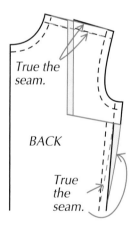

True the seam.

BACK

True the seam.

Make the Shoulders Fit

In methods 2 and 3, the back shoulder will not match the front shoulder length. Do one of the following:

◆ Since the shoulder seam is somewhat bias, you can ease the excess into the front shoulder when you stitch the shoulder seam. Since many people with a broad back are also rounded, the extra back shoulder ease improves the fit.

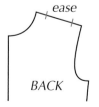

ease

BACK

◆ The other option is to add a dart, or deepen an existing back shoulder dart.

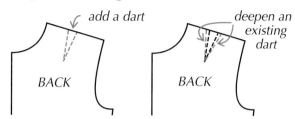

add a dart

deepen an existing dart

BACK   *BACK*

Breaking the Rules for Back Comfort

One rule is **"never add to the center back because the neck will get larger."** However, you can add to the center back and keep the original neck size by sewing pleats, tucks, or gathers to control the excess fullness.

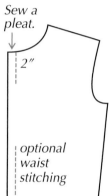

Add here.

BACK

Sew a pleat.

2"

optional waist stitching

Make a box pleat, an inverted pleat, or a knife pleat:

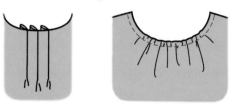

Or try several tucks or gathers:

These are excellent choices for people who have to reach a lot, as when driving a car.

Broad Back Alterations in Other Styles

Raglan
Kimono

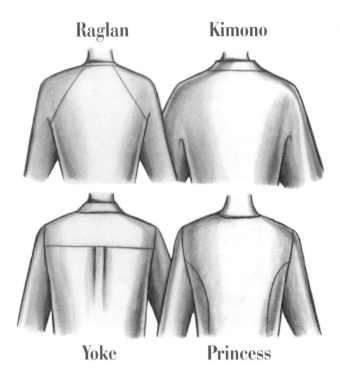

Yoke
Princess

Yoke

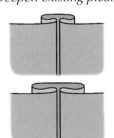

fold

← 1/2"-1"

center back

BACK

Place the back pattern piece on the fabric with the center back 1/2"-1" from the fold to add from 1"-2" ease across back.

Add a pleat or deepen existing pleats until the back matches the yoke edge.

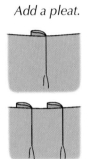

Add a pleat.   *Deepen existing pleat.*

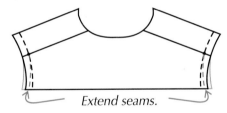

If you prefer, you can gather the edge to match the yoke edge. Most yokes stop above the shoulder blades. If the yoke is deeper, you may need a little width in the shoulder blade area. Let out the armhole seam as shown and pin the back to fit, adjusting tucks or gathers.

Extend seams.

Raglan

Ease excess into sleeve.

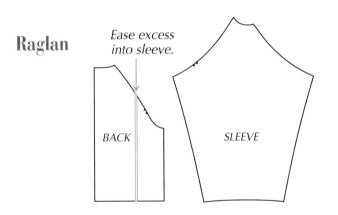

BACK

SLEEVE

Cut-On (Kimono)

Dart or ease excess to fit front shoulder.

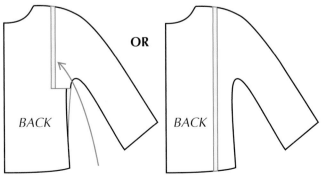

OR

BACK

BACK

Spread sleeve section to avoid adding hip fullness.

Spread this way for added hip fullness as well.

Shoulder Princess

Let out the seam only where you need more room.

Armhole Princess

Adjust the same as you would a one-piece back. Ease or dart out excess back shoulder fullness to fit the front.

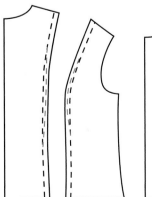

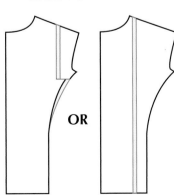

OR

Narrow Back—Two Clues

1 You have **vertical wrinkles in the back of your garment**. If the garment is full across the back, first check to see if you are using the right size. Many of our full-busted students buy a size too large, making the back too big. It would be better to buy the smaller size for a better back fit and then alter the bust to fit.

2 **The back armhole seam goes out into your arm** when you try on the basic bodice. Measure from the seamline to where it should be to determine the amount you will need to alter.

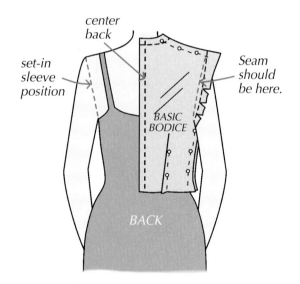

set-in sleeve position

center back

BASIC BODICE

Seam should be here.

BACK

Don't confuse narrow shoulders with a narrow back. See page 162.

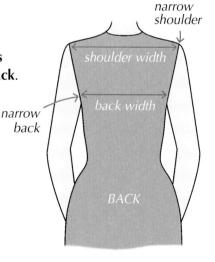

narrow shoulder

shoulder width

back width

narrow back

BACK

Most people are narrow only in the upper back. Cut and lap the pattern tissue as shown. Then true the side seam (page 113).

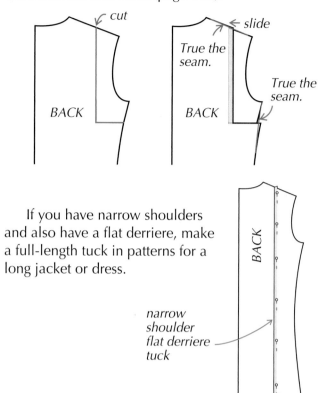

cut

BACK

slide

True the seam.

BACK

True the seam.

If you have narrow shoulders and also have a flat derriere, make a full-length tuck in patterns for a long jacket or dress.

BACK

narrow shoulder flat derriere tuck

Make the Shoulders Fit

Narrow the back shoulder darts or reduce back shoulder ease until the adjusted back fits the front.

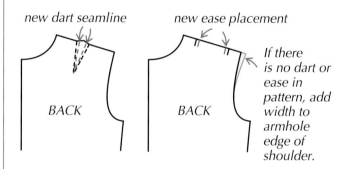

new dart seamline

BACK

new ease placement

BACK

If there is no dart or ease in pattern, add width to armhole edge of shoulder.

What About Too Much Center Back Curve?

We have fit jacket patterns with too much curve in the upper center back. If you find this in your pattern, it does not necessarily mean you are narrow. To remove the excess, simply pin-fit it out.

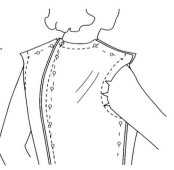

Narrow Back Alterations in Other Styles

Raglan

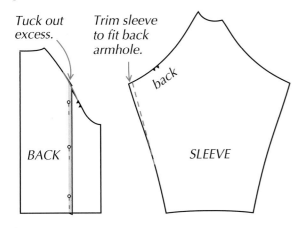

Tuck out excess.

Trim sleeve to fit back armhole.

back

BACK

SLEEVE

Cut-On (Kimono)

A narrow back generally won't show in this loose style. If you do feel you need an adjustment, try this to narrow the back without changing the shoulder width.

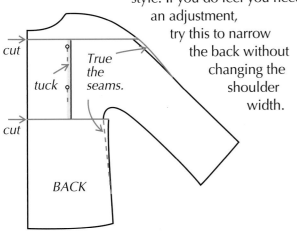

cut

True the seams.

tuck

cut

BACK

Yoke

Designs with back pleats or gathers:

If you are narrow, reduce or eliminate the fullness. Place the pattern center back over the edge of the fold.

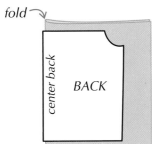

fold

center back

BACK

Pin the back to the yoke, pinning in pleats or gathering as needed to fit. This makes the back less full.

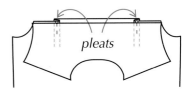

pleats

Generally, the yoke doesn't need narrowing because the back width is usually in the shoulder blade area below the yoke. If the yoke seam is below the shoulder blades, take in the armhole seam as shown here and pin the back to fit, adjusting tucks or gathers.

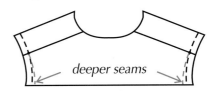

deeper seams

Yoke designs with no pleats or gathers:

Tuck the back, and narrow the armhole seam allowance in the lower back yoke.

center back

BACK

center back

YOKE

Narrow here.

Shoulder Princess

Adjust the seam where needed. If you are narrow just in the shoulder blade area, shoulder width is not affected.

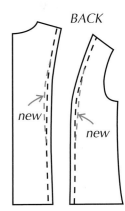

BACK

new

new

Armhole Princess

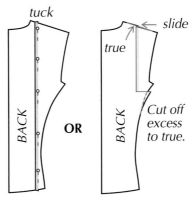

tuck

slide

true

BACK

OR

BACK

Cut off excess to true.

Remember to adjust ease or the size of the dart in the back shoulder to fit the front shoulder.

Prominent Shoulder Blades

The bigger the body bumps, the deeper the darts need to be—front and back. In the extreme case of a fitted bodice, do the following:

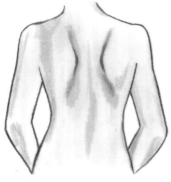

First widen the entire back...then deepen the darts.

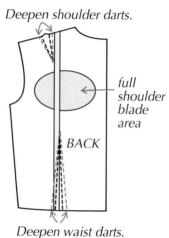

widen

Deepen shoulder darts.

BACK

full shoulder blade area

BACK

Deepen waist darts.

Some thin people have very high prominent shoulder blades.

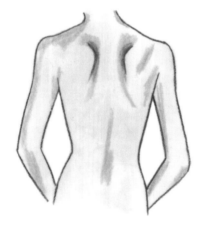

Widen the back shoulder and add or increase the shoulder dart or ease. This gives room for the bump *and* camouflages it.

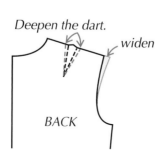

Deepen the dart.

widen

BACK

Round Back

There are different types of round backs requiring different pattern adjustments:

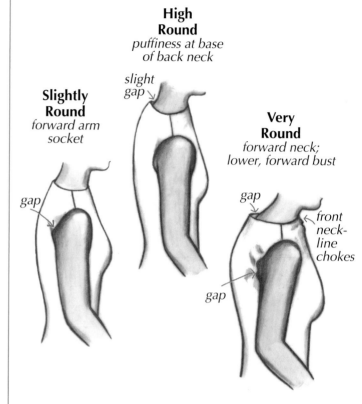

High Round
puffiness at base of back neck

slight gap

Slightly Round
forward arm socket

gap

Very Round
forward neck; lower, forward bust

gap

front neck-line chokes

gap

Slightly Round Back

The clue is that you have a small gap in the back armhole.

Add or deepen the back shoulder dart and the gap goes away.

Widen the back shoulder to match the front.

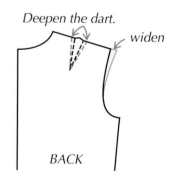

Deepen the dart.

widen

BACK

High Round Back

This is the computer-generation alteration. With so much close work, our shoulders move forward and our upper back gets rounded. A clue is that blouses or jackets want to ride to the back, making the front neckline too tight. Also, the back neck seam doesn't reach to the top of your neckbone and may stand slightly away from your neck.

You need to move the neck/shoulder seam into the proper position so your garment front will fit correctly. This is why we tell you to fit the back first.

About 1" below the neckline seam, draw a line across the back pattern from the center back to the armhole or shoulder seamline. Cut to the seamline from the center back and cut to the seamline in the seam allowance for a "hinge." Below are examples with two different shoulder slopes.

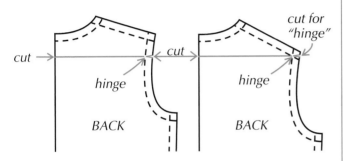

NOTE: The exact position of the line will also vary depending on the pattern's design. For example, if the neckline seamline is 1/2" lower than the normal neckline, draw the line 1/2" below the seamline. If the seamline is 1" to 4" below the normal neckline, draw the line directly on the seamline. A high round adjustment cannot be made in a design with a very low back.

Raise the upper section at the center back. (The amount is generally only 1/4"–3/8".) Fill in with tissue.

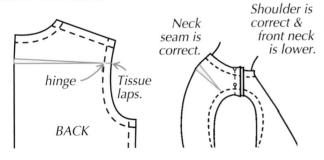

The center back is now slightly curved at top. There are three options for handling the curve:

◆ If you place the center back along the fold when cutting out and ignore the curve, the neck will be slightly larger (usually 1/16"–1/8"). Ease the extra fullness into the collar or facing.

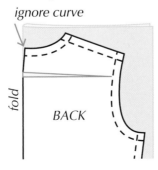

◆ **OR** add a center back seam so you can maintain the curve. If you have to lift the upper back section more than 3/8", this is a good choice.

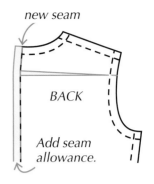

◆ **OR** add a neck dart. Slash the pattern as shown to spread for the dart. Straighten the center back edge. When you stitch the neckline dart, the upper curve returns in order to fit your body.

Straighten center back by slashing and adding a dart.

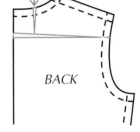

High Round Back in Other Styles

Raglan

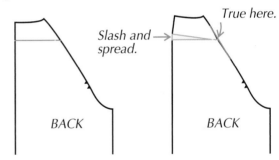

NOTE: We haven't found it necessary to alter the sleeve as well in the raglan styles we've used.

Cut-On (Kimono)

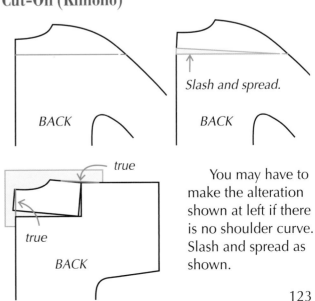

You may have to make the alteration shown at left if there is no shoulder curve. Slash and spread as shown.

123

Yoke

To alter a yoke for the high round back, draw a horizontal line 1" below the neck seam and a vertical line from that line to the neck at center back. Cut on those lines to seamlines. Cut seam allowances to seamlines, forming "hinges."

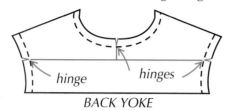

hinge   *hinges*

BACK YOKE

Raise the neckline at center back and add tissue.

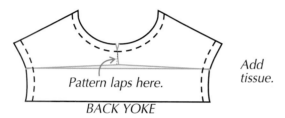

Pattern laps here.   *Add tissue.*

BACK YOKE

NOTE: This applies to any garment without a center back seam.

Very Round Back

This used to be called the dowager's hump. Let's just call it a *very round back!*

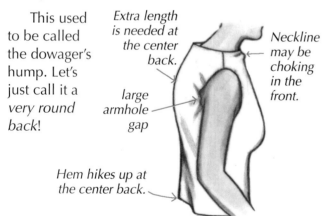

Extra length is needed at the center back.

large armhole gap

Neckline may be choking in the front.

Hem hikes up at the center back.

Practice this alteration using our basic fit pattern for McCall's because it has a horizontal line printed on the back in the area where you need to alter. On other patterns, draw a line about 6" below the base of the neck or at the center of the place where your back is most round.

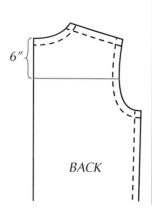

6"

BACK

You'll need a friend to help with this! Pin the front to the back and try on the tissue.

1. Pull the tissue down at center back until the **horizontal** line is straight. (You may need to unpin the shoulder seam.)

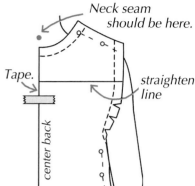

Neck seam should be here.

Tape.

straighten line

center back

2. Tape the tissue to your skin.

3. Slash the tissue from the center back to the armhole seamline. Raise the upper back tissue to the correct neckline position.

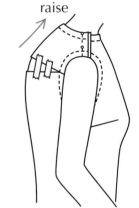

raise

4. Tape across the opening to preserve the adjustment for the next step.

5. Remove the pattern. Unpin. Place on top of alteration tissue. Add more tape to secure alteration tissue. Trim away the excess alteration tissue.

Trim away excess tissue.

BACK

NOTE: In some cases it may be necessary to slash at the middle of the round back and again at the high round to get enough length over the back.

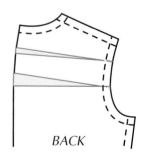

BACK

See Olga, pages 206-207.

Three Ways to Handle the New Center Back Curve

Since the center back pattern edge is no longer straight, you have three options:

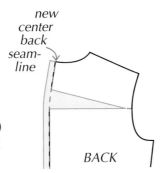

new center back seamline

BACK

 Add a center back seam allowance (if there isn't one already) so you can sew it to fit your back curve. This is our preference.

OR

 Add a neck dart if your fullness is more toward the center back. Draw a line from the neck edge to the upper horizontal line. Slash and spread to straighten the back edge. A neckline dart is created.

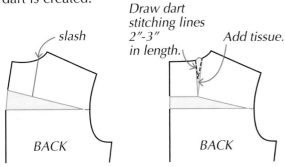

slash

Draw dart stitching lines 2″-3″ in length.

Add tissue.

BACK

BACK

OR

 Add a shoulder dart if your roundness is more toward the shoulder blades. Draw a line from the shoulder edge to the horizontal line. Slash and spread to create the dart and straighten the back edge.

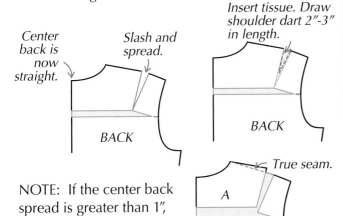

Center back is now straight.

Slash and spread.

Insert tissue. Draw shoulder dart 2″-3″ in length.

BACK

BACK

True seam.

A

BACK

NOTE: If the center back spread is greater than 1″, you may have to disconnect section "A" to get the center back straight.

Very Round Back in Other Styles

Raglan

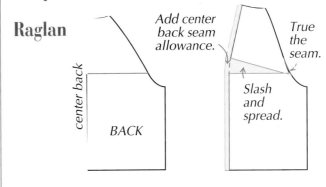

Add center back seam allowance.

True the seam.

center back

BACK

Slash and spread.

Cut-On (Kimono)

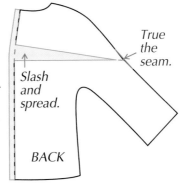

Add center back seam allowance.

Slash and spread.

True the seam.

BACK

Yoke

Add length at the center back, tapering to nothing at the side seams on the yoke and lower back pattern pieces. The seam will appear straight when on the body. Avoid plaids.

YOKE BACK

BACK

Shoulder Princess

Lap pieces and proceed as for a one-piece back.

Armhole Princess

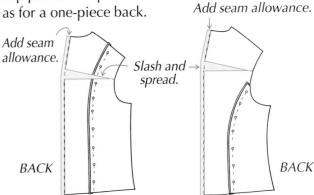

Add seam allowance.

Add seam allowance.

Slash and spread.

BACK

BACK

Forward Head

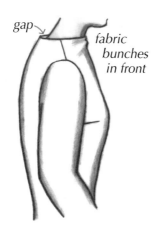

gap

fabric bunches in front

This often is seen with a very round back (page 124). The back is long and the upper chest is shorter than usual.

Cut and lengthen the back. Make the spread even across the back. Tuck the front the same amount.

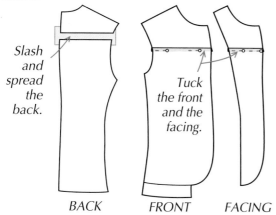

Slash and spread the back.

Tuck the front and the facing.

BACK   FRONT   FACING

Set in the sleeve matching shoulder dot with shoulder seam. Underarm seams technically won't match unless you put less ease in back and a little more in the front of the sleeve. See page 172.

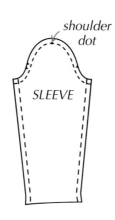

shoulder dot

SLEEVE

We did the following for one of our students. It worked like a charm. She needed a high round adjustment, which adds only at the **center** back, but she was short in the upper chest so we took an **even** tuck across the chest. See Karin on pages 209-210.

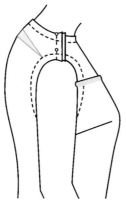

Straight/Erect/Sway or Flat Back

We are lumping these alterations together as they each require less length at the center back.

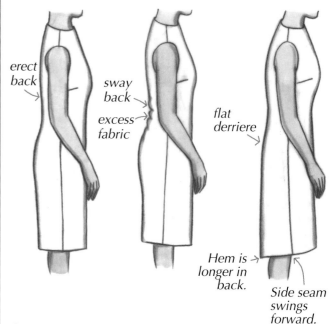

erect back

sway back

excess fabric

flat derriere

Hem is longer in back.

Side seam swings forward.

Solutions

One-Piece Dresses

Take one or more horizontal dart-tucks at the center back of the tissue, tapering to nothing at the side seam.

The tuck can be high or low, depending on where you see the fullness. Usually it falls between the underarm and the waist. Take it where it feels right. If you have an erect upper back and a flat derriere, one tuck may be too deep. Make two tucks instead.

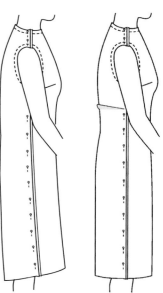

NOTE: Marta has been known to sew a horizontal waistline dart tuck in ready-made, one-piece dresses and hide it with a belt—a great quick fix.

Dresses with Waistline Seams

Tissue fit the top first and dart-tuck the center back of the tissue if necessary until the waistline seam is at the bottom edge of the elastic.

Then fit the skirt tissue. Pull up at the center back until the hem is level. Mark the new waistline seam at the bottom edge of the elastic.

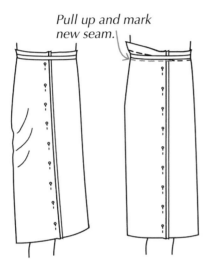

Pull up and mark new seam.

Now you have your correct waistline seam marked on both the bodice and the skirt.

Skirts

Follow the same procedure as for the skirt of a dress pattern with a waistline seam.

Straighten Back Grainline

The horizontal dart-tuck will distort the grainline on the pattern. To straighten, connect the arrow points with a new vertical line.

If the garment has a center back seam, it will be slightly curved. We'd recommend straightening it, then deepening it when you stitch if you desire.

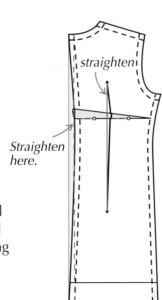

straighten

Straighten here.

If there is no center back seam, place the center back at the top and bottom on the fold of the fabric. The waist area won't touch; don't worry. The extra added width is minor and won't affect the overall fit.

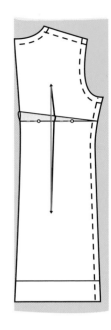

NOTE: It isn't necessary to do this alteration on a blouse that will be tucked in, unless you will occasionally wear the blouse out. However, it "feels" better when the alteration has been done.

The Size of the Tuck Can Vary with Fashion from One Pattern to Another

Generally, if you take a 1/4" tuck in a bodice, you may need a deeper tuck in a full-length dress pattern. Always try on the unaltered tissue first. Pinch out a tuck until the garment hem is level.

Confusion Guaranteed!

This person has a high round back AND an erect or straight back.

We lengthened the upper back and shortened the lower back with a dart-tuck, tapering to nothing at the side seam.

If the amounts of the spread and the tuck were equal, your body would measure the same as the pattern, yet your garment wouldn't fit. That is why using measurements doesn't always work.

Straight/Erect/Sway or Flat Back Alterations in Other Styles

Princess Styles

It is difficult to pin in the tuck across the back and center back pieces while the tissue is on your body. First, determine the amount of tuck required by pinching a horizontal tuck at the center back until the hem is even.

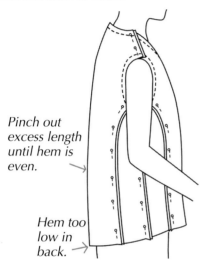

Pinch out excess length until hem is even.

Hem too low in back.

Now you will need to remove the excess tissue with a dart-tuck all the way through the back and the side back, tapering to nothing at the side seams.

Lap the back over the side back seam allowances, matching the stitching lines. You can then easily draw two lines tapering from your pin marks to nothing at the side seams.

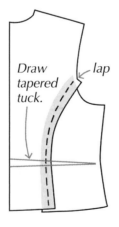

Draw tapered tuck.   *lap*

Separate the pattern pieces. Then bring the lines together in each piece, forming a tuck. Tape in place.

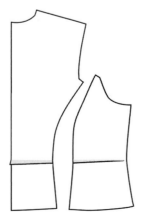

Make dart-tuck on both pattern pieces using lines drawn.

A One-Piece Back

Occasionally a pattern is designed with a one-piece back such as this recent Palmer/Pletsch pattern for McCall's for a tunic with an asymmetrical hem.

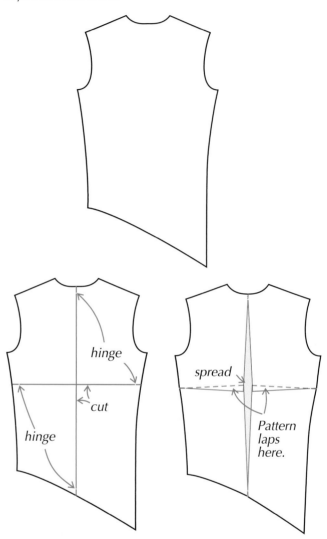

hinge

cut

hinge

spread

Pattern laps here.

If you also need a high round back alteration, see "Yoke" on page 124 for how-to's.

CHAPTER 15

The Neck & Chest

It's important to know that neck and chest areas can affect each other. For example a V-neckline falls in the chest area, so your chest affects its fit.

Neck Adjustments

Changing the size of the neck opening is easy to do when tissue-fitting. **Evaluate neck fit AFTER you've altered for round back** as neck position will change.

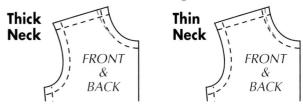

before · *after* — *neckline too high* / *neckline now lower*

Thick Neck

A deeper seam allows more neck room.

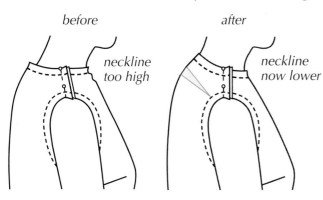

original stitching line

new stitching line

FRONT & BACK

Thin Neck

A narrower seam makes neck opening smaller.

new

original

FRONT & BACK

Make the same change on the facing.

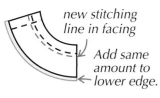

new stitching line in facing

Add same amount to lower edge.

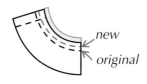

new

original

NOTE: On some styles the change is needed only at the sides of neck, not along the entire neckline.

Thick Neck

FRONT & BACK

Thin Neck

FRONT & BACK

Collar

Measure the new neckline with the **tape measure standing on its edge**. Double this measurement for the entire collar edge.

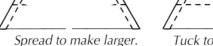

Start at center back.

BACK

Double this measurement for the entire collar edge.

Lap shoulder seam.

FRONT

fold

Make the collar neckline edge the same size by spreading or tucking to match the garment seamline measurement.

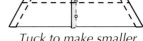

Spread to make larger. · *Tuck to make smaller.*

Uneven Neck

Sew a basic pattern in muslin. Staystitch the neckline at 5/8". Clip as necessary to make the neck fit comfortably. Mark the new seamline at the bottom of the clips.

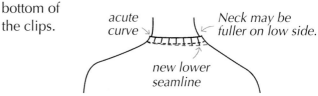

acute curve

Neck may be fuller on low side.

new lower seamline

Neck Base is Low in Front

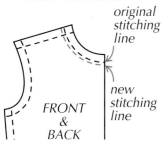

FRONT

new

If the back feels fine, but the front feels like it is choking you, simply lower the front neckline. Also see "Forward Head," page 126, and "Round Back", pages 122-124.

Muscular Neck

If the muscles in the neck are well developed or thicker, you may also need to adjust the shoulder seam at the neck base.

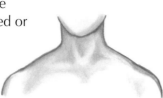

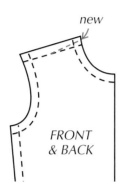

new

FRONT & BACK

Facing

new

Collar

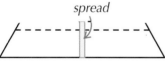

spread

Measure neckline seam of altered pattern with tape standing on its edge (see page 129) and measure collar neckline seam. Spread the center back neckline of the collar the amount you need to add.

Short Neck

collar too tall

Long Neck

collar too short

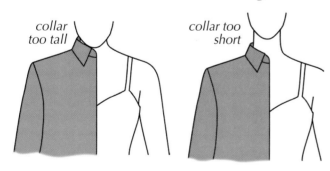

Tuck collar and band to remove width.

Spread collar and band to add width.

tuck

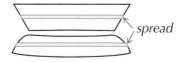

spread

It's OK to Redesign a Neckline

Square, bateau, V-neck, U-neck, button-up or convertible shirt collars are all fashion styles. Personal preference joins fit in the alteration process.

First, try on the tissue pattern. Decide what changes you'd like to make. How much do you want to raise or lower, widen or narrow the existing neckline?

A wide, deep "V" will just fall off of the shoulders if they are extremely sloping. Narrow and raise the neckline by adding tissue.

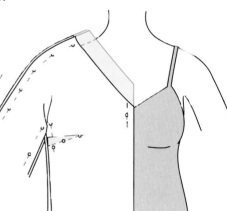

The following examples show other possibilities:

Too Wide

Add tissue.

Too High

Remove tissue.

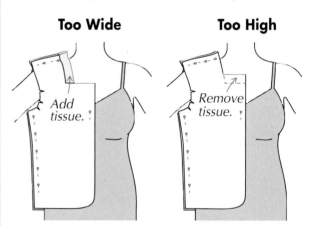

Too Wide & High

Add tissue.

Remove tissue.

Too Wide & Low

Add tissue.

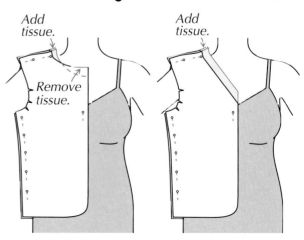

Too High

Too Low

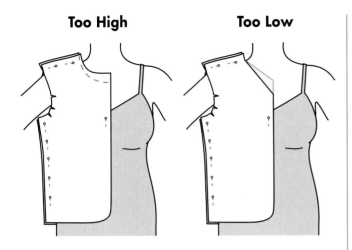

Don't forget that the finished neckline will be lower, because you will use up a seam allowance when you add the facing or collar! Therefore, **after determining the new neckline position, add a seam allowance.**

Make the same neckline adjustments on the facing.

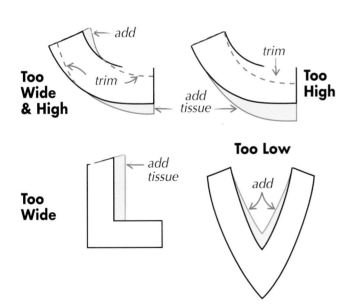

Too Wide & High

← add

trim

Too High

add tissue →

trim

Too Wide

add tissue

Too Low

add

OR
Use the new neckline to draft a facing pattern. Trace the neckline cutting edge and then measure 2″ from the edge to draw the facing cutting line.

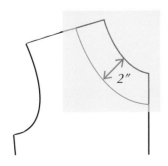

2″

Chest

Gaping Necklines

Many gaping necklines are caused when a full-busted person buys a pattern that is too large. It is better to choose the size using the high bust measurement and adjust for the fuller bust.

Hollow Chest
You may have what is called a *"hollow chest."* It curves in and is often accompanied by forward shoulders.

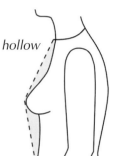

hollow

Remove extra length with a dart-tuck. Generally, no more than 1/4″ (1/8″ tuck) at widest point is necessary.

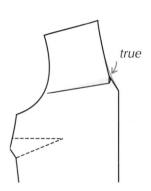

true

For maximum accuracy, redraw the neck and armhole as necessary to its original position.

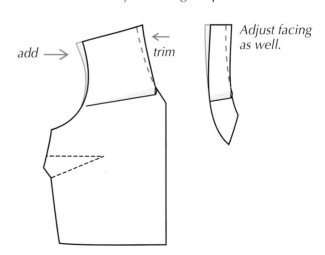

add →

← trim

Adjust facing as well.

NOTE: See page 244 for filling in a hollow chest area with padding. This works very well in jackets.

Gaping Neckline Alterations in Other Styles

True seams as necessary.

Shoulder Princess

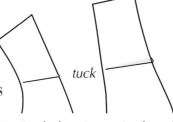
tuck

NOTE: Armhole princess is altered the same as the fitted front (page 131).

Raglan

tuck

FRONT

Cut-On (Kimono)

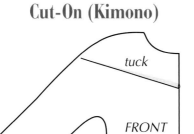
tuck

FRONT

"Gaposis" of the Roll Line on Jackets

To eliminate the excess fabric that is commonly seen along the lapel edge, making it gap or pull away from the body, simply ease the roll line to twill tape cut slightly shorter than the roll line.

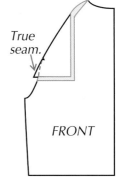
gaps

If it gaps a large amount, shorten the roll line by taking a dart-tuck in the pattern, tapering to nothing at the armhole. (Be sure to make this change on interfacing and facing pieces, too.) This does not change the position of the roll line. It still begins and ends at the same points but hugs the body better in the finished garment.

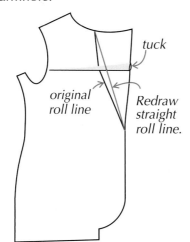
tuck
original roll line
Redraw straight roll line

Rounded Chest

This has been called "barrel" and "pigeon" chest.

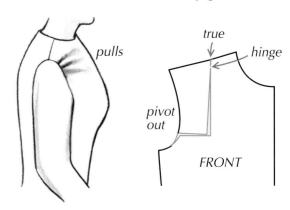
pulls

true
hinge
pivot out

FRONT

Shoulder Princess   ### Armhole Princess

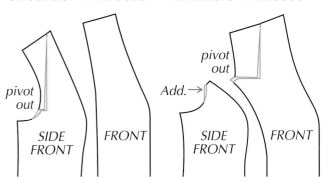

pivot out

SIDE FRONT   *FRONT*

pivot out
Add.→

SIDE FRONT   *FRONT*

Raglan

True seam.

FRONT

Since the raglan front doesn't go up to the shoulders, it needs widening in the armhole seam area that is at chest level. Cut out a section and move it out. Ease the excess length into the sleeve.

Yoke

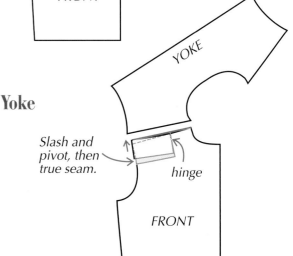

YOKE

Slash and pivot, then true seam.

hinge

FRONT

CHAPTER 16
Darts

There were few darts in the fashions of the '80s and early '90s. However, when fashion cycles back to a closer fit, darts reappear. They may even become design details! We've recently seen darts stitched on the outside of the garment, then pressed and topstitched in place. Interesting!

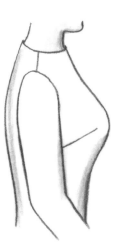

We also saw an Ann Klein vest with three bust darts. The lowest one extended to the center back, creating a seam for the look of a back band.

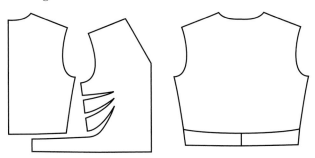

The most common darts are either horizontal or vertical. In very fitted bodices you find both.

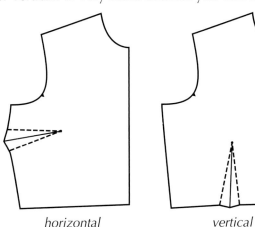

horizontal   *vertical*

Bust Dart Rules

1

Darts should point to the bust but stop about 1″ from the point (apex) on most figures. The fuller busted you are, the further from the bust point your dart should be.

Think of a circle drawn around your bust point. It would be larger if you are full-busted. If you are **very small-busted**, a dart may come to within 1/2″ of your bust point. If you are **full-busted** it can stop 1″-3″ from the apex.

2 **Multiple Darts**

If there are two darts coming from two different seams, the dart with the greater angle should end closer to the bust point.

*In **Couture, The Art of Fine Sewing**, Roberta Carr discusses interesting designs with more than one dart.*

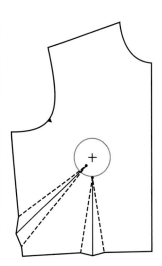

133

To Raise or Lower a Dart

You may need to raise, lower, shorten or lengthen darts until they point to the bust point (apex). Pin the pattern pieces together, then:

Try on the tissue and **mark your bust point (X)** gently with a soft tip pen.

NOTE: Remember that patterns are designed for a 20-year-old with a B-cup bust. As we mature, we generally get fuller and lower.

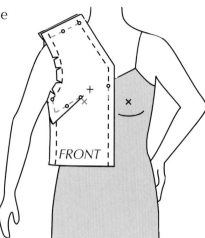

FRONT

To raise the dart, raise the point and redraw the stitching lines.

To lower the dart, drop the point and redraw the stitching lines.

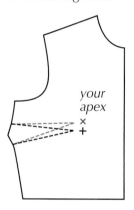

your apex

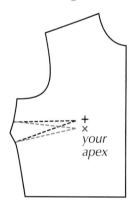

your apex

OR

1. Draw a box around the dart and cut out the box.

2. Move the dart, keeping the cut edges parallel, until the dart points to your apex.

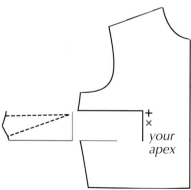

your apex

Fill with tissue.

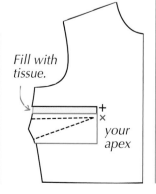

your apex

Shorten or Lengthen Darts

To Shorten

To Lengthen

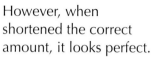

Sometimes a dart that is too long seems too high.

However, when shortened the correct amount, it looks perfect.

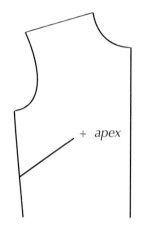

+ apex

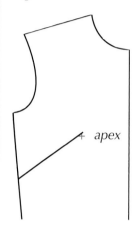

+ apex

French Darts

French darts are slanted and can begin above or below the waist.

Some French darts are curved as shown for body shaping. Draw a curved dart with a French curve.

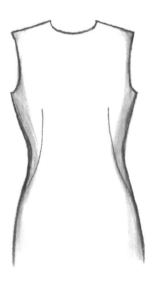

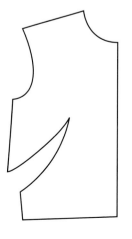

Make a sample from fabric cut on the same grain as the pattern and see if you like it before you cut the garment out of expensive fabric.

Shaped Darts

Dart stitching is traditionally straight from seam edge to the point, and yet your body is probably curved, not straight.

Dart shapes should match your body shape. People with small waists but full in the high hip need short curved darts to avoid puckers.

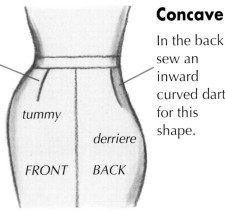

Convex

In the front, sew an outward curved dart for the cushion below the waist.

Concave

In the back sew an inward curved dart for this shape.

tummy

derriere

FRONT *BACK*

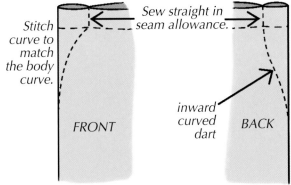

Stitch curve to match the body curve.

Sew straight in seam allowance.

FRONT

inward curved dart

BACK

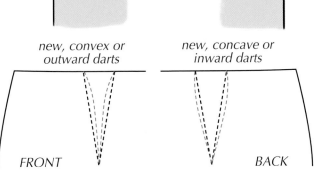

new, convex or outward darts

new, concave or inward darts

FRONT

BACK

For more on marking, sewing and pressing perfect darts, see Chapter 24, "Sewing Techniques that Affect Fit," beginning on page 235.

Darts in Plaids and Stripes

If a vertical dart is off-grain, plaids and stripes won't match after the dart is stitched.

Draw a box around the tissue dart and cut it out.

Shift the box until the dart is vertically straight. Tape the box in place.

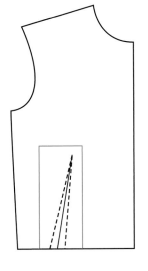

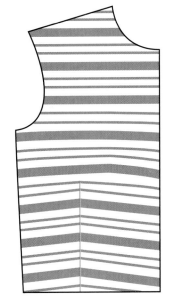

Now the dart will chevron when stitched.

Learn to Move Darts

You too can be a designer in the simplest of all drafting techniques—moving and changing darts. Darts can come from anywhere as long as they point to the bust point (apex).

Moving darts is like magic! Knowing how to move darts is wonderful, particularly if you are full busted! Practice on old patterns by altering and tissue-fitting to see the results.

How to Move a Dart

If you want to move a dart that is already on the pattern tissue, **extend the existing dart lines to the apex**.

Practice Moving Darts

One evening of practice will change your life by giving you the skill and confidence to do this! Make copies of the bodice front below (enlarge if you wish) and start designing.

1. Cut out the horizontal dart, **which has already been extended to the apex**.

2. Cut on any other line coming from the apex and close the horizontal dart. A new dart opens up.

3. Add tissue and draw in new stitching lines.

1.

apex

2.

apex

Draw lines to extend the dart to the apex.

3.

Cut out extended dart.

4.

Close old dart.

New dart appears.

At new dart position, draw a line and cut up to apex.

5. After moving the dart, place tissue under the new dart opening and tape in place. Then draw the dart stitching lines so the dart ends approximately 1" from the apex.

1"

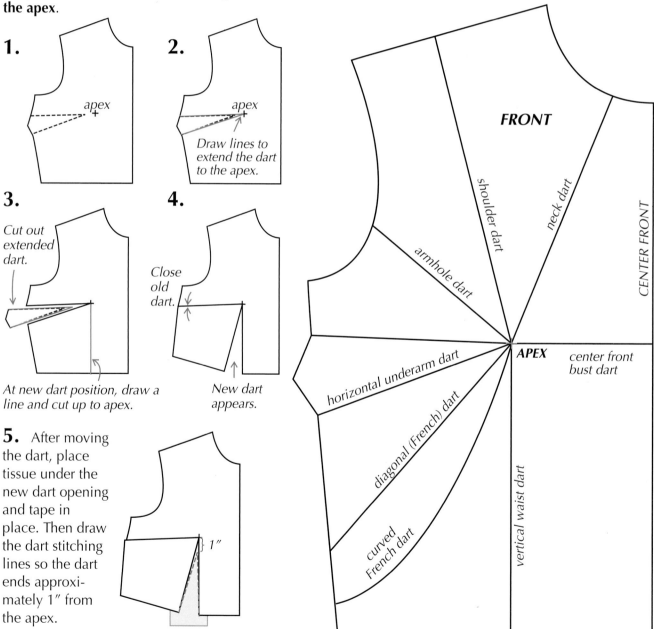

FRONT

shoulder dart

neck dart

CENTER FRONT

armhole dart

horizontal underarm dart

diagonal (French) dart

curved French dart

vertical waist dart

APEX

center front bust dart

Permission granted to photocopy this page for personal or teaching use only.

© Palmer/Pletsch Inc.

136

Creating Princess Seams

To create a princess seam, transfer part of the horizontal dart to an armhole dart and the rest to a vertical waist dart.

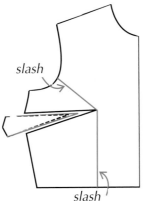

slash

Extend and cut out dart (page 136).

slash

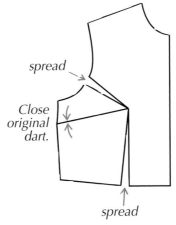

spread

Close original dart.

spread

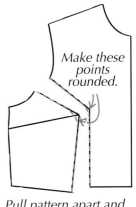

Make these points rounded.

Pull pattern apart and add seam allowances to both pieces.

Adding a Yoke

Add a yoke with tucks or gathers. Move the dart to the yoke seam, then ignore it! Just gather the bodice into the yoke instead of darting.

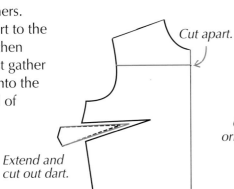

Cut apart.

Extend and cut out dart.

This new seam will have a slight curve that will disappear when you add tucks or gather it to fit the yoke edge.

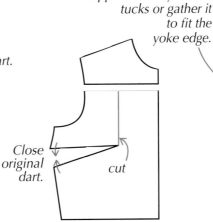

Close original dart.

cut

Add seam allowances and tuck or gather bodice to yoke here along seamline.

Open, then fill with tissue.

Creating a Bustier

A bustier is a sleeveless strapless bodice. It is either elasticized or boned and worn instead of a blouse for summer or evening wear. Test this first in muslin before cutting from fashion fabric.

1. Draw a line from apex to center front. Cut out the extended horizontal dart.

2. Close the horizontal dart and open the center front.

3. Turn the center front into gathers for soft shaping and bust fullness.

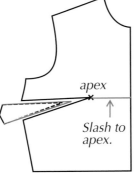

Extend and cut out dart.

apex

Slash to apex.

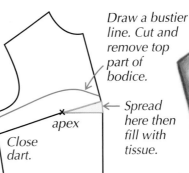

Draw a bustier line. Cut and remove top part of bodice.

apex

Close dart.

Spread here then fill with tissue.

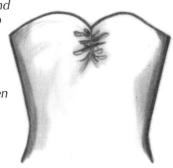

Eliminating Horizontal Darts on Jackets with Lapels

A full bust adjustment adds a horizontal dart. Some designs may look strange with this new dart. In that case, transfer some of the dart to under the lapel and/or to a vertical dart.

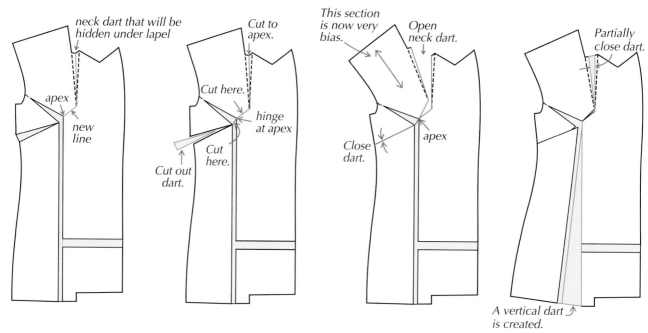

neck dart that will be hidden under lapel

apex

new line

Cut to apex.

Cut here.

hinge at apex

Cut here.

Cut out dart.

This section is now very bias.

Open neck dart.

Close dart.

apex

Partially close dart.

A vertical dart is created.

1. Draw a line through the center of the neck dart (or where you would like one) to its point, then draw an angled line to a hinge at apex. (Do not re-angle the neck dart to point to the bust, since then it wouldn't hide under the lapel.)

2. Cut through the center of the neck dart or on the neck dart line you added. Angle and continue cutting to, but not past, the apex hinge. Cut out the horizontal dart, then cut from the tip of that dart up to the apex.

3. Close the horizontal dart so the neck dart opens up. If the neck dart is now too wide, transfer some of it to a vertical dart below the bust.

4. To transfer some of the neck dart width to a vertical dart, cut from the hem up to the apex. Close the neck dart until shoulder area is less bias. A vertical space below the bust will open up.

5. You have now created extra width across the tummy. What can you do with it?

- If you have a full tummy, don't do anything. You'll need the room.

- OR remove the extra width at the side front seam.

- OR sew the vertical dart.

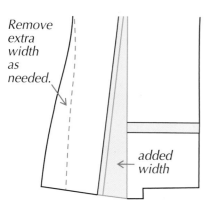

Remove extra width as needed.

added width

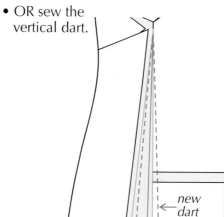

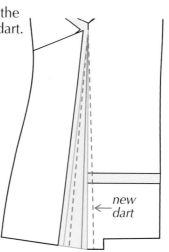

new dart

Designer Tip

Instead of one deep vertical dart, sew two—or THREE! See page 140 for a few ideas.

Dart Extensions— Do You Need Them or Not?

If you've added a horizontal bust dart to a pattern, you'll need to add an extension or you may not catch the edge of the dart when you sew the side seam.

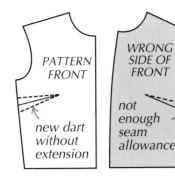

PATTERN FRONT

new dart without extension

WRONG SIDE OF FRONT

not enough seam allowance

1. Add tissue to the side seam edge of the pattern tissue in the dart area as shown.

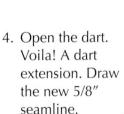

2. Fold the dart stitching lines together and press down.

3. Cut straight along the edge of the pattern.

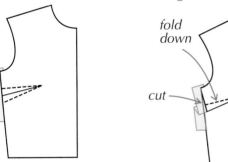

fold down

cut

4. Open the dart. Voila! A dart extension. Draw the new 5/8" seamline.

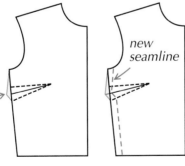

dart extension

new seamline

If you have enlarged an existing dart, extend the cutting lines until they intersect for the new extension.

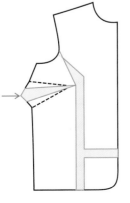

Quick Tip

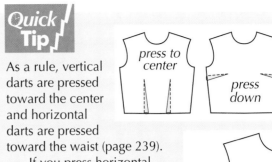

press to center

press down

press up

As a rule, vertical darts are pressed toward the center and horizontal darts are pressed toward the waist (page 239).

If you press horizontal darts up, it is more youthful and you don't need a dart extension at the edge.

Transfer Darts in Skirts

Turn a straight skirt into an A-line by eliminating the darts.

For a Wide A-Line: Cut up to the original dart point. Then cut out the original dart and bring the edges together.

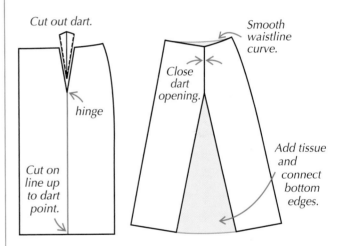

Cut out dart.

Smooth waistline curve.

Close dart opening.

hinge

Cut on line up to dart point.

Add tissue and connect bottom edges.

For Less A-Line: Extend the dart downward. The more you extend the dart, the less fullness you will add at the bottom edge.

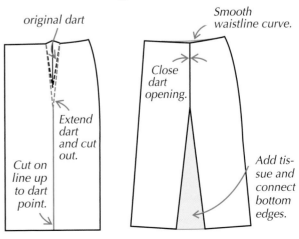

original dart

Smooth waistline curve.

Close dart opening.

Extend dart and cut out.

Cut on line up to dart point.

Add tissue and connect bottom edges.

139

CHAPTER 17
Bust

A good rule to remember:

The bigger the body bumps, the more length, width, and deeper darts they will need.

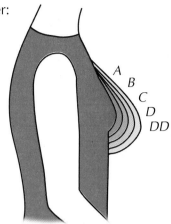

This certainly applies to a woman's chest. Pati used to think that people with small busts needed to take deeper darts to make the front smaller. Then she realized that men's clothing doesn't have darts! If you are flat-chested, you need **narrower** darts and less length and width over the bustline.

As teachers, we are most rewarded when we empower a full-busted person to pick any style and make it fit. However, it wasn't always that way. During their department-store teaching days, a woman with a DD bust-cup size wanted to take a class. Neither Marta nor Pati had full bustlines and didn't know how to fit her so they told her the class was full. Today, everyone is welcome in their classes, even those larger than a DD bust-cup size! Pati and Marta have learned how to fit anyone!

Different bra styles can drastically change the fit of your clothes. Have a trained bra fitter, available in most department stores, help you find your best bra. Then, stick with that style.

Patterns are designed for a B-cup bra size. "Cup size" in bras can be deceiving. For example, when buying a bra, if you go up a band size, the cup size given to you will be the same size as before, but called a size smaller.

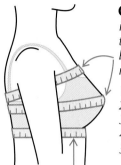

Cup Size
is determined by the difference between these two measurements.

1" = A
2" = B
3" = C
4" = D
5" = DD

Band Size *(32, 34, 36, 38 etc.)*
Take your chest measurement below the bust and add 4" for your band size.

You can see that a 38A is the same as a 32D:

Bra Cup Size Chart

32A	32B	32C	32D
34A	34B	34C	34D
36A	36B	36C	36D
38A	38B	38C	38D

SAME SIZE CUPS

Some people are wearing a B-cup bra size, but they have a full rib cage, so they really need the bust room of a D. See "Dorothy" on page 228.

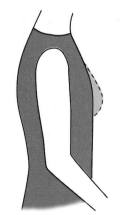

A B-cup with an average rib cage

A B-cup with a fuller rib cage may need to alter to a D-cup size

Remember how to use both the high bust and bust measurements to determine your size (page 24).

Amount of Alteration Depends on Style

Don't automatically do a bust alteration. Try on the tissue first! The dress shown below is 4" larger than the body measurement in the bust and the blouse is 9" larger. The blouse may require no alteration or much less than the dress. The fuller bust simply "uses up" some of the ease in the blouse.

Fitted Dress 4" Bust Ease

Classic Blouse 9" Bust Ease

Try On the Tissue

Prepare the pattern tissue as described on page 112. Pin seams and darts, wrong sides together. Try on as you'll wear it (i.e. with shoulder pads or over a blouse). Check and alter the back to fit first, then alter the front. If you are full-busted you'll usually see a gap in the armhole or drag lines pointing towards the bust. Also, the pattern's center front won't reach yours.

Measure from the pattern center front to your center front. *That* is the amount you'll need to widen the front pattern piece.

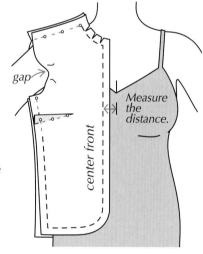

gap

center front

Measure the distance.

NOTE: If the dart is too high, don't worry. It will be lower after completing the alteration.

 If you are thick in the waist, put one pin only at the top of the side seam during tissue-fitting.

Full Bust–Darted Front

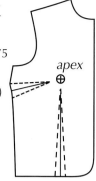

apex

(We first used this technique in the Palmer/Pletsch **Painless Sewing** book in 1975 and it has been our favorite ever since.)

Darts should point to bust (apex) but stop about 1" from it. The apex is generally marked on the pattern tissue. It can be an arrow or a circle with crossmarks.

STEP 1

With pattern right side up, draw three lines on the pattern tissue:

Draw **Line 1** from one-third of the way up the armhole to the apex and then straight down from the apex. (If there is an existing vertical dart, as shown, this line will usually go through the center of it.)

Draw **Line 2** through the center of the side dart, extending it to the apex.

Draw **Line 3** anywhere below the apex in the section shown.

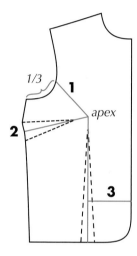

1/3 **1** *apex* **2** **3**

STEP 2

Cut on Line 1 from the lower edge up to, **but not through**, the armhole seam.

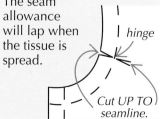 In the armhole area, cut the seam allowance to, BUT NOT THROUGH, the seamline from both sides (so armhole won't get larger when you spread the tissue). The seam allowance will lap when the tissue is spread.

hinge

Cut UP TO seamline.

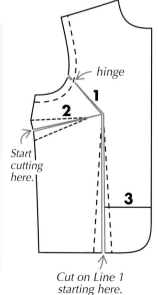

hinge **1** **2** **3**

Start cutting here.

Cut on Line 1 starting here.

STEP 3

Cut on Line 2 up to Line 1, leaving a tiny hinge.

STEP 4

Pin the pattern front to a cardboard cutting board as shown. This anchors the stationary front section.

Pull the pieces apart at the horizontal **arrows** along Line 1 the amount determined during your tissue-fitting.

Keep the long edges of Line 1 parallel. To do this, and to keep the pattern **totally flat**, the armhole goes up and the side panel drops down as Line 2 opens up forming a deeper dart.

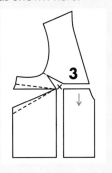

Now, anchor the two side sections with pins as shown.

 Angling pins AWAY from the center of a cut tissue section keeps it in place. It CAN'T move.

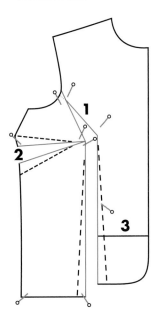

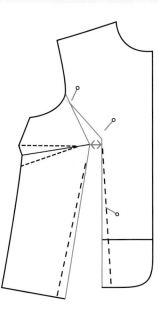

OR, if its easier for you, cut on Line 1 and spread the tissue the amount you need at the horizontal arrow in the illustration at left. Then cut on Line 2 and make Line 1 edges parallel.

STEP 5

Cut on Line 3 and lower until the bottom edges of the pattern sections are even. Anchor as shown.

 If you want a lower "V" in a vest, Line 3 CAN be at the apex as shown here.

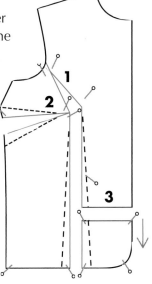

STEP 6

Fill in the openings with tissue. Make sure all pieces are **flat** with **no wrinkles**. Tape in place, **beginning in the middle and working to the outer edges**.

Don't remove pins until all pieces are securely taped.

You now have deeper darts, more width across the front and a higher armhole which won't gap after the dart is sewn!

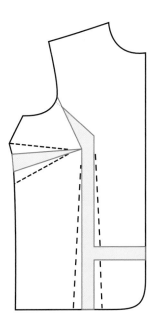

Quick Tip Steps 1-6 can be done on top of one large sheet of tissue to save time. After altering and taping, trim away the excess tissue.

STEP 7

Try On for Dart Position

Pin in the horizontal dart. Pin the back to the front at the shoulder and side seams. Try on, pinning the pattern to your center front, and mark your apex.

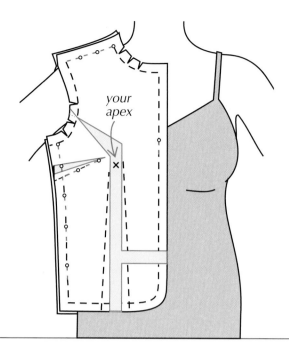

your apex

At this point, if dart does not point to your bust, move as shown.

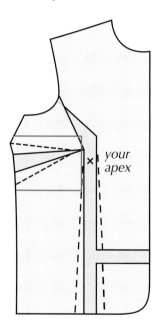

your apex

DRAW a BOX around the dart.

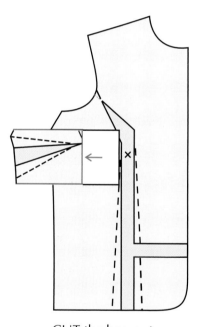

CUT the box out.

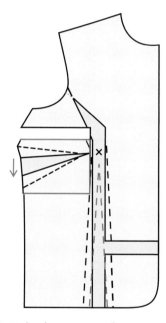

MOVE the box up or down until the dart points to your apex, keeping cut edges parallel. Raise or lower the point of the vertical dart to 1″ below the apex and redraw the dart.

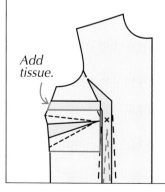

Add tissue.

NOTE: Altering for a full bust automatically lowers the horizontal dart. However, if you are really low-busted (1½″ or more), lower the dart to 1″ above bust apex **before** altering. Don't make darts too low as they often drop 1/4″ to 1/2″ in fabric.

Vertical Dart Options

◆ Don't stitch the vertical dart if you are full in the waist.

◆ Pin in the vertical dart along the original stitching lines for a deeper dart. You may have to reposition the dart so it is under your apex. However, some vertical darts are designed not to be directly under your apex but slightly toward the side seam. It is your choice. The pattern is the manuscript, you are the editor.

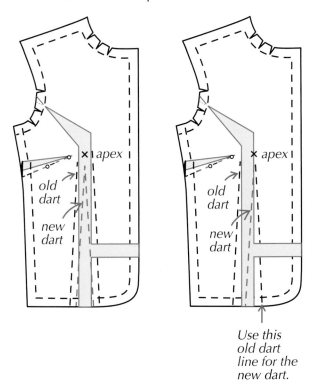

◆ Redraw the stitching lines at an equal distance from both sides of the dart center as desired. Two different examples are shown below.

old dart

new dart

apex

old dart

new dart

apex

Use this old dart line for the new dart.

For additional vertical dart options in a jacket, see page 138.

Where Do I Draw Line 1 When the Vertical Dart Is Not Below Apex?

Choose one of the following methods of bust adjustment:

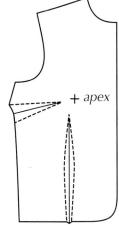

+ apex

Method

Draw Line 1 through the apex and alter as usual. See page 142.

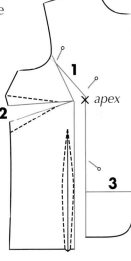

× apex

Method

Draw Line 1 through the center of the vertical dart, rather than the apex, and alter, using the same method.

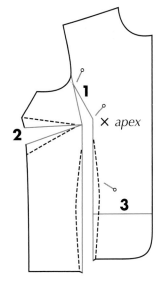

× apex

Either way works; however, in method 2, the horizontal dart will be narrower (1/4" in size 18). This is pretty minor, but we want you to know there will be a slight difference when you change the pivot point to an area other than the apex.

The "Y" Bust Dart Alteration

Use this technique for a full bust alteration when more than 1½" is needed to bring the center front of the pattern to your center front.

1. Draw lines 1, 1a, 2, and 3 on pattern tissue as shown. 1a goes to approximately one third of the way up the armhole.

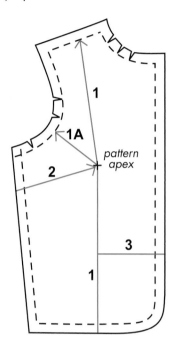

2. Cut line 1 from lower edge to apex. Continue cutting to center of shoulder seam. Move the side section of the front half the total amount needed. Anchor with pins above the apex.

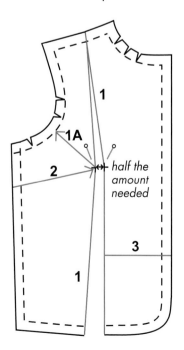

3. Cut on 1a from the apex to the armhole. Move the side front the other half of the total amount needed. Anchor with a pin in the just under the armhole.

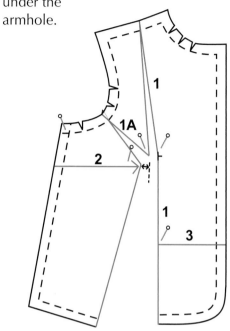

4. Cut on line 2 and open until the lower part of the side section's line 1 is parallel to the front from the apex to the bottom.

5. Cut line 3 to make the center front and side even at the hemline. Use the lengthen/shorten line above the waist to do this if it is available. Remember to "hinge" the Line 1A cut at the armhole seamline (see page 113) so you don't change the length of the armhole seam.

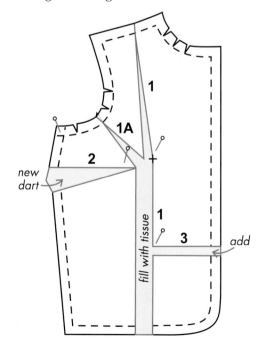

Altering No-Dart Fronts

If the pattern has no horizontal bust dart and if you need one, pin the shoulders and side seams together and hold the front pattern piece up to you. Measure the distance from the pattern center front to your center front.

Remove tissue. Draw a line from the side seam to the apex mark where you visualize a dart. Proceed as directed for "Altering a Darted Front," on page 142.

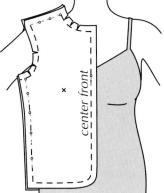

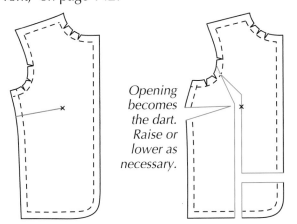

Opening becomes the dart. Raise or lower as necessary.

"Smooshing Out" Small Darts

This easy solution is something Marta does that you probably won't find in most fit textbooks! She was a costume designer in her former life, so we allow it. In other words...if it works, do it.

When Marta uses a pattern with a small horizontal bust dart that is not wanted, she **folds it out, tapes to secure it, and irons the bubble at the dart point flat**. Now she can cut out a dartless front.

Against the rules? Yes. But it works in loose styles for A-, B- and C-cup bra bodies. **Don't try this if you are larger than a C-cup.** Those darts are usually too deep to smoosh. Also, this is not for fitted garments.

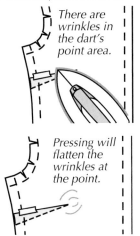

There are wrinkles in the dart's point area.

Pressing will flatten the wrinkles at the point.

Altering for a Small Bust

To fit a small-busted figure, you basically do just the opposite of a full bust alteration. Where you spread for a full bust, you lap for a small bust.

Measure from your center front to the center front of the pattern. That is the amount you need to reduce the bust. If the garment is loose-fitting, don't bother. Let the ease or fullness camouflage your small bustline.

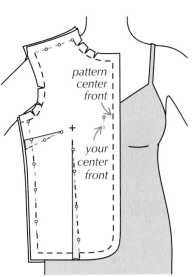

pattern center front

your center front

To alter, draw the same lines as for the full bust (Step 1, page 142).

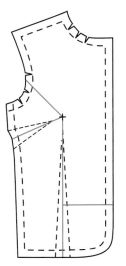

Cut and lap the pattern tissue instead of spreading. You'll reduce width and center front length and the bust dart will become narrower.

See Anastasia on page 200 for a "real people" example.

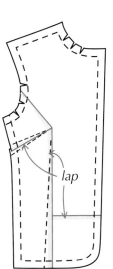

lap

Altering Princess Seams

Princess seams offer great opportunities for fit. The curved seams may be adjusted to follow the curves of each individual body.

There are two main types of princess seams. The shoulder princess seam usually falls over the center of the bust. The armhole princess seam usually falls to the side of the center of the bust toward the underarm seam.

ARMHOLE PRINCESS

SHOULDER PRINCESS

Get the Tissue Ready

Press the tissue with a dry iron set at the wool setting.

With tissue right side up, tape the following:
- armholes
- bust area on front
- back necklines

Use small pieces of tape around the curves.
Clip seam allowance to, but not through, the tape in the curves.

Shoulder Princess

BACK

SIDE BACK

SIDE FRONT

FRONT

Armhole Princess

SIDE FRONT

FRONT

Raising or Lowering Bust Fullness

Armhole princess is shown but alterations also apply to shoulder princess.

1. Pin the shoulder seams of the front and back pattern pieces with **wrong sides together**.

2. Try on the tissue, matching your center front to the pattern's center front. (We don't pin side seams because you probably couldn't get the pattern to your center front.)

3. Is the pattern's bust fullness in the right place? If not, raise or lower it. **If you are full-busted,** you must get the fullness in the right place **before** enlarging the bust.

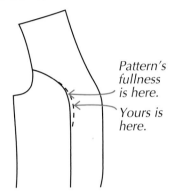

Pattern's fullness is here.

Yours is here.

NOTE: Most patterns mark apex or print finished bust measurement on tissue at bust level.

4. Remove the tissue and press it from the wrong side so you don't melt the tape.

5. Draw a box as shown on both the front and the side front above and below bust notches.

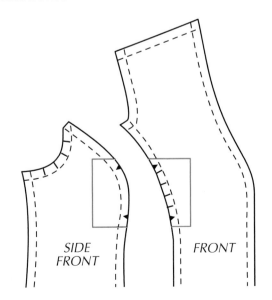

SIDE FRONT

FRONT

6. Cut out the boxes.

7. Lower or raise the boxes. **True the seams as shown:**

Lowering

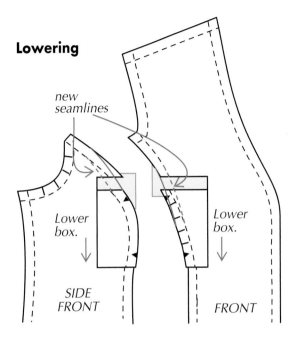

new seamlines

Lower box.

Lower box.

SIDE FRONT

FRONT

Raising

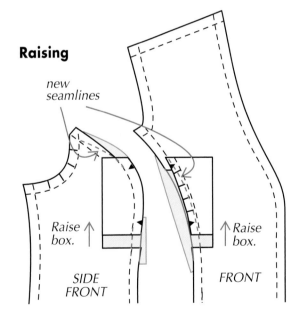

new seamlines

Raise box.

Raise box.

SIDE FRONT

FRONT

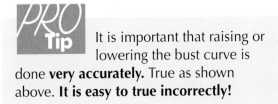

PRO Tip It is important that raising or lowering the bust curve is done **very accurately.** True as shown above. **It is easy to true incorrectly!**

Determine Amount of Full Bust Adjustment

Shoulder princess is shown but alterations also apply to armhole princess.

1. Pin the front and the back pattern pieces **wrong sides together**. Try on the tissue. Pull it **snugly** over your bust.

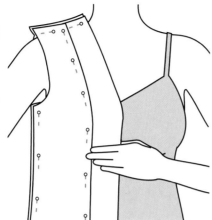

2. If you can't get the pattern center front to meet your center front, unpin the princess seamline in the bust area until the center fronts line up.

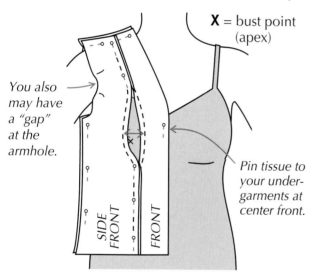

X = bust point (apex)

You also may have a "gap" at the armhole.

SIDE FRONT

FRONT

Pin tissue to your undergarments at center front.

3. Measure the opening from seamline to seamline at the widest part. That is the amount you will add for the needed width.

Breast spacing affects the princess seam position. Which are you?

Ideally, the princess seamline should be over the apex (X) or toward the side seam. If the seamline on the front piece is toward the center front side of your bust, as shown, you will add to the front pattern piece.

To determine the amount to add, with center fronts matching, measure from the seamline to the apex (X).

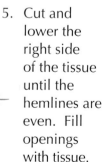

FRONT

Adding Width to the Front

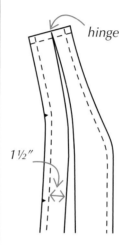

hinge

1½"

1. Unpin the tissue and press from the wrong side.

2. To move the seam over to the correct position, slash the pattern from the bottom edge to the bust area 1½" in from the side front seamline. Continue slashing at an angle up to the middle of the shoulder as shown.

3. Half-way between the bust notches, **cut horizontally up to, but not through,** the vertical cut edge. This spread will be minor.

4. Spread pattern until the side front seamline is near your apex and the two long edges are parallel at arrows. This step adds length. See the note below. See Debbra, page 201.

5. Cut and lower the right side of the tissue until the hemlines are even. Fill openings with tissue.

NOTE: We do not recommend adding to the bottom when evening up hemlines, as this may alter the lower edge if it is rounded, pointed or otherwise shaped.

Adding to the Side Panel

This is the more common princess adjustment. You may add to both the front and the side. However, **if the seamline on the front panel** is on or slightly toward the side seam from the center of your bustline, add all of the fullness to the side front piece.

STEP 1

On the side front, draw Line 1 as close as possible to the front stitching line. In the full bust area, Line 1 angles, aiming at a point 1/3 of the way up the total armhole, from the underarm.

as close as possible to front stitching line.

Draw Line 2 where a side dart would go and point it toward the full bust.

Draw Line 3 anywhere below the bust notches.

For the armhole princess, the 1/3 measurement applies to the entire armhole as if the front were sewn to the side front panel.

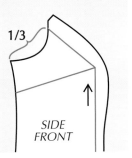

STEP 2

Cut on Line 1 from **lower** edge up to, **but not through**, armhole seam.

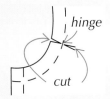

Cut the seam allowance to, BUT NOT THROUGH, the seamline to create a hinge.

Cut on Line 2 **up to, but not through**, Line 1.

Pin the pattern front to a cardboard cutting board as shown. This anchors the stationary section.

Pull the pieces apart along Line 1 at the horizontal arrows the amount determined during tissue-fitting.

Keep the long edges of Line 1 parallel.

For the pattern to remain totally flat, the armhole moves up and the side panel drops lower, as Line 2 opens up, forming space for a dart.

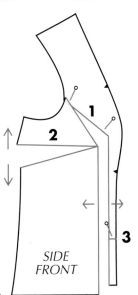

Now, anchor side sections as shown.

Cut on Line 3 and lower until bottom edges are even. Anchor as shown.

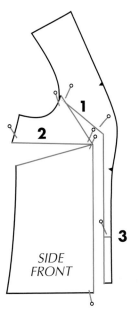

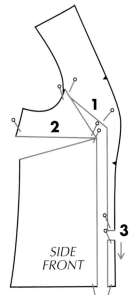

STEP 3

With pins still in, fill Line 1 and 3 areas with tissue. Make sure all pieces are flat and there are **no wrinkles** in the tissue. Tape in place.

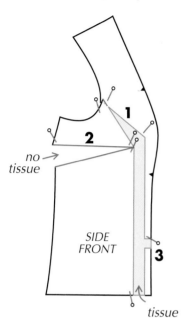

STEP 4

Draw Line 4 from the fullest bust point to the dart point. Cut on that line.

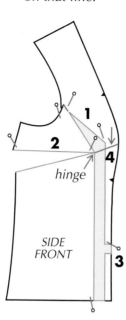

STEP 5

To eliminate the horizontal dart, tape dart edges together at Line 2.

You have now widened and lengthened the side front edge for your fuller bust. Fill the area at Line 4 with tissue. Measure the spread at Line 4 **at the seamline**, not at the cut edge. This is the amount you will lengthen Line 5 on the front piece.

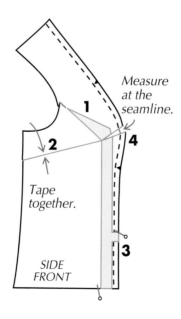

 If you needed more than 1" width at Line 1, the armhole will be very curved. It's okay! Try it on. You will be pleased.

STEP 6

Lengthen the front pattern piece at Line 5 (halfway between notches) the same amount as the opening at Line 4 **seamline**, so that bust fullness notches match on the front and side front pieces.

At Line 6, lengthen the same amount as Line 3. Fill openings with tissue and tape in place.

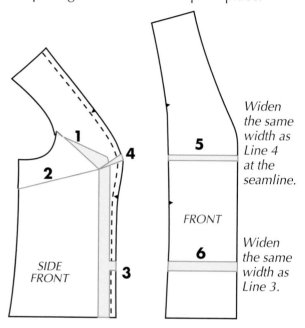

NOTE: If you also widened the front (page 150), measure the side front seams with the tape measure on its edge and make the front seamline the same length.

STEP 7

Pin pattern pieces together again and try on. The front fits, and, the armhole gap is gone!

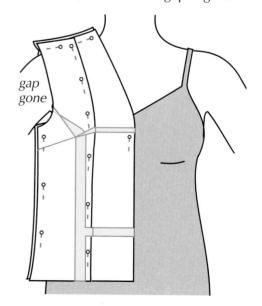

Alternate Alterations for Just a Little Extra Room (1/2" or Less)

Shoulder Princess

If you need just a little more room in the bust, 1/2" or less, this may be an easier alteration. By letting out the seam over the bust, you are adding to both the front and the side front.

Add an equal amount of tissue to the side front and front between bust notches to allow for a 5/8" seam allowance on each.

Measure the entire length of the new stitching lines by standing the tape measure on its edge. If the side front is longer, lengthen the front to match.

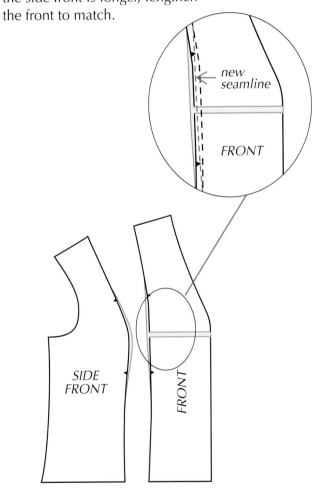

new seamline

FRONT

SIDE FRONT

FRONT

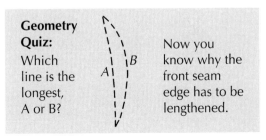

Geometry Quiz: Which line is the longest, A or B?

A   B

Now you know why the front seam edge has to be lengthened.

With this alteration you'll get the width and length you need, but you may still have an armhole gap, especially if you try adding more than 1/2" this way.

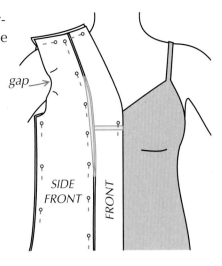

gap

SIDE FRONT

FRONT

To remove the gap, move the side front inward as shown until the gap disappears.

Remove the excess tissue, leaving a 5/8" side front seam allowance. Add the same amount of tissue to the armhole as shown.

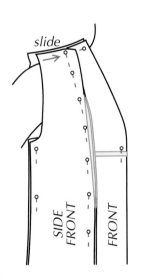

slide

SIDE FRONT

FRONT

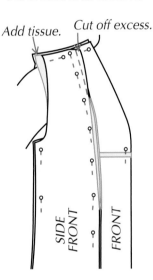

Add tissue.   Cut off excess.

SIDE FRONT

FRONT

Armhole Princess

Alter following the same as for shoulder princess. However, before drawing the lines, see the PRO TIP on page 151, column one.

NOTE: We often only add to the side front and lengthen the front so seams match.

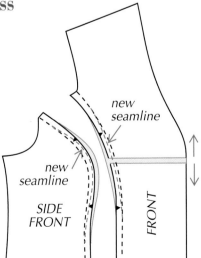

new seamline

new seamline

SIDE FRONT

FRONT

Try on the pattern. You may still have a gap at the armhole.

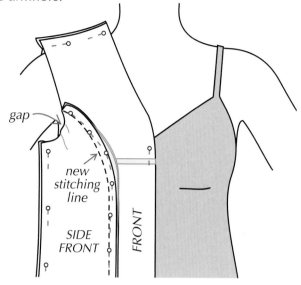

gap

new
stitching
line

SIDE
FRONT

FRONT

To remove the gap, take a deeper seam in the side front, then check the armhole width. Is the seam coming to your armhole crease?

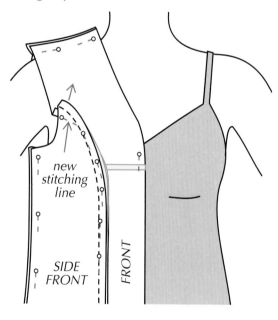

new
stitching
line

SIDE
FRONT

FRONT

Add tissue to the armhole until you like the look and it fits your armhole curve.

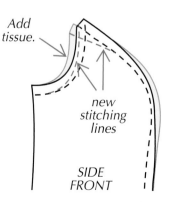

Add
tissue.

new
stitching
lines

SIDE
FRONT

Altering a Princess Seam for a Small Bust

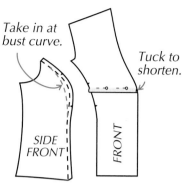

Take in at
bust curve.

Tuck to
shorten.

SIDE
FRONT

FRONT

When you are small-busted, lessen the bust curve on the side front. Then add a tuck between bust notches to shorten the front so seamlines match in length.

Princess Droop

The center panel may droop. On page 152 we told you to lengthen the center front to match the side front seams in length. Sometimes this makes the front too long. Why?

The seams on the front have to be staystitched and clipped in order to be easily pinned to the sides. See how-to's for sewing inward to outward curves, page 243. This clipping can cause this seam to grow in soft or loosely woven fabrics.

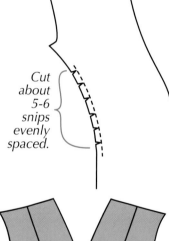

Cut
about
5-6
snips
evenly
spaced.

The solution is to take a chance. You can't always tell ahead of time. BUT, you can always "unstitch" to just above the droop lines, let the front relax, and then cut off the excess at the bottom and re-stitch.

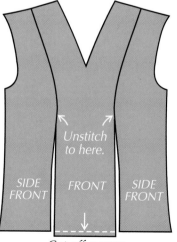

Unstitch
to here.

SIDE
FRONT

FRONT

SIDE
FRONT

Cut off excess.

Bust Adjustments...Fashion Challenges

Fashion changes! That's the reason computerization of fit may never be economical for anything but classic designs. The rules we've given you apply to 90% of the styles, but fashion itself, creative as it is, changes the rules. Just remember, **"If it works, it's right!!"**

When you have a design challenge, make a mini sample of the pattern piece out of paper and play with your options.

A Princess Dart Instead of a Seam

In this design, darts create an armhole princess seam.

the unaltered pattern

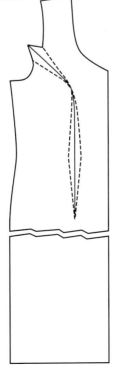

Princess Dart Method

1. Draw the bust alteration lines on the tissue just as you would for the princess line (see page 151).

2. Make alterations.

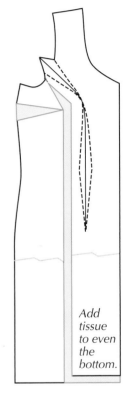

Add tissue to even the bottom.

3. Extend the new horizontal dart to the apex. Cut out that horizontal dart. Cut through the center of the armhole dart to the apex hinge.

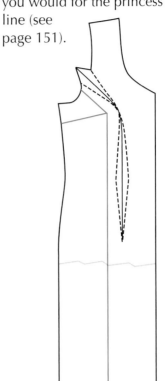

Cut up to apex.

Remove dart.

apex hinge

4. Close the horizontal dart and open the armhole dart.

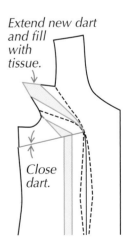

Extend new dart and fill with tissue.

Close dart.

5. If the dress is now too full in the hips, take the side seams in or add a second vertical dart (toward the side seam). Pin the extra dart to fit your shape.

Princess Dart Method

1. Extend the vertical dart center line to the bottom edge.

2. Cut the pattern apart. Draw lines for bust alteration on side front. See page 151.

5. Close the horizontal bust dart. Tape in place. You've now added length and width over the bust.

6. Lengthen front to match side front. Tape fronts together. Fill in the deeper armhole dart area with tissue.

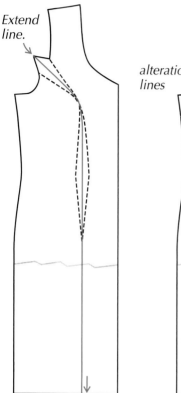

Extend line.

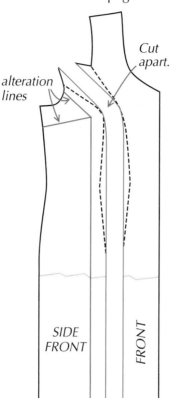

alteration lines

Cut apart.

SIDE FRONT

FRONT

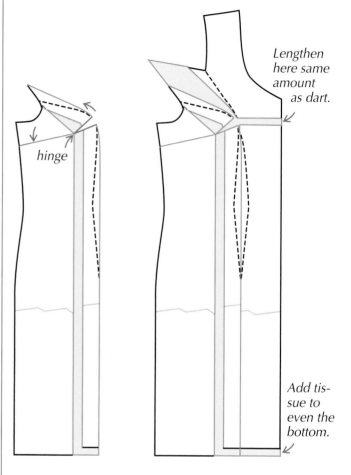

hinge

Lengthen here same amount as dart.

Add tissue to even the bottom.

3. Alter and add tissue to the vertical opening only.

4. Draw a line from the tip of the dart to the center of the bust curve (apex).

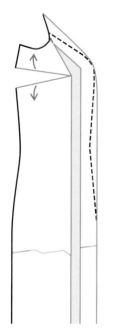

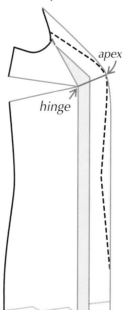

apex

hinge

Now, which method is the best? The first method has less cutting and we liked the shape of the altered front better. The second method would probably be easiest for someone very full-busted. However, either method works. Use the one that seems best for you.

Fronts with Cap, Cut-On, or Kimono Sleeves

This technique works especially well if the armhole is deep.

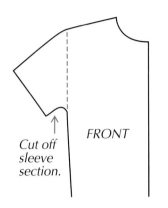

↑ Cut off sleeve section.

FRONT

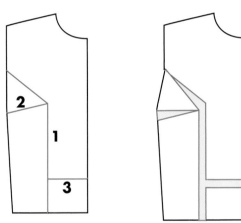

Draw lines. See page 142. (If armhole is quite low, slant line 2 to avoid having it in the sleeve!)

Alter.

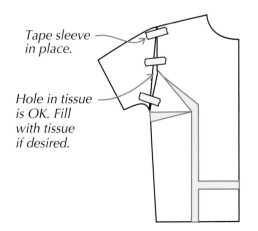

Tape sleeve in place.

Hole in tissue is OK. Fill with tissue if desired.

If you are full in the bust area, and don't want to cut off the sleeve, try this:

Draw a line at dart level (or through an existing dart) (1) and one vertically through the apex to the shoulder and the hem (2).

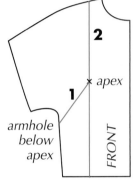

2

1 × apex

FRONT

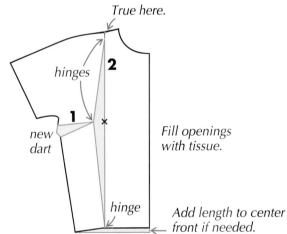

2

1 × apex

armhole below apex

FRONT

NOTE: If the bottom of the armhole is below the bust area, draw the dart line (1) at a deeper angle.

True here.

hinges

2

1 ×

new dart

Fill openings with tissue.

hinge

Add length to center front if needed.

See a "real people" example on page 219.

Fronts with Raglan Sleeves

Alteration will be similar to the cut-on sleeve. The altered front will look like the one to the right.

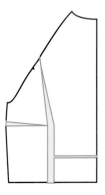

Fronts with Armhole Darts

If a pattern has an armhole dart, alter for a full bust the usual way. Then eliminate the new horizontal dart by transferring it to the existing armhole dart, making it deeper.

Extend the dart center line to the apex. Draw other adjustment lines (see page 142).

Alter for full bust, but don't add alteration tissue yet. Anchor pattern with pins where shown.

Cut armhole dart open and close horizontal bust dart. Armhole dart will widen. Anchor underarm piece.

Fill in with tissue, tape in place, then redraw the armhole dart.

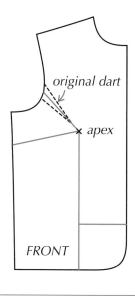

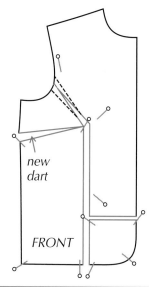

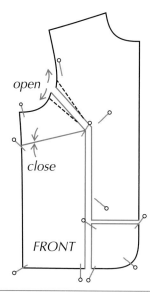

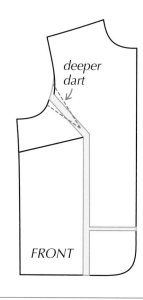

Front of a One-Piece Dress

When adding or changing a dart, sometimes it is easier to alter only the upper portion of the pattern.

Cut the dress off at or below the waist.

Draw the bust alteration lines, make alterations (see page 142), then tape the pattern back together.

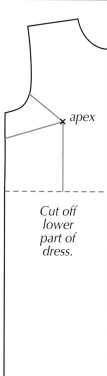

Cut off lower part of dress.

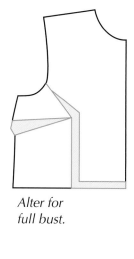

Alter for full bust.

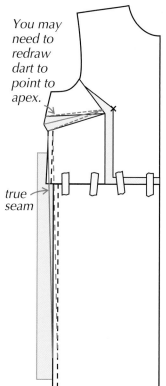

You may need to redraw dart to point to apex.

Tape back together and fill with tissue.

true seam

You have now added a horizontal bust dart.

158

A Full Bust Alteration Adds a Horizontal Dart. Keep It? Eliminate It? Or Move It?

Very full-busted people usually need the shaping a dart gives, but keeping the dart depends on several things:

◆ It can depend on your fabric. Maybe the one-piece dress on page 158 is to be sewn in a sheer fabric and you don't want the dart layers to show through.

◆ It can also depend on fashion. In the '80s, fashion was baggy and darts were out. In the '90s, fashion became fitted. Darts became necessary.

◆ It can depend on the design lines of the pattern. A jacket with a side panel altered would leave a very short horizontal bust dart coming from the side front seam, but it does appear in fashion today.

Removing a Dart in a One-Piece Dress

To eliminate a dart from a pattern like the one-piece dress on the previous page, transfer the dart to a vertical dart that you don't sew. Remove any excess at the side seams when you fit-as-you-sew.

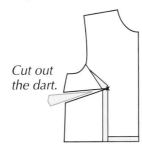

Extend line to apex.

Cut out the dart.

After altering the pattern, extend the dart to the apex. Cut from the bottom edge to the apex.

cut

Close the horizontal dart, transferring it to a vertical dart. Tape the top to the skirt, draw a new side seam line, and draw 1" side seam allowances to give you some adjusting room if you need it.

The front side seam will become slightly longer than the back, usually not more than 3/8", which can be trimmed off at the hem edge.

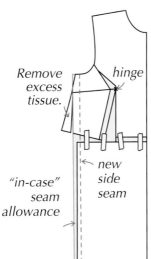

Remove excess tissue.

hinge

"in-case" seam allowance

new side seam

trim

When You Don't Want an Underarm Dart in a Shirt or a Shirtdress

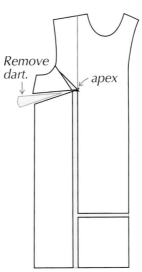
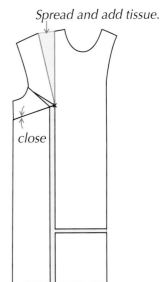

Remove dart.

apex

close

Spread and add tissue.

Alter for full bust and then extend the dart to the apex and cut the dart out. Draw a line from the shoulder to the apex.

Cut from the shoulder to the apex and spread to close the underarm dart. Fill with tissue. Pleat or gather front shoulder to match back shoulder.

To move a horizontal dart in a jacket to hide it under the lapel, see page 138.

Make a Shirt More Slimming

If you are full-busted and have narrow hips, an undarted shirt may stand out too far in front. If you've altered a shirt for a full bust then transferred the horizontal dart to a vertical dart, you may want to sew that dart.

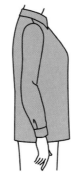

The shirt will now be more slimming AND you'll have less bulk to tuck in.

Vertical dart controls excess fullness.

Shirt stands out in front.

159

CHAPTER 18

Shoulders & Armholes

Good shoulder fit flatters your figure. Compare your shoulder width and slope to the pattern company basic as discussed on page 67. The normal slope from the base of the neck is about 2". It will be less for small sizes and more for large sizes. (It is 1⅝" for a size 10.) When you try on the basic bodice tissue, it will be noticeable if you are not the same slope as the pattern on both sides. See page 77.

Square Shoulders

You will recognize square shoulders by diagonal wrinkles in the tissue pointing to the shoulders.

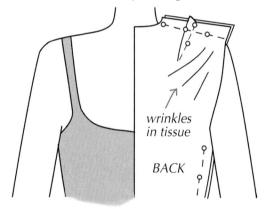

wrinkles in tissue

BACK

If you look at the back, you will see horizontal wrinkles at the base of your neck. This is not easy to see in tissue. If you sew a basic pattern in muslin or gingham (page 85), you'll be able to see it better. Plus you'll see if the slope of one shoulder is different from the other.

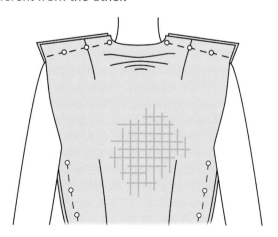

Sloping Shoulders

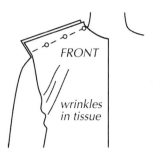

FRONT

wrinkles in tissue

If you are sloping in the shoulders, you will see these drag lines.

Altering for square and Sloping Shoulders

To alter the garment shoulders to make them more square, raise the seam at the shoulder. Raise the armhole the same amount. For sloping shoulders, lower the shoulder stitching line and the underarm the same amount.

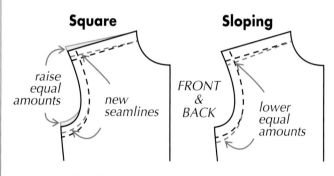

Square

raise equal amounts

new seamlines

Sloping

FRONT & BACK

lower equal amounts

Designer Tip

In some garments you can get the same look the designer intended by correcting square or sloping shoulders with shoulder pads.

If too square,

eliminate or decrease size of pad.

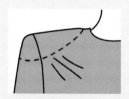

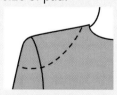

If too sloping

add or increase size of pad.

In jackets with traditional set-in sleeves, we don't raise the underarm in the square shoulder alteration. It makes the sleeve easier to set in.

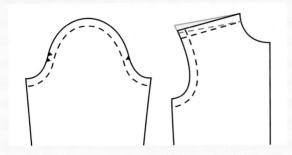

However always raise the underarm on shirts, because the sleeve cap and the armhole are nearly the same size.

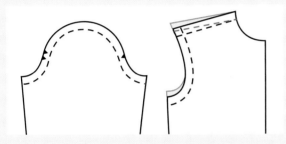

If your cap height is in between, and you've squared the shoulders without raising the underarm, cut a larger seam allowance at the top of the sleeve cap, tapering to nothing at the notches. This amount is half of the square shoulder. If you raised the shoulder 1/2" add 1/4" to the cap of the sleeve.

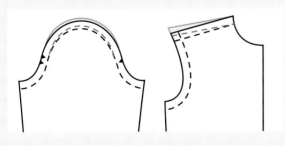

flat cap   *average cap*   *high cap*

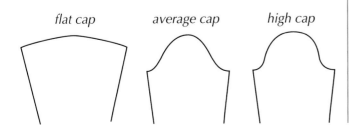

Uneven Shoulders

Uneven shoulders are usually caused by carrying books, groceries, babies or shoulder bags on one side of the body. It's better to even them up than to emphasize an uneven body! If you have uneven shoulders, fit the high side in order to make sure you cut enough fabric length for that side.

Neck angles are different.

Low shoulder may also be wider.

Arm appears longer, but it's really just lower.

The Shoulder Pad Solution

Then use a thicker shoulder pad on the low side to even them up. See page 244 for information on layered shoulder pads.

thin pad   *thick pad*

You can also extend the pad out to widen a shoulder (page 244).

The Sewing Solution

If you are not using a shoulder pad, sew the shoulder and underarm deeper on the low side.

Fit your high side.

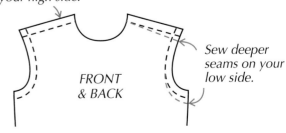

FRONT & BACK

Sew deeper seams on your low side.

Broad and Narrow Shoulders

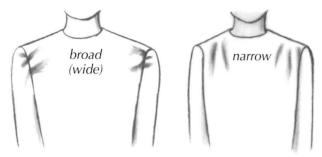

broad (wide) *narrow*

Are your shoulders broad (wide), average or narrow? Pattern shoulder width is from 4¾" on a size 10 to 5¼" on a size 20 on a basic fit pattern.

Don't get broad and square mixed up. They are two different things.

Using a basic fitted bodice in your correct size, you can tissue-fit (page 77) or sew and try on (page 85) to see how your body compares to patterns.

If you are narrow in the shoulders and would like to appear broader, use raglan shoulders pads (page 244).

For shoulders wider than the pattern:

add

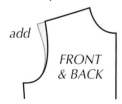

FRONT & BACK

For shoulders narrower than the pattern:

take in

FRONT & BACK

Forward Shoulders

If your clothes fall back off your shoulders, you probably have forward shoulders. This is more common than in the past due to more desk and computer work. Even sewing can affect your posture. Forward shoulders are often seen with a slightly rounded upper back (high round). Do the high round back alteration first if you need it, as it will change the position of the shoulder seam at the neckline. The shoulder seam should lie in a straight line from the base of the neck to your shoulder pivot point.

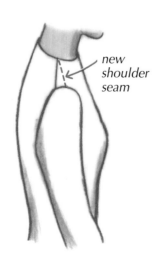

new shoulder seam

To pivot the shoulder seam forward, raise the seamline on the back pattern piece and lower it on the front at the armhole edge, tapering to nothing at the neckline on both pieces.

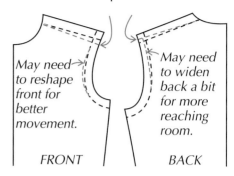

May need to reshape front for better movement.

FRONT

May need to widen back a bit for more reaching room.

BACK

Do not move the sleeve shoulder dot. Set the sleeve into the armhole and it should hang perfectly. The underarm seams won't necessarily match unless you put more sleeve ease in front and less in back. (Who's looking?)

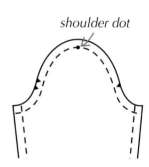

shoulder dot

NOTE: Your posture, the amount of forward shoulder rotation, and how your arm hangs all affect sleeve fit. If there are wrinkles in your sleeve after you set it into the new armhole, you may need to adjust the sleeve rotation. See "Cap Rotation," pages 172-173.

Forward Shoulder on a Yoke

Simply move the shoulder dot forward the amount necessary.

normal shoulder line *new dot*

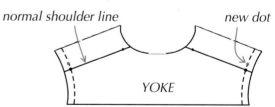

YOKE

Forward Shoulders in Cut-On and Seamed Raglan Sleeves

When Pati tissue-fitted the dresses on page 47, she first pivoted the whole seam forward, but it hit in a funny place at her wrist.

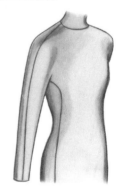

Therefore, she decided to just move the seam in the shoulder area forward and liked the results.

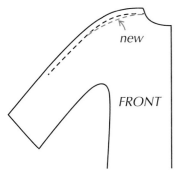 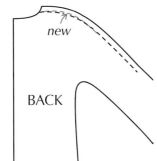

FRONT   BACK

If the raglan sleeve is darted instead of seamed, just move the end of the dart forward and redraw the dart.

Redraw dart.

Head Sits Forward on Body

On most people the shoulder seam lines up with the back of the ear. If your head sits forward on your body, you may want to move the entire shoulder seam forward rather than pivoting it forward from the neck. Sometimes you move the seam forward equal amounts at neck and shoulder and sometimes one end is moved less than the other. It depends on your shape.

You can see where the seam is during tissue-fitting and decide.

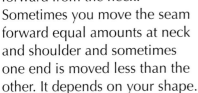

new seam

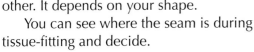

BACK   *FRONT*

new

FIT Tip Do the high round back alteration first (page 122) if you need it. It changes the shoulder seam position.

Forward and Square Shoulders

If you have square shoulders *and* forward shoulders, **always** do the forward shoulder adjustment first (the red line in the illustration). Then, do the square alteration (the grey line). That line will be your final stitching line.

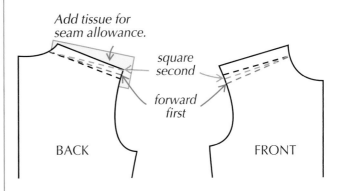

Add tissue for seam allowance.

square second

forward first

BACK   FRONT

Tip for Jacket Linings

Raise underarms 1/4" on front, back, and sleeve to float over jacket seam.

Lower shoulders and sleeve cap to make room for shoulder pads. The amount depends on the size of the shoulder pad. Pin-fit the lining inside the jacket to find the correct shoulder seam.

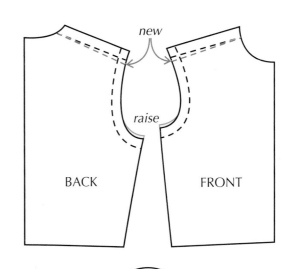

new

raise

BACK   FRONT

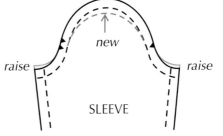

raise   *new*   *raise*

SLEEVE

Shoulder Adjustments for Other Styles

NOTE: If a garment has shoulder pads, adjust these styles by moving the shoulder pads or changing pad width.

Cut-On/Kimono

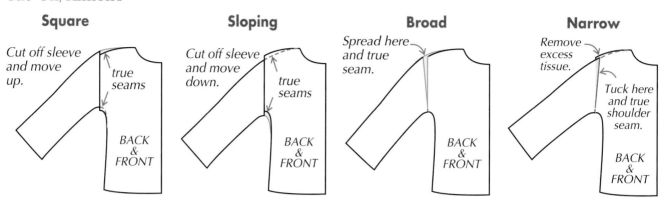

Square
Cut off sleeve and move up.
true seams
BACK & FRONT

Sloping
Cut off sleeve and move down.
true seams
BACK & FRONT

Broad
Spread here and true seam.
BACK & FRONT

Narrow
Remove excess tissue.
Tuck here and true shoulder seam.
BACK & FRONT

Princess

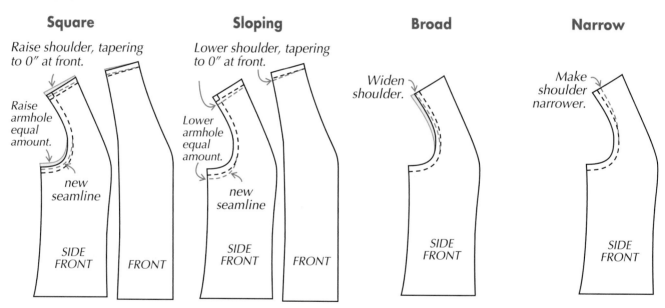

Square
Raise shoulder, tapering to 0" at front.
Raise armhole equal amount.
new seamline
SIDE FRONT
FRONT

Sloping
Lower shoulder, tapering to 0" at front.
Lower armhole equal amount.
new seamline
SIDE FRONT
FRONT

Broad
Widen shoulder.
SIDE FRONT

Narrow
Make shoulder narrower.
SIDE FRONT

Extended Shoulder

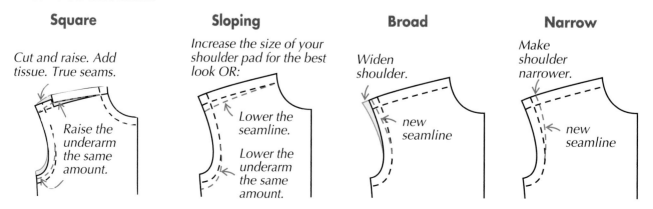

Square
Cut and raise. Add tissue. True seams.
Raise the underarm the same amount.

Sloping
Increase the size of your shoulder pad for the best look OR:
Lower the seamline.
Lower the underarm the same amount.

Broad
Widen shoulder.
new seamline

Narrow
Make shoulder narrower.
new seamline

164

Yoke

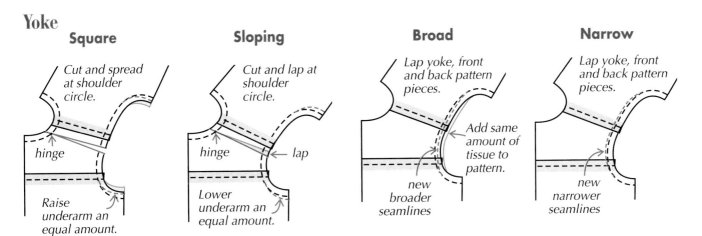

Square

Cut and spread at shoulder circle.

hinge

Raise underarm an equal amount.

Sloping

Cut and lap at shoulder circle.

hinge ← lap

Lower underarm an equal amount.

Broad

Lap yoke, front and back pattern pieces.

Add same amount of tissue to pattern.

new broader seamlines

Narrow

Lap yoke, front and back pattern pieces.

new narrower seamlines

NOTE: For dropped shoulder, add amount needed at the shoulder position, not at the edge.

Raglan   There are three styles of raglan sleeves:

This one-piece style appears in sweatshirts and oversized garments. Shoulder alterations are not necessary.

This style is the most common in fitted garments, but is also used in some oversized styles.

This style has a dart, and is not often seen today.

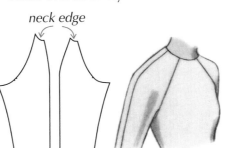

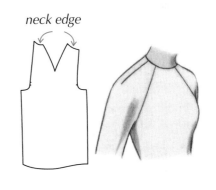

neck edge

neck edge

neck edge

For two-piece or darted raglan styles alter as follows:

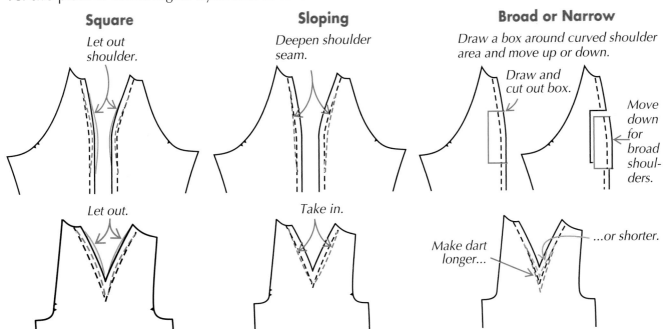

Square

Let out shoulder.

Let out.

Sloping

Deepen shoulder seam.

Take in.

Broad or Narrow

Draw a box around curved shoulder area and move up or down.

Draw and cut out box.

Move down for broad shoulders.

Make dart longer...

...or shorter.

CHAPTER 19
Sleeves

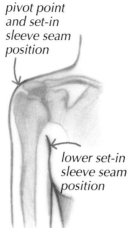

pivot point and set-in sleeve seam position

lower set-in sleeve seam position

The shoulder seam of a fitted garment meets the top of a set-in sleeve at the middle of your pivot point. If the garment has shoulder pads, the seam is usually extended 1/4" to 3/4" beyond the pivot bone.

Sleeves come in different shapes. Often, the armhole also changes shape to accommodate the sleeve. See the illustrations on the next page.

Sleeve Variations

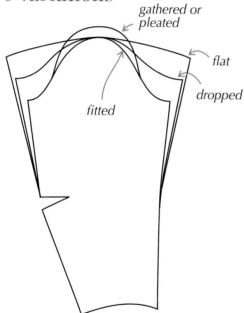

gathered or pleated

flat

dropped

fitted

Armhole Variations

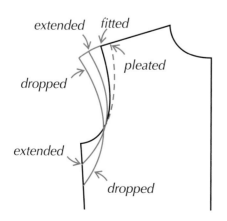

extended *fitted*

pleated

dropped

extended

dropped

Sleeve Anatomy

Fitted Sleeve

Most of the sleeve ease is in the upper third of the cap. 1"-1¾" is normal for a fitted sleeve cap.

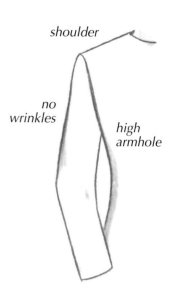

shoulder

no wrinkles

high armhole

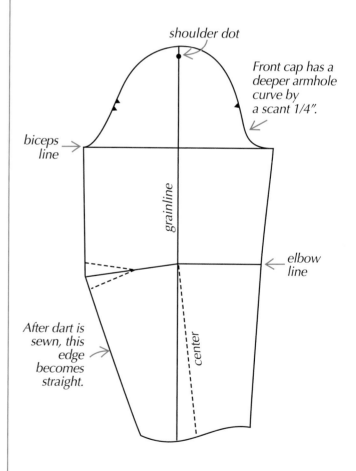

shoulder dot

Front cap has a deeper armhole curve by a scant 1/4".

biceps line

grainline

elbow line

After dart is sewn, this edge becomes straight.

center

Extended Shoulder

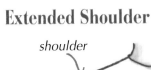

shoulder

less cap ease

Drape lines are normal.

deeper armhole

flatter, wider cap with 1/2" ease

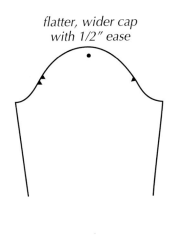

extended shoulder line

armhole for fitted sleeve

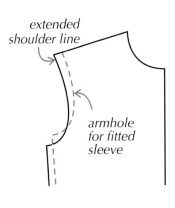

Dropped Shoulder

shoulder

Lots of drape lines are normal.

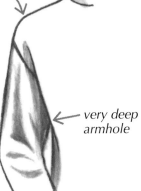

very deep armhole

flat cap with 0-1/4" ease

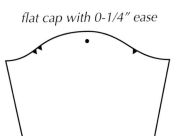

dropped shoulder line

lower armhole

armhole for fitted sleeve

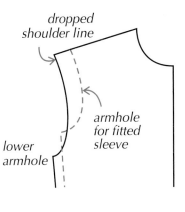

Gathered or Pleated

Cap is puffy if seam is pressed toward sleeve.

Cap is flat if seam is pressed toward garment and edgestitched.

pleated or gathered sleeve sets in further

shoulder

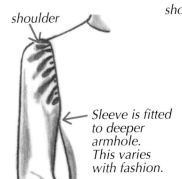

Sleeve is fitted to deeper armhole. This varies with fashion.

shoulder

tall, wide cap

armhole for fitted sleeve

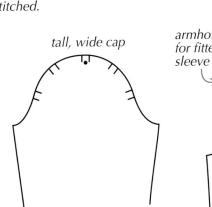

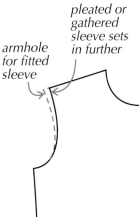

Adjusting at the Sleeve Cap

Dropped shoulders or oversized designs will always have drag lines in the sleeves. We call it "drape." Any style sleeve with a slightly flatter sleeve cap will have those "drape" lines. You will see deep drape lines in shirt sleeves.

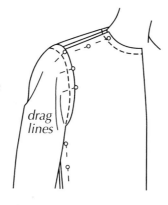

drag lines

If the sleeve is fitted and drag lines show up when tissue fitting, gently pull sleeve down from shoulder seam until drag lines diminish. Measure the resulting gap at the shoulder between the sleeve cap seam and the bodice armhole seam.

Raise the cap this amount by adding tissue to create a better fit and a better-looking sleeve.

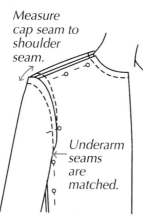

Measure cap seam to shoulder seam.

Underarm seams are matched.

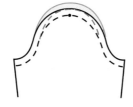

If you now have too much cap to ease in smoothly, adjust the armhole a little deeper. See page 171, "Very Large Arms."

Sleeve Width

Pin sleeve seams together and pin the sleeve to the bodice tissue at **the underarm only**. The top of the sleeve doesn't need to be pinned to the shoulder.

Can you pinch 1" of tissue? That would be 2" of ease, since you are pinching a double thickness of tissue.

Minimum sleeve ease is 1", but that may be too fitted for you unless you are using a knit. For woven fabrics, 1½"-2" of ease is more comfortable.

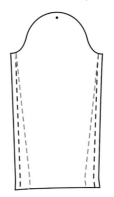

NOTE: It is perfectly okay to make a sleeve narrower at the bottom if it is designed looser than you prefer. We do this often to make our hips appear smaller. A narrower sleeve means less width at the hip when arms are down.

Sleeve Length

Get the sleeve *width* right before judging the length. Pin the sleeve to the bodice at the underarm *only*! For a shaped sleeve, adjust length above or below the elbow as needed until the elbow mark is at your elbow and the hemline is at the bottom of your wrist bone.

A Shaped Sleeve

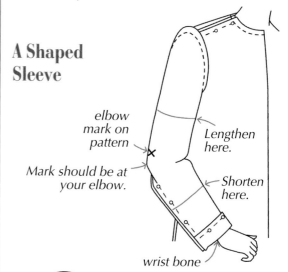

elbow mark on pattern

Mark should be at your elbow.

Lengthen here.

Shorten here.

wrist bone

Spread to add.

+ elbow

Tuck to shorten.

A **straight sleeve** is usually **tapered** to the wrist, and the hem flares out to fit to the taper. The sleeve may be adjusted either above or below the elbow, but not at the bottom, as that would alter the correct hem shape.

168

Full Arms

If your sleeve is too tight, you will need to add fullness for a more comfortable and attractive fit.

1. Draw a straight line from the shoulder dot to the hemline. Draw a perpendicular line connecting underarm seam intersections.

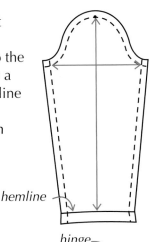

2. Cut through seam and hem allowances to stitching and hem fold lines. This will create hinges so seamlines won't change in size.

Cut to, but not through, hemline.

3. Cut on the lines you drew, up to the hinges.

4. Pin the sleeve bottom edge to the work surface as shown.

> **Quick Tip** Alter on a cardboard cutting board so you can pin into cardboard. The entire tissue must be on the cutting board. Pins should be at opposite angles at each end of a cut or slash so tissue won't move.

5. Spread the amount needed at arrow ($\leftrightarrow$) by pulling underarms apart. Do not tape yet!

6. Anchor with pins at B, and then at C.

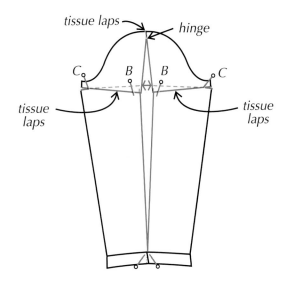

7. True the sleeve cap. Make sure the tissue is **totally flat, then** anchor at D and E.

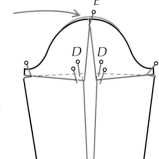

8. Insert tissue under the open area.

9. **When, and only when, tissue is completely flat**, tape the sections in place. Remove the pins.

NOTE: When adjusting for a full arm in **short sleeves**, follow same procedure, spreading pattern piece as if there were a pivot point at the wrist (steps 6 and 7, above). The tissue will not touch at the bottom edge of the short sleeve pattern piece, for if it did, the sleeve would be too tight. Try on the pattern piece to check the adjustment.

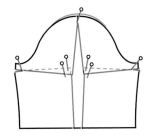

> **Quick Tip** You can do this alteration on top of one large sheet of tissue and trim excess away when you have finished making changes.

169

Thin Arms

If you have thin arms, follow the directions in step 1 on page 169 to mark the sleeve. Then cut and lap the vertical sections to remove excess fullness. Fill with tissue.

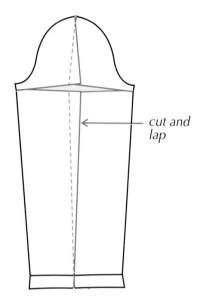

cut and lap

Two-Piece Sleeves

If you have a two-piece sleeve, lap the seams and draw a line at the underarm across both pieces so you'll know where to lap for thin arms or spread for full arms.

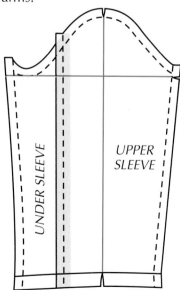

UNDER SLEEVE

UPPER SLEEVE

Cut and spread (or lap) upper sleeve only.

Variations

Full or Thin Wrists, Elbows or Lower Arms, as Well as Thin or Full Upper Arms

Lap or spread evenly from the underarm to the lower edge. This can be done for one or both arms.

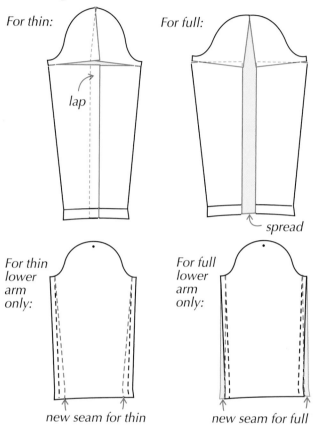

For thin:

lap

For full:

spread

For thin lower arm only:

For full lower arm only:

new seam for thin

new seam for full

Are Your Arms Two Different Sizes?

If one of your arms is larger than the other, trace the sleeve onto Perfect Pattern Paper so that you can tissue-fit a sleeve to each arm.

So you won't cut two right sleeves, place patterns **right side up** on the **right side** of a single layer of fabric with single (or double) notches facing each other.

Cut both on the right side of the fabric.

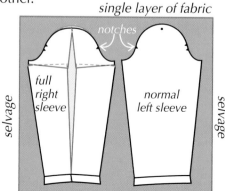

single layer of fabric

notches

full right sleeve

normal left sleeve

selvage

selvage

Full Arms and Torso

When both arm and underarm area of torso are full, add to the underarm of both sleeve seams and to the front and back bodice pieces as needed. (Make all additions equal.)

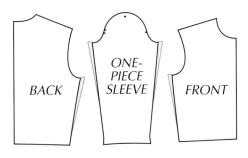

For a two-piece sleeve, spread only the undersleeve at the under-arm to add the total amount needed.

UNDERSLEEVE

Very Large Arms

If you need to spread a sleeve more than 1", you may need to raise the cap back to its original height.

1. Trace the original cap onto tissue before altering.

2. Make the alteration. Use the original sleeve cap cutting line, allowing some "in-case" seam allowance for fitting. (Your "in-case" seam allowance at the cap may or may not be used.)

True seam.

NOTE: Spread evenly to bottom to enlarge lower arm as well (page 170).

Your sleeve cap seamline is now much larger than before. In some fabrics it's difficult to ease more than 1½" into the armhole. Deepening the armholes will make them larger.

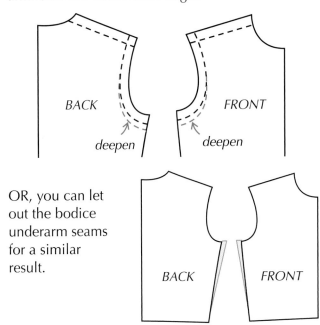

OR, you can let out the bodice underarm seams for a similar result.

Very Large Arms and Torso

If you have very full arms and are full in the torso and have already altered the sleeve, add "in-case" seam allowances to the underarms of the sleeves as well as to the bodice.

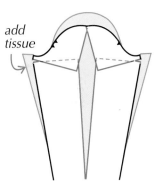

add tissue

Another Option for Very Large Arms

Sleeves with a seam down the center are ideal for people with full arms.

One of our students had very full upper arms with most of the fullness toward the back. Using a sleeve pattern with a center seam made it easier to fit her arm. See how we did it on page 172.

Cut and spread as you would to enlarge a one-piece sleeve (page 169), but do it on the **back** piece where the fullness is needed. Let out the center seam where needed for upper and lower arm fullness.

In our student's case we also needed to add to the side seams of her bodice, so we added the same amount to the underarm seam of her sleeve.

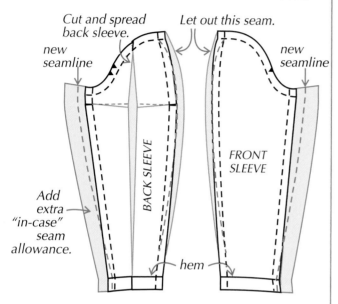

Cut and spread back sleeve.

Let out this seam.

new seamline

new seamline

Add extra "in-case" seam allowance.

BACK SLEEVE

FRONT SLEEVE

hem

This combination of alterations allowed us to expand her sleeve 4" in width at the fullest part of her upper arm with no distortion of the cap.

Cap Rotation

A wonderful revelation came to us in 1990 when we began seeing the need for the forward shoulder adjustment (page 162).

We initially moved the dot on the cap forward the same amount so the underarm would match the bodice, but the sleeve didn't hang correctly due to the forward arm rotation.

Then we decided to try setting the sleeve in by match- ing the original sleeve shoulder dot with the *new* shoulder seam on the garment. The sleeves hung perfectly.

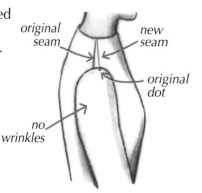

original seam

new seam

original dot

no wrinkles

Then, the question was, "What do we do with the underarm seams that won't match?"

If you go ahead and match them, you ease more in the front of the sleeve and less in the back. It's pretty minor and generally works quite well.

OR

◆ Allow them to not match! Who on earth will be looking under your arms?

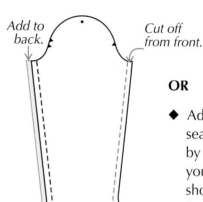

Add to back.

Cut off from front.

OR

◆ Adjust the underarm seam on the sleeve by the same amount you rotated the shoulder seam forward. Then the underarm seams will match!

Shoulder Pad Tips

no pad   pad

sleeve shorter

When you plan to wear shoulder pads in the garment you are making, always tissue-fit with them in or sleeves will end up too short when you add the pad later.

If the upper arm is full, use a raglan pad for camouflage. This also helps balance full hips.

More shoulder pad tips can be found on pages 160, 161, 166, 234 and 244.

Move raglan pad out until edge lines up with fullest part of arm.

Another Shoulder Wrinkle Solution

If there are still wrinkles in your sleeve (perhaps you have not moved the shoulder seam), you probably need to rotate the sleeve in the armhole. The wrinkles will guide you. Rotate the cap until the sleeve falls the same way your arm does and the wrinkles disappear.

Forward

Rotate sleeve toward the front.

Backward

Rotate sleeve toward the back.

Sewing Adjustments to the Cap

A poorly sewn sleeve makes a garment look "home-made" rather than "custom-made."

Diagonal Pulls

To eliminate diagonal pulls, add height to the cap.

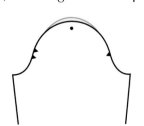

Puckers or Sagginess

To eliminate puckers or sagginess, reduce cap height and width.

puckers   *sagginess*

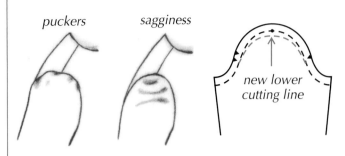

new lower cutting line

Pulls in Front and Back

If there is stress across the cap, widen cap.

Add width to cap.

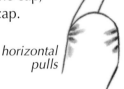

horizontal pulls

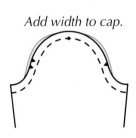

Pulls in Back Only

If back of arm is full, add to sleeve in the same location.

Add here.

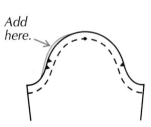

If you can't ease the extra fullness into the armhole, also add to the back bodice as shown.

BACK

Add here.

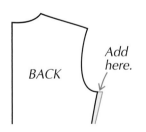

For more sleeve sewing tips including "pin-basting" see page 241.

Armhole Depth

In the late '80s the fashion trend began to shift toward a closer body fit. As a result, the armholes became very snug compared to what they had been with the oversized look.

Rule of Thumb

As clothing gets more fitted, you need higher armholes so you can move your arm comfortably. A low armhole in a *fitted* jacket restricts movement.

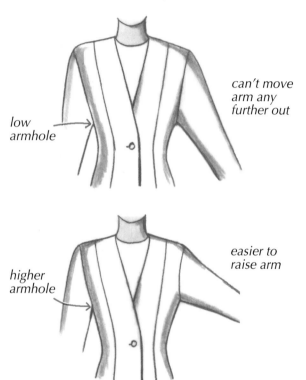

low armhole

can't move arm any further out

higher armhole

easier to raise arm

Changing Armhole Depth

A fitted armhole is about 1/2" from your actual underarm with your arm down and 1½" with your arm out to the side. A closer fit will be uncomfortable unless it's in a knit body suit.

You could lower the armhole on the pattern if it is too high.

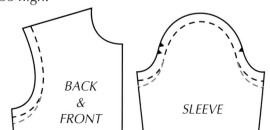

BACK & FRONT

SLEEVE

OR, wait until you try on the garment after you have trimmed the underarm seam to 1/4". If too tight, stitch 1/4" lower at the underarm, tapering to nothing at the notches. Trim to 1/4". Try on. Repeat if needed until the armhole is comfortable.

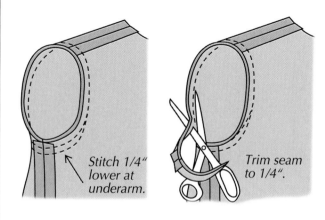

Stitch 1/4" lower at underarm.

Trim seam to 1/4".

Sewing Adjustments to Armhole

It is not a crime to reshape the armhole. Remember, **the pattern is the manuscript; you are the editor**.

If the back pulls at the armhole, set the back part of the sleeve further out into the back bodice seam allowance. **You can do this while sewing.** That extra 1/4" at each armhole edge is 1/2" extra room across the back.

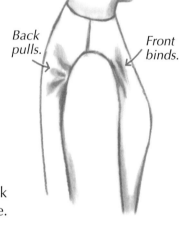

Back pulls.

Front binds.

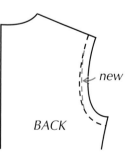

new

BACK

If the front binds or restricts movement, reshape where necessary. See "Forward Shoulders," page 162.

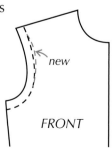

common reshaping for forward shoulder

new

FRONT

Sleeveless Dresses

The front and back underarm in a sleeveless dress is usually cut higher.

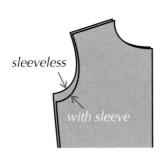

sleeveless

with sleeve

For a sleeveless dress you can also reshape the armhole for modesty or to hide extra flesh.

Sleeve Adjustments in Other Styles

Raglan Sleeves

This sleeve was originally used in a loose over-coat made for British Field Marshal Lord Raglan after an injury to his arm made a regular set-in sleeve impractical.

There are three ways to structure raglan sleeves—darted over the shoulder, seamed at shoulder, or seamless at shoulder (page 165).

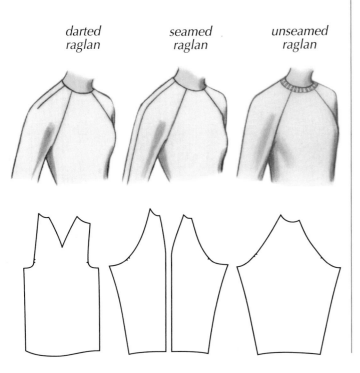

darted raglan   *seamed raglan*   *unseamed raglan*

To help you under-stand raglan sleeves, in a simplistic way, we'll show you where they come from. Part is from the shoulder of the basic bodice and part is from a basic sleeve.

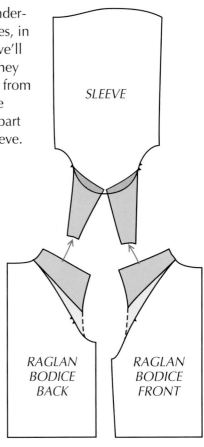

SLEEVE

RAGLAN BODICE BACK   *RAGLAN BODICE FRONT*

In loose-fitting raglan garments, the dart is removed for a seamless, dartless sleeve.

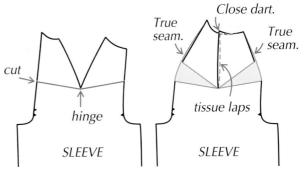

cut   *hinge*   *SLEEVE*

Close dart.

True seam.   *True seam.*

tissue laps   *SLEEVE*

If you close the dart at the top of a raglan sleeve, the shoulder seam gets longer. Add the same amount to the armhole of the bodice.

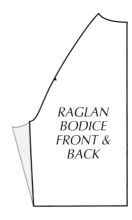

RAGLAN BODICE FRONT & BACK

An alternative way to make armhole seams match on both sleeve and bodice is to do a dart transfer (page 136).

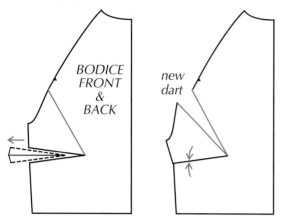

Move dart from here...   ...to here.

Raglan Sleeve Alterations for Full or Thin Arms

Raglan sleeves can be altered using the same technique as for the fitted sleeve.

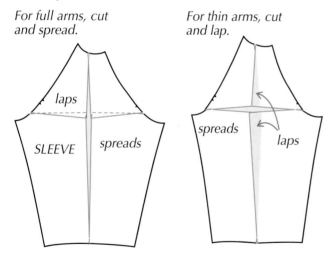

For full arms, cut and spread.

For thin arms, cut and lap.

A seamed raglan can simply be widened or narrowed as needed through the seam over the arm.

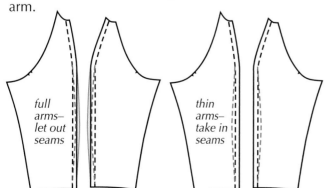

full arms— let out seams

thin arms— take in seams

Today, most raglans are undarted or seamed. A darted raglan is rare. It can be altered like a non-darted raglan, but be sure you adjust the size of the dart at the neck to keep the neckline seam the same size as before the alteration.

You can also split a darted raglan down the middle of the dart and continue to the sleeve hem. Add an even seam allowance from the dart stitching lines and to the cut edges below. Then alter as for a seamed raglan.

See "Shoulder and Armholes," page 160, for more information.

Cut-On (Kimono) Sleeves

The following are the common cut-on shapes. The sleeves can be long or short.

Japanese Style   Traditional Style

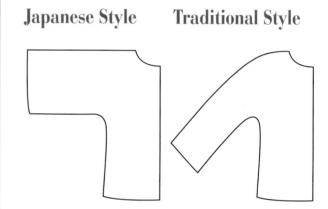

We will only address the more fitted style, as the Japanese style is very forgiving. Here you can see the differences in the cut-on styles.

Full Arm Adjustment   Thin Arm Adjustment

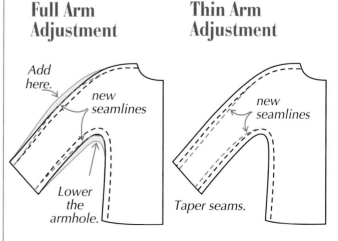

Add here.

new seamlines

Lower the armhole.

new seamlines

Taper seams.

CHAPTER 20

Waist, Hips, Tummy & Thighs

Tissue-fitting, then sewing a straight skirt is the quickest way to learn to fit your waist, hips, tummy and thighs. In this chapter we'll take you through the process. Also see pages 43, 82 and 101 for skirt tissue-fitting, and pages 186-229 for more skirt fitting on real people.

Try On the Tissue

Pin side seams and darts **wrong** sides together. Point pins down so they won't fall out. Also, do not use pins above the waistline and you won't get poked!

Tie elastic around your waist (usually at the top of your hip bones). Make sure pantyhose elastic is exactly at your waist.

We like to fit the right side of the body so that the tissue is printed-side out. **But if your left side is larger**, fit it instead. The skirt will then be cut large enough for your largest side when cutting double. Take in the smaller side to fit.

Try on the tissue. Put bottom edge of the elastic on the waistline seam. Match the skirt center front and back to yours.

 Generally, the belly button marks your center front.

RIGHT FRONT

LEFT FRONT

Waist & Hip Width

Small Waist

Pin the side seam deeper in the waist area until it fits your shape.

You could also deepen the darts. Or, make two narrower front or back darts. They will fit better than one deep dart, especially if you are flatter in front.

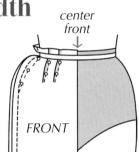

center front

FRONT

Thick Waist

1. If you can't get the pattern centers to meet yours, first unpin the front dart. Does the skirt fit and look better?

If you are flat in the derriere, let out the back darts as well.

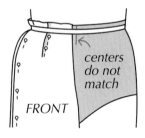

FRONT — *centers do not match*

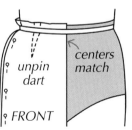

unpin dart — *FRONT* — *centers match*

2. If you still need more room, unpin the waist at the side seam. This will show you how much tissue to add at the upper side seam edges.

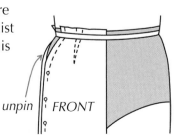

unpin — *FRONT*

3. Add the same amount of tissue to the front and back in the waist area. Add more than you'll need.

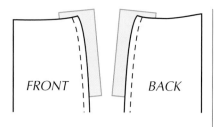

FRONT   BACK

4. Try it on again and pin to fit your body.

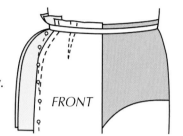

FRONT

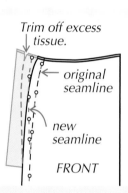

FIT Tip The tissue added to the front and the back MUST be shaped the same. For accuracy, pin the tissues together on the original seamlines. Mark new seamlines. (Ink will penetrate both layers.) Cut both layers on the new cutting line.

Trim off excess tissue.

← original seamline

new seamline

FRONT

Full Hips

1. If you can't get the tissue centers (front and back) to meet yours in the hip area, unpin the side seams until the centers meet. Now you can see how much tissue to add.

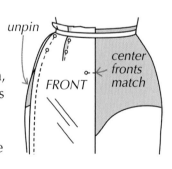

unpin

FRONT

center fronts match

2. At this point it's easiest to simply add **equal amounts** of tissue to the front and back at the side seams from the waist to the hem. Add more than you might need, as you can trim away excess later.

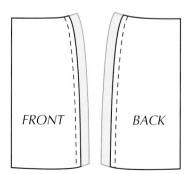

FRONT   BACK

3. Try on and pin to fit your shape. You may choose to pin straight down from the fullest hip area, or taper back to the original seamline at the hem for a more flattering line. See page 233. After you mark the new seamline, trim to an even seam allowance.

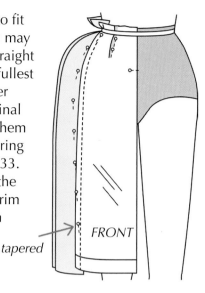

FRONT

tapered

Small Hips

Try on the tissue and pin to fit your shape.

Full, High Hips

Many of us have "fluff" (extra fullness) just below the waistline. If your skirts always have little wrinkles just under the waistband, your skirts are too tight there. The lower, larger part of the skirt rides up to make room for your full high hips, causing the wrinkles.

skirt rides up

Sew to match the actual shape of your body. The side seams will need to curve up to the waistline. However, don't continue curving into the waistline seam allowance. Sew straight up from the waist in the seam allowance.

Sew straight here.

Don't continue to sew curve in waistline seam allowance.

"In-Case" Seam Allowances

After adjusting for waist and hip width, always make 1" side seam allowances on straight skirts. They are larger "in-case" you need them.

178

The Front

Full Tummy

Pull down at the center front until the side seam is straight and the hem is level.

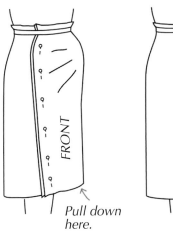

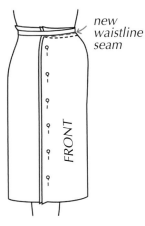

Pull down here.

new waistline seam

Mark new waistline seam at bottom of elastic. Add tissue to pattern for more tummy room.

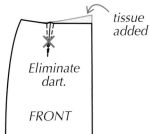

tissue added

Eliminate dart.

FRONT

FIT Tip
You probably won't want front darts if you have a full tummy, because they fall in the hollows on both sides of the tummy and will pucker.

Prominent Hip Bones

Hip bones often protrude on thinner people. You can camouflage them by adding a little width at the waist and ease or gather the skirt to the waistband over those areas.

add

FRONT

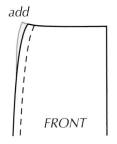

FRONT

Or, try angling the dart toward the prominent bone for a pucker-free dart and a smoother fit.

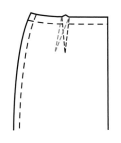

FRONT

The Back

Full Derriere

BACK

The side seams swing toward the back and may curve at the fullest part of the derriere. Also, the wrinkles point to the problem.

Pull down at the center back until the side seam is straight and the hem is level.

Add to the side seam of the back only, and raise the waist seam at the center back. Add an extra waist dart or deepen existing darts as needed.

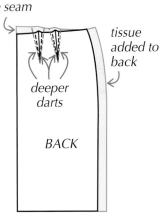

raise seam

tissue added to back

deeper darts

BACK

Try the tissue on again with the center fronts and backs matching yours. Pull the center back down until the hem is level. Then have a friend help pin-fit the side seam to your shape and to make sure the side seam is straight.

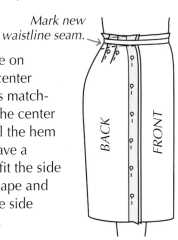

Mark new waistline seam.

BACK   *FRONT*

You can also slash into the pattern in several places. We experimented with techniques used in the past. Most of the methods change the center back or side seam shape.

The alteration at the right, from a book called **Fitting & Pattern Alteration** by Judith Rasband, did not.

Slash and spread as shown.

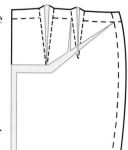

Flat Derriere

The side seams swing toward the front and there is bagginess below a flat derriere.

baggy wrinkles

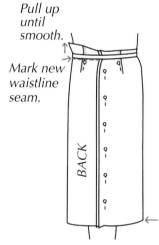

Pull up until smooth.

Mark new waistline seam.

BACK

Pull up at the center back until the hem is level, the bagginess is gone, and the side seam is straight. Mark the new waistline seam.

← *Hem is now straight.*

If the skirt fits, yet the entire side seam is forward, re-pin side seams narrower. Make a vertical tuck in the back to remove the excess width.

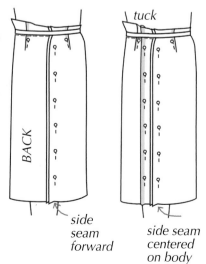

tuck

BACK

BACK

side seam forward

side seam centered on body

If you take a tuck in the back, you may then need to eliminate or make narrower the back darts and/or add to the waist at the side seams.

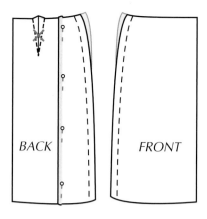

BACK   FRONT

Sway Back

You will see wrinkles just below the waistband in the back.

wrinkles

Pull up until wrinkles disappear.

Mark new waistline seam.

Back "Pillows"

Do you have those little areas of fluff on both sides of the back just below the waistline? You'll need more length over them. See Marta's skirt, page 82. We pulled the tissue down right above those pillows.

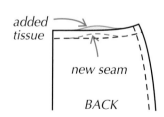

BACK

The waist seamline on your back skirt may end up looking like this:

added tissue

new seam

BACK

You may also need up to three curved darts on each side of the back. See convex darts on page 135.

Thighs

Full Thighs

If your thighs are just "full" you may be able to alter by just adding a little width to the side seams.

If they protrude at the sides, the following alterations work wonders. See Janice, on page 229, for a "Real People" example. Spreading the side seam adds length over the fuller thigh "bump."

Remember one of the fit rules on page 122, "The bigger the bump, the more length you need to cover it."

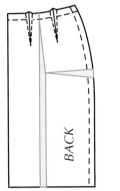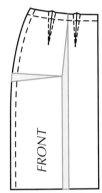

Thin Thighs

We've never had to do a "special" alteration for this on skirts, only on pants. Generally, just taking in the skirt side seams is the answer! (Lucky you!)

Refining Front Darts

If you have a full tummy, you are probably flat or even a little hollow on both sides of it, right where the darts are. The darts will pucker. See page 239 for sewing darts.

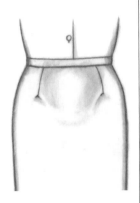

Simply eliminate the darts and ease the waistline to fit the waistband.

Or, if you want the design detail of the dart, sew an "essence" of a dart.

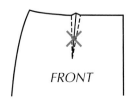

FRONT

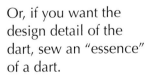

essence of dart

Dippy Waistlines

People with a full tummy who have eliminated their front darts may see dippy wrinkles just below where the darts are marked. If so, pull the tissue up at the waistline in the dart area. We call this "tweaking." Mark new seamline below the elastic.

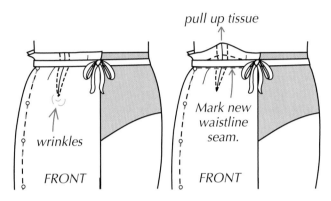

pull up tissue

wrinkles

FRONT

Mark new waistline seam.

FRONT

Getting Things Straight & Level

Side Seam Isn't Straight

Usually, this happens when a person has both a full tummy and a flat derriere. See page 183. A portion of the side seam may not be straight.

If the front dart is eliminated, the top of the side seam may lean to the back.

If so, remove the dart depth from the side front, then re-fit.

Does side seam lean?

BACK FRONT

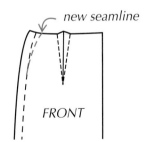

new seamline

FRONT

Or, try easing some of the dart fullness across the front into the waistband for a softer look over the tummy. See Marta on page 104. Place most of the ease where the dart used to be. The fuller the tummy, the less ease you will have.

181

If the tummy is VERY FULL, the top of the side seam may lean to the front even after unpinning the dart. Straighten by adding to the front and taking off of the back.

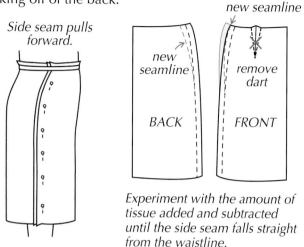

Side seam pulls forward.

new seamline

new seamline

remove dart

BACK

FRONT

Experiment with the amount of tissue added and subtracted until the side seam falls straight from the waistline.

Hem Level Tells All

If you have uneven hips, a full tummy or derriere, or a sway or flat back, your hem won't be level at the bottom.

We used to measure hems from the floor to get them level. This didn't correct fitting wrinkles. Now we level from the waistline. Bias skirts are the only ones we still level from the floor.

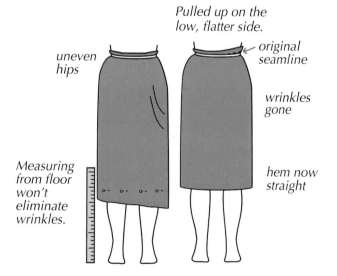

uneven hips

Pulled up on the low, flatter side.

original seamline

wrinkles gone

Measuring from floor won't eliminate wrinkles.

hem now straight

Uneven Hips

One high, full hip is common. It is often caused by poor posture—carrying things just on one side, for example. If you have a baby, try to alternate sides when carrying it. This is also true for grocery and shoulder bags. If you have back problems, it is likely you also have uneven hips.

To find out if you have a high hip, tie elastic around your waist (which is usually at the top of your hip bones). If you are wearing pantyhose, make sure the top edge is at your waist!

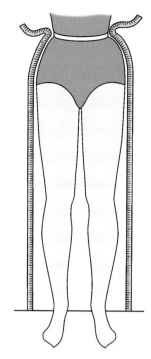

Have someone measure you from the bottom of the elastic to the floor on both sides. The longer side is usually fuller or rounder as well.

As we mentioned on page 177, if you have a noticeably fuller hip, you should tissue-fit that side first.

If you want to perfect the fit of a straight skirt, after tissue-fitting your high side, cut your pattern out of 1/4" gingham and pin-fit it to you. The checks make it very easy to spot needed changes.

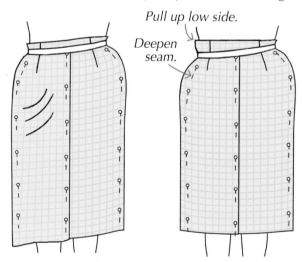

Pull up low side.

Deepen seam.

After fitting, mark all seams for your fullest side with red and for your smaller side with green.

This way you can cut both sides at once. You'll cut to fit the bigger side and pin to fit the smaller side. OR, tissue-fit using TWO patterns so you can fit each half accurately. We did this on Connie on page 211, because she was so uneven all the way around, not just at the sides.

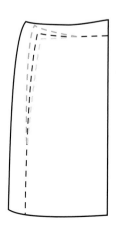

Low in Back, High in Front

The goal is for your skirt's side seam to be straight and the hem level. If the hem isn't level, the side seam won't be perpendicular to the floor. Check your side view! Adjust at the waist until the seam hangs straight.

flat derriere

full tummy

side seam curves toward front

For example, when one has a full tummy and a flat derriere, the waist is likely to be very high in front and low in back. It's where your waistband will want to sit.

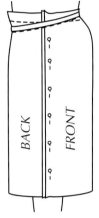

Pull up the tissue.

Mark the new waistline below the elastic.

BACK *FRONT*

Pull down in the front until the hem is level and the side seams are straight.

Add tissue to the center front if needed.

side seam now straight and hem level

Low in Front, High in Back

This may be due to poor posture, a full tummy, or genetics. Pull up in the front until the side seam is perpendicular to the floor and the hem is level. Eliminate front darts. The bottom of the elastic is the new waistline seam.

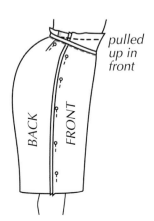
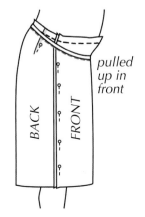

pulled up in front

pulled up in front

BACK *FRONT* *BACK* *FRONT*

Length

Lengthen or shorten a straight skirt at the bottom. If it has a detail such as a vent or is tapered at the hem, then lengthen above the detail.

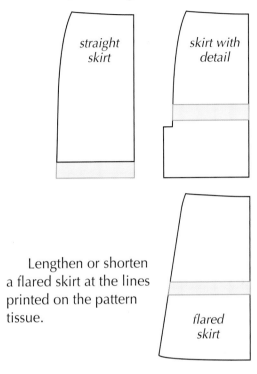

straight skirt

skirt with detail

Lengthen or shorten a flared skirt at the lines printed on the pattern tissue.

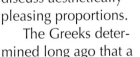

flared skirt

What Length is Good?

In our book **Looking Good** we discuss aesthetically pleasing proportions.

The Greeks determined long ago that a 2:1 proportion (one-third/two-thirds) was the most pleasing.

Skirts should stop at a length flattering to the leg. Avoid placing the hemline at the fullest part of your knee, calf or ankle.

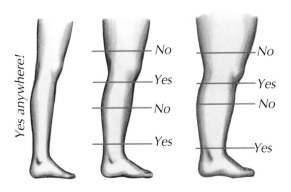

Yes anywhere!

No
Yes
No
Yes

No
Yes
No
Yes

183

Tweaking in Fabric

It is absolutely amazing how good your fit will be if you carefully tissue-fit. Even so, **it is always necessary to also fit-as-you-sew**.

However, if you always sew with the same fabric, cut perfectly accurately, and never change in weight, maybe you could eliminate fitting in fabric. (It won't happen! Trust us!)

It is very simple to fit in fabric when making a skirt.

Sewing Order

1. Sew darts (or baste, if unsure of fit).

2. Sew center back seam, and insert the back zipper.

3. Fit; **pin with wrong sides together** and try on with elastic at the waistline seam.

If the skirt is too tight you will see horizontal wrinkles.	Re-pin sides where you see the wrinkles until they disappear.

If it is too loose, you will see vertical wrinkles.	Re-pin sides where you see the wrinkles until they disappear.

Adjust the waistline until the hem is even, side seams are straight, and wrinkles are gone. Mark below the elastic for waistband stitching line.

Mark the side seams at pins with chalk or water-soluble marker.

 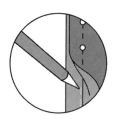

NOTE: If you have side seam pockets, fit first. Mark the side seams. Then sew the pockets to the seam allowance 1/4" from the seamline. See page 243 for more tips.

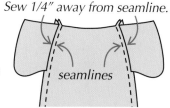

Sew 1/4" away from seamline.

seamlines

4. **Re-pin with the right sides together** and sew on the chalk marks. Generally, the length of the zipper opening is not affected.

5. Attach the waistband and complete the hem.

Fitting a Skirt with a Yoke

Chances are, your waist is fuller than a 20-year-old's waist. Try on the yoke. Have someone slash it at the waist and spread the pattern until it fits. Tape over the slashes. Remove the yoke tissue and place on a piece of alteration tissue. The tape will stick to the tissue under the slashes.

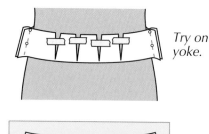

Try on yoke.

Place on tissue.

If your waist is smaller, split and lap the tissue instead. For fuller, high hips, split from the bottom to the top and spread the lower edge.

Quick-Fit the Waistband

1. Tissue-fit the waistband. Fold the waistband pattern piece in half. To see if it is long enough, wrap it around your waist, over the skirt seam allowance (and over the top you will wear if you plan to wear it tucked in).

2. If you do not have at least 2" extensions at each end of the pattern piece to allow for seam allowances and a generous under-lap, add tissue to both ends. It's just plain safer!

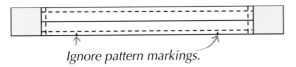

Ignore pattern markings.

3. Try on the skirt without the waistband pinned to it. Fold the waistband over the interfacing and wrap it around the waist just like when you tissue-fitted.

4. When the waistband feels comfortably snug, pin ends together. Distribute skirt ease under band evenly.

Chalk where the ends meet.

pin

Chalk the waistband at skirt's matching points: front & back darts, tucks, side seams, center front and center back.

◆ If your waistline is uneven and you have, for example, more fullness on the sides than in the front, or more fullness on one side, adjust the skirt under the waistband until the ease is distributed over the **fuller** areas.

◆ These wrinkles tell you to move some of the ease toward the side seams.

◆ If your hip area is considerably larger than your waistline, make the skirt waist-line larger than the waistband and ease into waistband over the full areas.

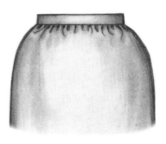

When you need to ease in a lot of the skirt to a waistband, after matching chalk marks, pin remaining edges together with a FEW pins first.

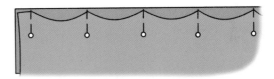

Then add as many pins as necessary to help the skirt material lie flat.

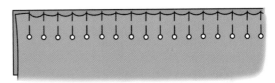

If you sew with pins next to the feed dogs, sew slowly. If you need to sew **over** the pins (which is dangerous but sometimes necessary, as with the waistband shown above), then the feed dogs will help ease in the fullness and help avoid puckers.

Quick Tip A quick way to ease a lot of skirt into the waistband is to machine baste on the waist seamline of the skirt. Pull on the bobbin thread to ease the skirt to fit the band. Now you won't have to sew over pins.

PRO Tip When lining a skirt, before sewing on the waistband, attach lining with the same basting stitch used in the Quick Tip.

CHAPTER 21

Real People

People who need fit help are not perfect size 10 twenty-year-olds. They are you and me, with time-tested bodies. In some cases they're well-aged (like the fine fabrics we've collected) and are often beginning to reflect their ancestry. With that in mind, we set out to find some "real people" for our book. It was easy, because when people came to our fit classes at our sewing school, we also analyzed them for their book potential! We appreciate the real people shown in the following pages for being willing to share themselves and their fitting challenges with other sewers.

Even if your challenges are not exactly the same as those modeled in this chapter, we're confident that reading through the fitting process for each one will show you how to make fitting decisions for your own body in a variety of pattern designs.

Dorothy

FLATTERING A RECTANGULAR SHAPE

Dorothy, a retired nurse and an avid sewer, is on the front cover of this book. She is 38¼" in the high bust and 39" in the full bust. This makes her a size 16 by either measurement. She has a B-cup bra size, but she is thick also through the rib cage and waist. We wanted to give her rather **rectangular figure** a flattering **hourglass** look so we chose a jacket pattern with a shoulder princess line.

The Front Before

Dorothy tries on her jacket tissue and it is tight across the bust as well as the hips. However, the **bust fullness** is too high for her so it must be lowered first (page 149). Then we can accurately see how tight it is in the bust area.

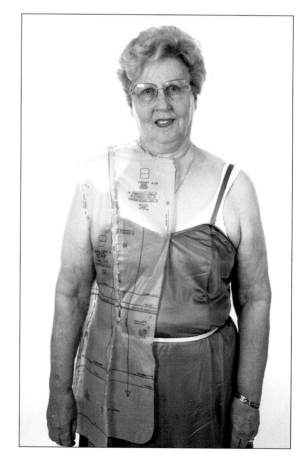

The Back Before

Let's take a look at the back before we alter the front. Remember, if someone has a broad back, that alteration could solve the front problem. This wasn't the case with Dorothy because she has an average back width.

The back doesn't hang straight. It swings to the side and is longer in the center back because Dorothy has a **flat derriere**.

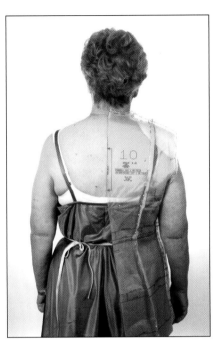

The Front After

We lowered the bust fullness and VOILA! It fits in width. We also let out the waist and hip area at the side seam for more room. The shoulder princess seam curves toward the center front at the waist to give an hourglass look.

The Back After

We took a dart tuck through both back pieces, tapering to nothing at the side seams until the back hung straight and the hem was level. See page 128.

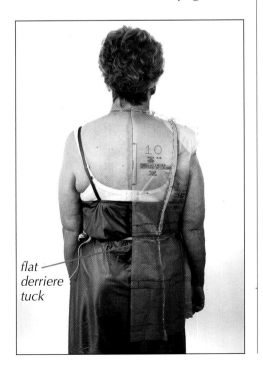

flat derriere tuck

The Sleeve Before

Dorothy slips on the sleeve tissue. She can barely pinch excess tissue, so the upper sleeve needs widening.

The Sleeve After

The sleeve is now wide enough after altering (page 169). The top of the cap (circle) isn't up to the shoulder seam, so we will cut a wider seam at the top of the cap just in case we need the added cap height.

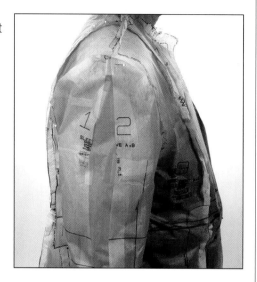

Pin-fitting in Fabric

The first fabric fitting is with seams pinned wrong sides together. Dorothy looks great in these two tones of wool crepe. We used a darker color on the sides of the jacket to give a thinner illusion.

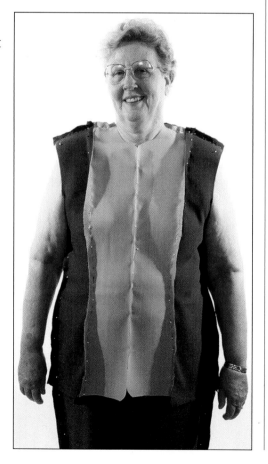

The back looks good, but a thicker shoulder pad on the left side will even up her shoulders and eliminate the hip wrinkle.

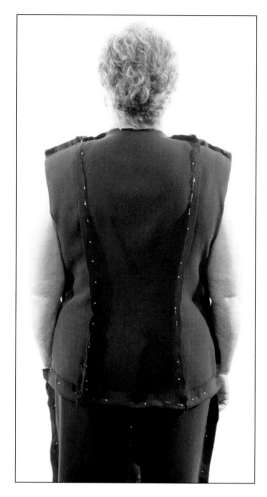

Marta pin-basted the sleeve to the armhole. If you've never done this, try it. It is a quick way to check sleeve fit and hang. The sleeve fits well, without wrinkles. See the finished jacket on page 191.

The Skirt Front Before

Dorothy tries on the skirt tissue pattern using elastic to hold it in place at the waist.

Ugh! Front darts! They rarely work on someone with a **full tummy** as there is usually a hollow on each side of the tummy. Darts will only pucker (page 179, 181 and 233). Note also the droop just under the dart.

The center front edge swings to the side. The tissue needs to be pulled down at the side. She's **rounder** at her sides and needs more length to go over that roundness. Many of us have this extra "fluff" just below the waist.

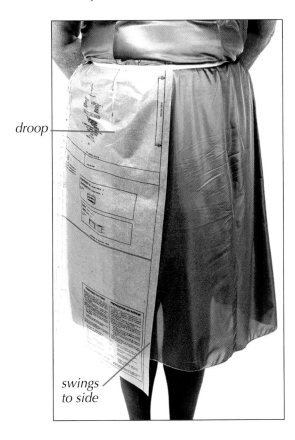

droop

swings to side

The Skirt Back Before

Let's "quick-check" the back before we do any altering to the front. The center back is not straight and the tissue is longer at the center back because she has a **flat derriere** (page 180).

swings to side

The Skirt Back After

We pulled the tissue up at the center back under the elastic until it hung straight and the back hem edge was level.

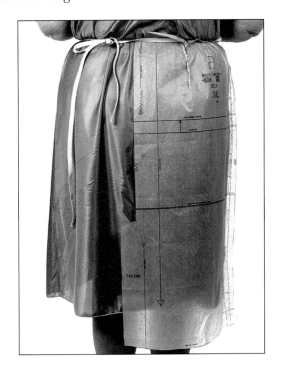

The Skirt Front After

We pulled the tissue down at the side front, eliminated the front dart, and pulled up on the tissue in the dart area. Now everything is smooth and hangs straight.

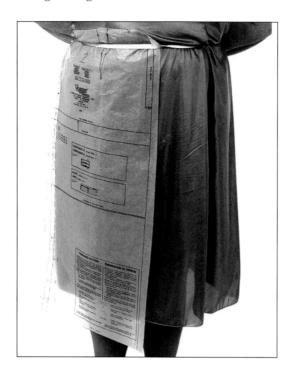

Pin-fitting in Fabric

We pinned the center back, back darts and side seams wrong sides together. The 1/4" elastic holds the skirt in place. The soft gathers in front look great in place of the darts.

The back looks great too. Wool crepe is wonderful. It molds to the body and hangs well.

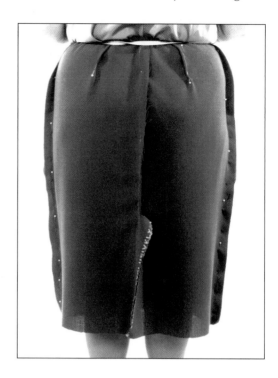

From the side view, you can see that the hem is level. Hems are "leveled" at the waist, not at the hem, except for bias cuts (page 182).

Dorothy's Finished Suit

Dorothy models her finished suit. Our goal was to create the illusion of a more hourglass shape using her admittedly rather rectangular body. The bit of curve at the waistline in the princess seam did the trick.

Designer Tip

If the princess line on the pattern is straight, redraw so it has more of an hourglass shape, curving in at the waist.

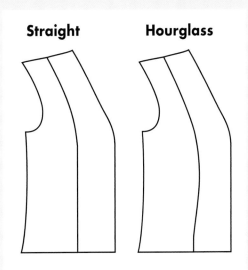

Straight   **Hourglass**

Mark new seamlines, and make seam allowances an even width.

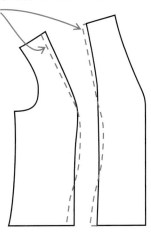

Marcy
A TALL PERSON

Our 5'10" friend Marcy is a Certified Palmer/Pletsch Instructor and co-author of our book, **The Business of Teaching Sewing**. Marta measures Marcy and finds her high bust 36½" (size 14) and her full bust 39½" (size 16). We will use a size 14 pattern (see Chapter 4, "Buy the Right Size").

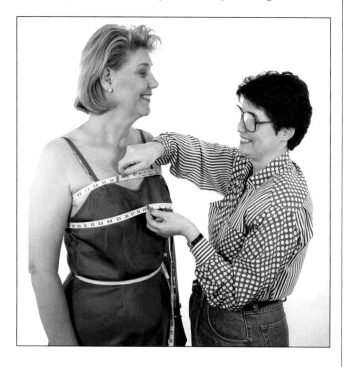

Fitting Marcy in a Sheath Dress

We started with a very fitted dress in order to clearly see how Marcy varies from a pattern. Since the pattern is multi-sized, we pinned along the size 14 stitching lines on the top, tapering out to the size 16 stitching line at the hips.

The Front Before

Look at the photo at the top of the next column. The tissue scrunches under Marcy's arm meaning Marcy needs more length (3/4") in the chest (page 115). The horizontal dart is high, but we need to do all lengthening first and then re-check the dart. The waist marking is 1½" above the waist elastic.

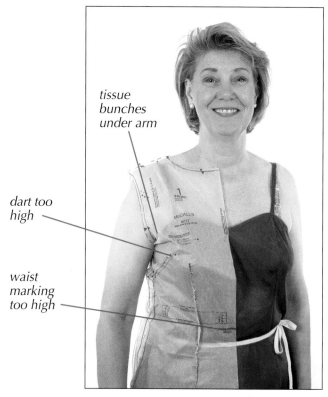

tissue bunches under arm

dart too high

waist marking too high

The Front After Length Adjustments

We lengthened the bodice in two places. The dart is now close to the right spot, but the center front is 5/8" from Marcy's center front. Also, there is a slight gap in the armhole. She needs a **full bust adjustment**. See page 142.

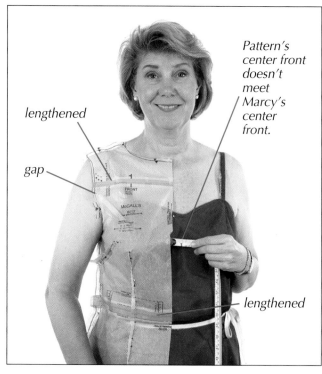

lengthened

gap

Pattern's center front doesn't meet Marcy's center front.

lengthened

The Front After Bust Adjustments

The tissue's center front comes to her center front and the deeper dart for the **full bust** removes the armhole gap. The dart also now points to her bust. The bust width was added all the way to the hem, giving her a little more hip/tummy room.

The Back After Length Adjustment

Before trying on the back tissue, the upper back was lengthened the same amount as the front. The center back swings toward the side. Marcy has an **erect back** and **flat derriere** (page 127). She needs less length at center back than allowed by the pattern.

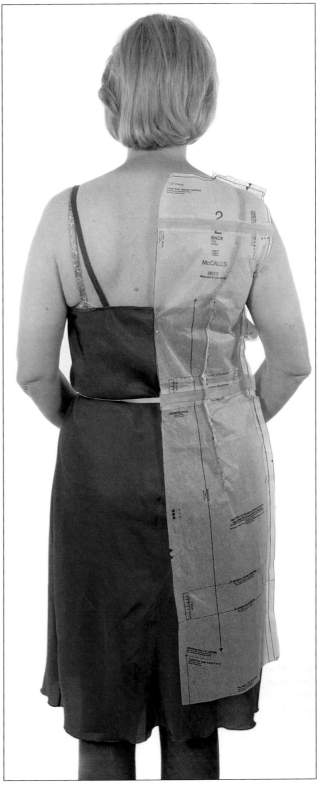

The Back After

We took a 1/4" tuck at the center back, tapering to nothing at the side seam to make the center back hang straight. We let out the side seams on the back and the front just below the waist. Many of us have acquired a little "fluff" in that area and need more room there.

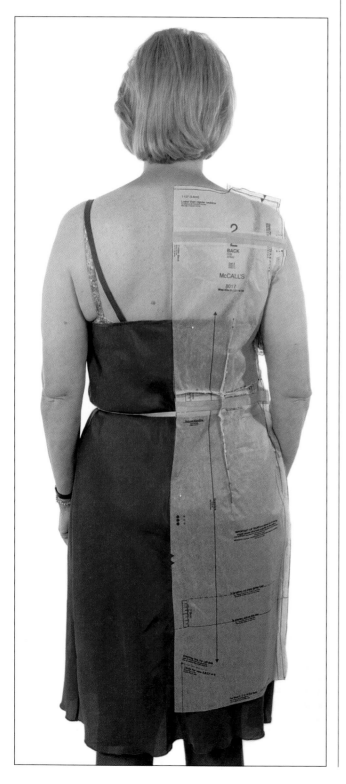

Joyce
SMALL WITH HIGH, FULL BUST AND SHORT LEGS

Joyce, a 25-mile-a-week runner, is also a Certified Palmer/Pletsch Instructor. Joyce's high bust is 30¼" (size 4) and her full bust is 34¼" (size 12). She had been sewing with a size 10 due to her full bust measurement. She is 5'3" and her **shortness** is below her waist.

We had to tissue-fit her in the size 6 bodice since the pattern doesn't come in a size 4. Because she is **full-busted**, we used the DD front from the McCall's Palmer/Pletsch fit pattern.

The Basic Bodice

The Front Before

The size 6 pattern is too wide across the chest in the mid-armhole area. This indeed means she is a size 4, which is a virtually non-existent pattern size.

The Back Before

The back is too wide. The neck seam is below her necklace at the base of her neck. The center back is too long just above the waist.

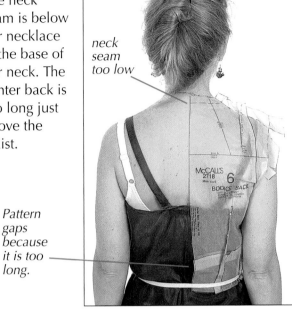

neck seam too low

Pattern gaps because it is too long.

The Front After

With an 1/8" vertical tuck the pattern now fits the width of Joyce's body. She is also **forward in her shoulders** so we pivoted the shoulder seam 3/8" forward (page 162).

Grading Down to a Size 4

To grade the pattern to a size 4, we will make a 1/8" vertical tuck in both the front and back pattern pieces, which will make the width 1" smaller all the way around (page 28). You can see the tucks in the after photos of the front and back.

The Back After

The 1/8" vertical tuck makes the back width correct. The back was also altered for a **high round back**. The neck seam now reaches the necklace. See pages 122-123.

Joyce has an **erect/sway back**. To make the center back hang straight, we took a horizontal 1/4" tuck at center back, tapering to nothing at the side seam. See pages 126-128.

Darted Vest Size 10

What if this pattern also doesn't come in a size 4 or even a size 6? No problem. We will make a size 10 vest pattern fit Joyce. This will be a common occurrence for Joyce, so she needs to become an expert at grading down!

The Front Before

The vest is too big. Joyce plans to wear the vest with a top that has shoulder pads. Therefore, all adjustments must be made with shoulder pads in place.

Grading Down

We tucked out 5/8″ vertically from the shoulder to the hem in the front and back. (Always try to avoid tucking through a dart.)

The Back

The back alterations were identical to the basic bodice.

The Front After

Since this is a B-cup front, we can now check bust fullness. The center front marking on the vest is 1¼″ from Joyce's, the amount of the necessary alteration.

After Full Bust Alteration

The full bust alteration automatically lowers the horizontal bust dart. In Joyce's case, it needs to be raised back to the original level. See pages 142-144.

bust dart too low

After Raising the Bust Dart

We cut around the dart, raised it, taped it in place and filled in the space with blue tissue.

Joyce is now ready to cut her perfect-fitting vest.

Princess Vest Size 10

The Front Before

Just as with Joyce's other patterns, the vest pattern is too big.

After Grading Down

We took 5/8" out of the front to reduce the width. After grading the width down, Joyce tried it on again and we measured from the center front to her center front—1¼" in this size 10. (The amount will vary with the ease in the design.)

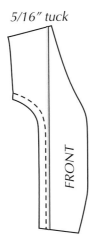

5/16" tuck

The Back

The back alterations were the same as on the basic bodice, except for needing to make a deeper tuck, since this is a size 10 pattern.

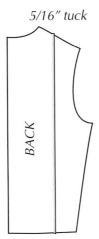

5/16" tuck

After Full Bust Alteration

After grading down we completed the **princess bust adjustment** (page 151). Since this alteration, unlike a darted front alteration, doesn't lower the bust position, it was correct on Joyce.

Because this alteration added width at the waist, which Joyce did not need, we deepened the seams until she liked the fit.

Size 10 Blazer

The Front Before

Once again the pattern is too large. Keep in mind that fittings must be done with the shoulder pads in place.

After Grading Down

We tucked 5/8" out of the front and back vertically through the shoulder **next to** the vertical dart.

We also made a 1/8" tuck in the side panel, making the armhole smaller. Since Joyce has size 4 arms, the same amount came out of the under sleeve.

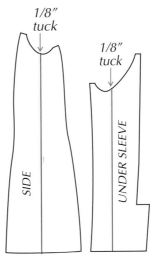

1/8" tuck

1/8" tuck

The distance from the pattern center front and Joyce's is now 1¼", the same as on the vest.

After Full Bust Alteration

We shortened the jacket below the waist because Joyce is **short between the waist and the knees** (page 32). The new jacket length is a better proportion.

Then we did the bust adjustment and transferred the new horizontal dart to the neckline dart (page 138).

After Bust Dart Transfer

The bust adjustment caused the upper front to become quite bias.

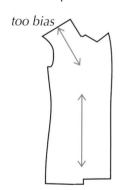

too bias

To straighten it out again, Joyce transferred part of the horizontal dart to a new vertical dart—the orange tissue in the photo. See page 138.

We then decided we liked the look of two vertical darts instead of just one deep dart. We lengthened the existing dart 1" and made the point of the second dart the same height.

The Back Before

The neck seam is too low—1/4" below the necklace due to a **high round back**. The back is too wide, which will require a vertical tuck.

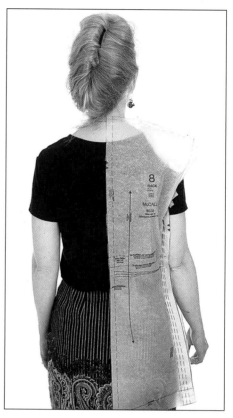

The Back Graded Down

As part of the grading down we narrowed the back 5/8", the same as the front. Note that the center back swings to the side because she has a **sway back** and doesn't need as much length above the waist as is in the pattern.

swings to side

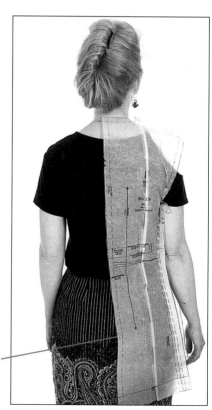

The Back After

We raised the neck 1/4" for the high round alteration (pages 122-123).

This pattern didn't have ease in the back shoulder, so we added about 3/8" to the back armhole to allow for back shoulder ease (or a dart). This eliminated the gap or droop in the back armhole.

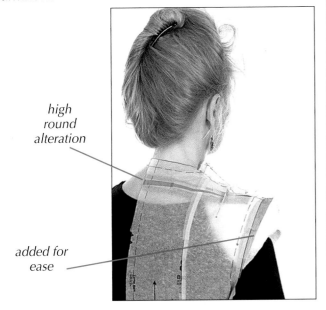

high round alteration

added for ease

To straighten the center back, we took a horizontal dart tuck above the waistline (page 128).

The side back seam was let out a bit. She needed the room for her runner's derriere.

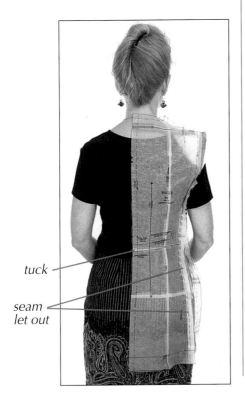

tuck

seam let out

The Sleeve Before

We pinned the sleeve to the jacket tissue, at the under-arm only.

The size 10 sleeve is way too full for her size 4 arms. It is also too long.

The Sleeve After

The sleeve was shortened 1". Joyce did this above the elbow because she wanted to maintain the taper at the lower edge.

The undersleeve was narrowed with a 1/4" vertical tuck. The upper sleeve was narrowed 1/2", (page 170). Because her entire arm is small, we took this tuck all the way down the sleeve through the wrist.

Wow! This looks like a lot of work, but it's well worth it for a beautiful fit in this classic jacket pattern. It can be made over and over again in various fabrics and colors—a great wardrobe addition.

Anastasia

SMALL BUST

Anastasia is Marta's daughter and at 20 is a student at the University of Oregon in the school of architecture. Her high bust measures 31½" and full bust 32", which puts her in a size 8 pattern.

The Front Before

Anastasia tries on the tissue and it is too full across the bust and too long at center front.

too long

The Intermediate Step

We pinned out the fullness so we knew how much to alter. The alteration itself is the opposite of a full bust alteration (page 146).

excess fullness temporarily pinned out

The Front After

The front has been cut and lapped for a **small bust alteration**. Now the front fits in width and length. We keep telling Anastasia it is much better to be small busted now because most people get larger as they mature. Plus, the only time she will need to do this alteration is when the garment is very fitted.

small bust alteration

The Back

Her back is a perfect size 8. See, there are some who fit the patterns— in at least one place, anyway.

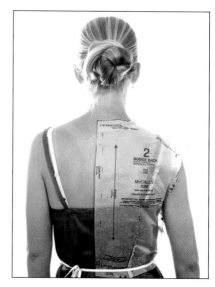

Debbra

FULL BUST ARMHOLE PRINCESS

Debbra, a beautiful professional model, is on our cover. She is also a talented seamstress. Her high bust is 39¾" and her full bust is 45". We will use a size 16.

The New Princess Bust Method

The Front Before

Debbra tries on the tissue. The pattern center front doesn't come to hers. She could measure the distance from the line on the tissue to the pin at her center front to see how much to add.

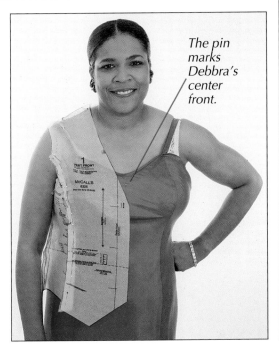

The pin marks Debbra's center front.

However, with a princess line, you can unpin the seam over the bust to see the actual amount. Measure across the opening from **seamline** to **seamline** for the amount to add.

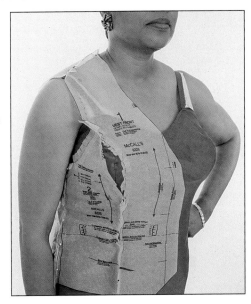

Can the extra room needed be added to the side panel or should some be added to the front and some to the side? How do you decide? The finished seam should be centered over the bust or slightly toward the underarm seam. Some styles are designed so the seam is even closer to the side.

The Front After

Debbra needed some width on both the front and side front pieces. Using our new princess bust alteration (page 151), we altered the side panel. Using the technique on page 150 we added width to the front. The fit, especially in the armhole, is perfect the first time!

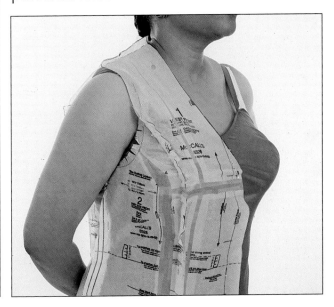

201

The Old Princess Bust Method

Why would we tell you about an old method when we've created a better method? Some people just don't like to cut into a pattern. This old method works if you know how to tweak it. You'll need several steps to complete the alteration.

First, we let out the seam over the bust, then added tissue and lengthened the front until the front seam was the same length as the side front. Now there is an armhole gap.

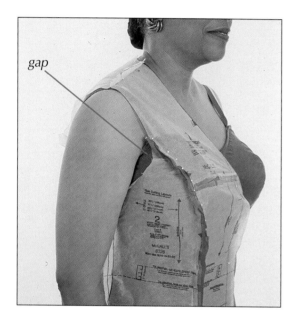

gap

One way to eliminate the gap is to move the front shoulder over. This removes shoulder width at the neckline, however, so you must add it back at the shoulder armhole edge. The lower armhole needs to be filled with tissue. See page 154.

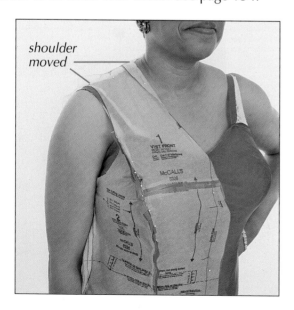

shoulder moved

Another way to eliminate a gap is to deepen the seam on the side front armhole. You will also need to fill in this space with tissue. See page 154.

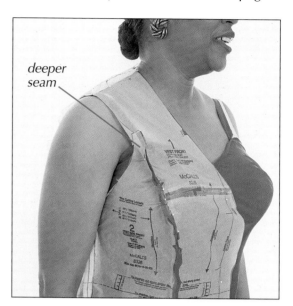

deeper seam

The Old Method Used with a Shoulder Princess

Debbra tries on the tissue. There is a gap in the armhole and the center front of the tissue doesn't come to hers.

Pin marks Debbra's center front.

We unpinned the shoulder princess pattern over her bust and matched the pattern center front to hers, then measured the opening from seamline to seamline.

We let out the seams over the bust and lengthened the front to match the side front. There is still an armhole gap.

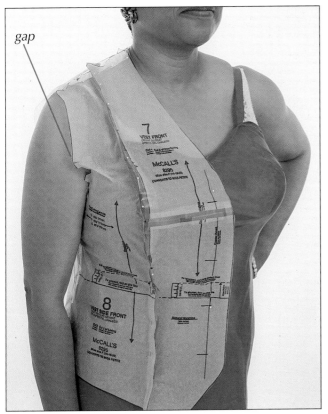

gap

The Front After

We moved the side front shoulder until the gap disappeared. Then we added tissue to the edge of armhole and marked the new seamline (page 153).

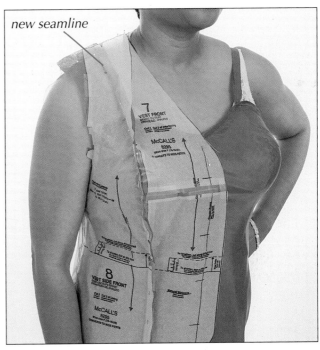

new seamline

Debbra's Finished Vest

Gretchen

PRINCESS BUST ALTERATIONS—LOW FULL BUST

Gretchen, a Certified Palmer/Pletsch Sewing Instructor and home-school mom, measures 42¼" at the high bust and 46¾" at the full bust. This makes her a size 20, based on her high bust measurement.

The Front Before

Gretchen tries on the tissue. She is **low busted**, so our first step is to lower the bust fullness. We can't tell how much width she needs until we do. Right now it appears she needs 1" more width at the center front.

We've lowered the bust fullness (page 149) and now the center front is only 1/2" from Gretchen's.

See page 149 for how to true seamlines when you lower bust fullness.

We unpinned the seam over the bust and the distance from seam to seam measures 1/2".

The Front After

We used the new princess bust alteration (pages 150 and 152) and added all the width to the side front. Now the bust and the armhole fit well.

Olga

ROUND BACK & SHOULDERS

Olga, a three-times-a-week swimmer and retired epidemiologist, takes writing classes. She tells us her age is "fourscore," but we don't believe it.

Due to scoliosis and some osteoporosis, Olga has the combination of a **curved spine** and a **rounded upper back** (see page 122).

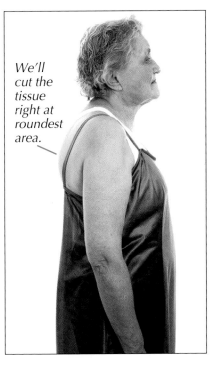

We'll cut the tissue right at roundest area.

You can see her **right back at the shoulder blade is fuller** than her left back. Her **right shoulder is also higher**. These observations will play a big part as we make our fit decisions.

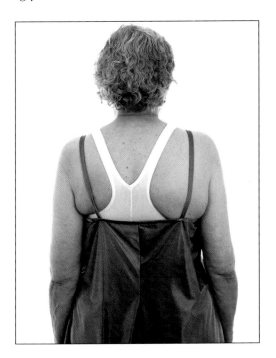

First, we measured high bust and full bust. Olga is 34½" in the high bust and 35½" in the full bust. Both measurements indicate a size 12 pattern.

Style and Fabric

Because one side of Olga's back is fuller than the other, it's not a good idea to choose fitted patterns that would only make this more apparent. We chose a straight cardigan—a style in which Olga is comfortable.

For the same reason, we didn't want a clingy fabric. We chose a wool coating and felt that by "tweaking" the seams and adding a little more shoulder pad to the left side we could visually even her figure out.

The Front Before

The tissue is snug through the hips.

In this close-up of the back, you see a gap in the armhole that will be removed by darting the shoulder. Also, the back neck seam is too low.

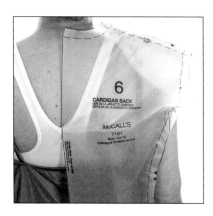

We cut the tissue across the shoulder blades from the center back to the armhole stitching line. We raised the neck seam to the correct position and simply taped the tissue to her back. See page 124.

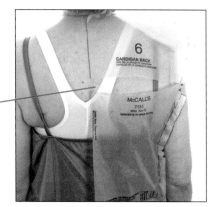

Vertically placed tape holds upper and lower edges of slashed pattern together.

The Back Before

The center back swings to the side.

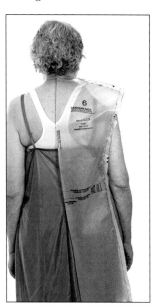

The Back After

We slipped off the pattern and filled in the back slash with alteration tissue.

Instead of straightening the center back, we added a center back seam which will curve over her roundness (page 125).

The horizontal tapered tuck at the waist straightened the lower center back.

We added width at the shoulder in order to dart the back shoulder seam to fit her full shoulder blade (page 122).

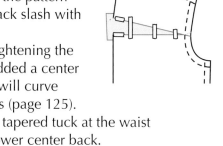

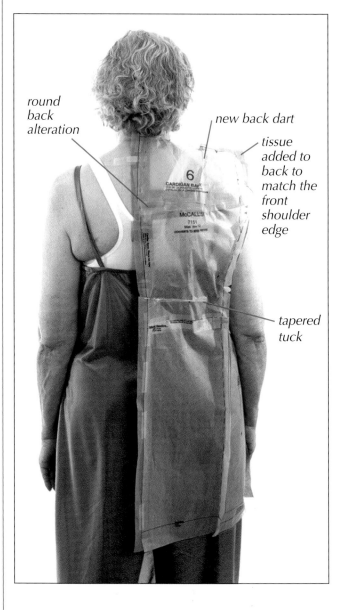

round back alteration

new back dart

tissue added to back to match the front shoulder edge

tapered tuck

We let out the side front hip seam for her **full tummy**. We didn't let out the side back hip seam because Olga has a **flat derriere**.

We shortened the jacket so it was better proportioned for her 5'-tall figure.

The sleeve fits well and needs no alteration.

Pin-fitting in Muslin

We decided to make a test muslin of the pattern because Olga's back is so much fuller on one side.

To even up her shoulders, we used a thicker shoulder pad on her **very sloping left shoulder** (page 161). Since she has a **short neck**, we didn't want much of a shoulder pad on her higher right shoulder or we'd visually shorten her neck. We used only one layer from a shoulder pad (page 244).

The neck of the garment stands away from Olga's neck in the back.

You can still see her **extra-full shoulder blade** on the right side. Wrinkles point to the fullest part.

We deepened the center back seam at the top and deepened both shoulder seams to eliminate the drag lines.

However, she still has drag lines at the hip. We decided we needed even more length at the top of her center back, but would use a slash closer to the neck, such as the slash used in a high round alteration (page 123).

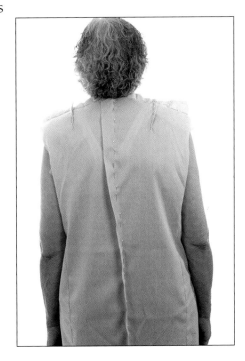

We slashed the muslin and raised the neck another 3/4". Drag lines are gone. Will the thicker coating fabric camouflage the full right back?

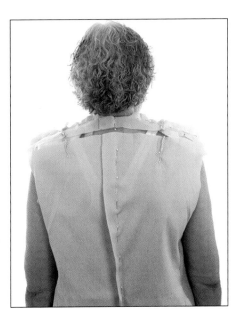

Many people have one shoulder higher than the other. This is easy to address, but, where thicknesses are different as on Olga, you really have to think about your fitting decisions. If she were to wear a fitted sundress, she would have to fit two separate pattern backs to ensure a good fit.

Pin-fitting in Fabric

The extra length added for her round back and the curved upper center back seam made the back fit beautifully. We also took the center back seam deeper through the hip area for her flat derriere.

To make her left shoulder even with her right, we had to use two shoulder pads on the left plus one layer of fleece next to the fashion fabric to smooth the edges of the pad. We used only one thin layer of a pad on the right shoulder.

Because her left shoulder blade is smaller than her right, we deepened the left back side seam through the shoulder blade area.

deeper seam

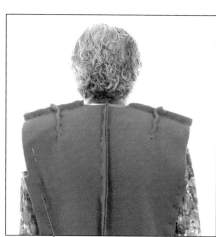

deeper seam

Olga in Her Finished Cardigan Jacket

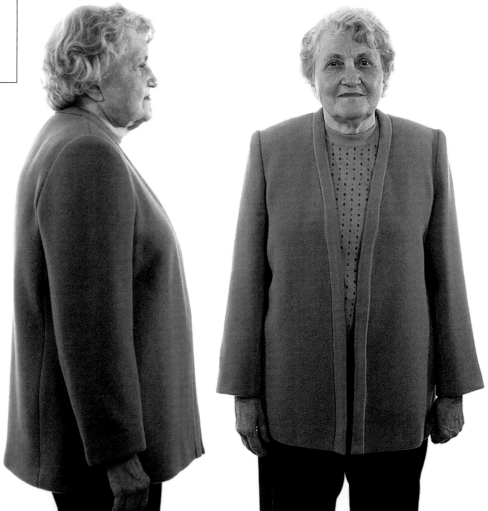

UNEVEN BACK & FORWARD HEAD

Karin is a Palmer/Pletsch Certified Sewing Instructor and she also teaches a variety of creative sewing classes. She uses the Palmer/ Pletsch liquid fabric stiffener, Perfect Sew, in her wonderful cutwork and embroidery. Karin has been trying to get the right fit for her body for years. Tissue-fitting gave her the key to success. Her **back is very uneven**, so we bought two basic dress patterns and fitted her "in the round."

The Side View Before

Normally we show you the front and the back first, but the clue to Karin's alterations came from the side view. She always felt like her clothes fit like straight jackets. The shoulder seam sits way back. The back neck gapes. This is because her **head sits forward** on her body. This makes her upper back longer than the pattern and her front chest shorter.

The Side View After

Marta slit the back of the pattern for a **high round** alteration (page 122-123) and raised the back. Karin said it felt like coming out of a straight-jacket. Now there was too much length in the front chest area, so we tucked the tissue from armhole to armhole to eliminate the excess. We also did a **forward shoulder** alteration. We moved the whole seam forward and pivoted it toward the front a little more at the armhole edge.

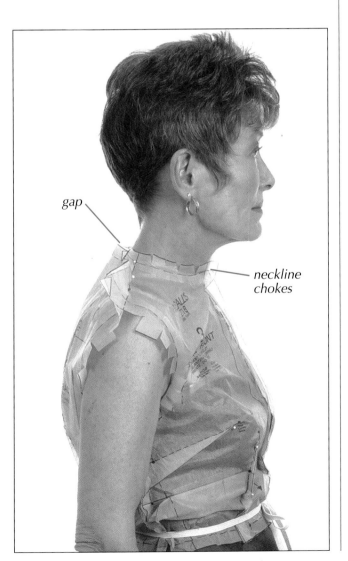

gap

neckline chokes

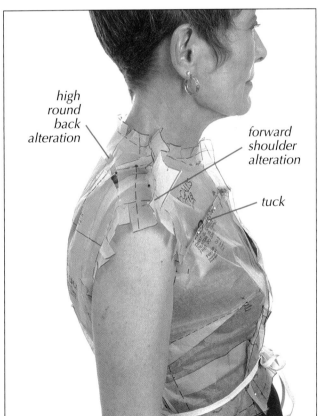

high round back alteration

forward shoulder alteration

tuck

The Front Before

We fitted Karin in a size 6 and from the front it appears nearly perfect except for the choking neckline.

The Back Before

Her **back right shoulder blade is fuller than her left**. You can see the excess tissue on the left and some drag lines.

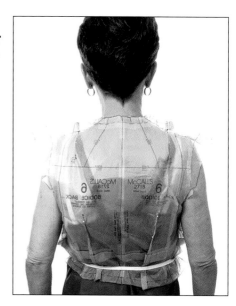

The Front After

We marked a lower front neckline seam for more comfort. This would only be necessary on a jewel or other high neckline. You can see also that the horizontal tuck goes all the way across the front.

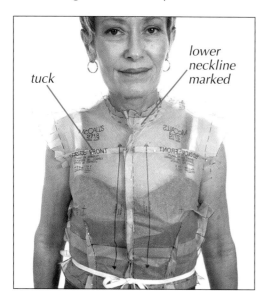

tuck

lower neckline marked

The Back After

In addition to the high round back alteration, we tucked out 1/2″ on the left back vertically to fit her smaller side. Karin has a **high right hip** so the elastic is higher on her right side.

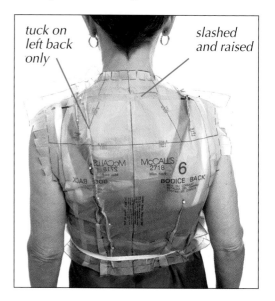

tuck on left back only

slashed and raised

Karin can cut her back double and trim 1/2″ (the amount tucked out) off the left side of the back and then to nothing at the shoulder so the back will match the front at the shoulder seam.

Karin has **small arms**, so to make the sleeve match the armhole, we made a vertical tuck in the sleeve front, removing the same amount as in the front armhole.

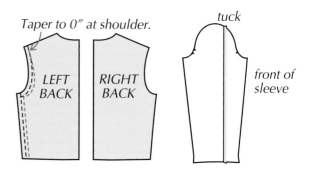

Taper to 0″ at shoulder.

LEFT BACK

RIGHT BACK

tuck

front of sleeve

Karin Now Fits a Shirt

Again, to check our fit, we decided to buy two patterns. We did the high round alteration on the yoke and made a tuck in the left back. The armhole seam on the back of the yoke will be taken in to fit.

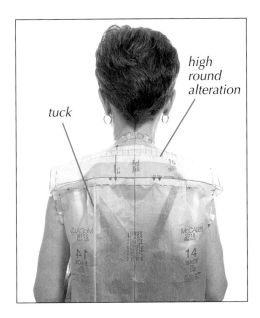

We tucked the front across the chest.

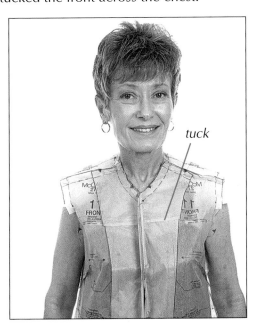

Since this solution is so simple, she can cut double and trim 1/2" off the side edge of the left shirt back later. She'll need to make a tuck down the front of the sleeve the same width as the one in the front armhole so the sleeve will fit into the smaller armhole.

UNEVEN HIPS

Connie Hamilton, a Palmer/Pletsch Certified Sewing Instructor and pant fit expert, usually camouflages her **uneven hips** by wearing a jacket while teaching.

Her **hips are much higher and fuller on her right side**. She is quite **uneven** (page 182). To complicate the issue, she recently had an operation and ended up **fuller on one side of her tummy** than the other. Rarely do we tissue fit both sides of a body. In Connie's case, we had to. These photos are of the altered tissue.

The Front Before

First, we bought two identical patterns and pinned them together. Her right hip is much fuller than the left, so we added Perfect Pattern Paper to the edges of the right side seam on both the front and the back. After centering the front and back on her body, we pinned the right side to fit.

As you can see in the close-up at the top of the next page, Connie also has a higher right hip. In order to get the centers perpendicular to the floor and the hem level, we pulled the tissue up on the lower left side. The bottom of the elastic will be the waistline seamline for her left side.

Also, we turned the darts into gathers. This totally camouflaged the side with the "tummy bump."

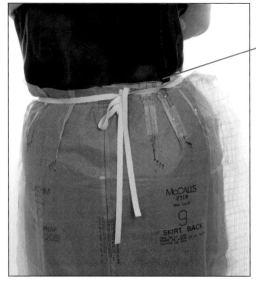

darts converted to gathers on front

The Back

The back posed some interesting challenges. If the darts were left as marked on the pattern, there would have been a lot of space between her right back darts and the side seam. We moved them toward the side to even up the visual space. Now the back darts are not in the same place on each side of the center back. Ideally, she should sew a skirt without a center back seam. A nice front wrap, button or trouser style would be perfect.

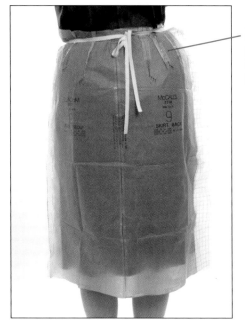

back darts moved toward right side

She is full just below the waist in the new dart area. We pulled the tissue down to add more length. Now the center back is straight.

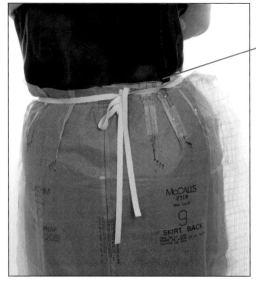

tissue pulled down

The Final Side Views

The left side seam is straight and the hem is level.

The right side seam is straight and the hem is level.

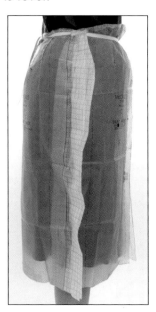

Connie is now ready to sew her perfect fitting skirt. She could cut singly for each side using all four pattern pieces she just fitted. Or, to save time, she could use the pattern that was fitted to her larger right side and transfer the stitching lines for the smaller left side onto it. Then she could cut large enough for the right side and simply sew the left side smaller.

Patty

LARGER THAN THE PATTERN SIZE RANGE

We loved working with Patty, a quality control inspector. She was a lot of fun and really appreciated what she learned. In fact, she wore the outfit we made for her to her wedding.

Her high bust measures 51″. Her full bust is 63″. (This would be size 40W if you just continue the Women's size range beyond what is in the pattern book or Misses' size 58, which is a 62″ bust.)

We used an XXL pattern size, which goes up to a 48″ bust. This is one size smaller than her 51″ high bust measurement.

The pattern is a unisex shirt which is cut a little differently than Misses'. Unisex patterns have less shape and longer sleeves for men, with a tuck line for women. We did the first fitting using the longer sleeve in case Patty needed it since she is tall.

The Front Before

We added length to the shirt to make it a dress, using the gridded Perfect Pattern Paper. We won't make any other judgments until we have graded the tissue up. We measured from the pattern center front to Patty's in the upper chest area at the approximate midpoint of the armhole to find the amount of width grade. (Don't do this in the full bust area. If you are more than a B-cup it won't be accurate.)

Notice how the tissue hikes up at the underarm. The armhole is too high so Patty needs length grading also.

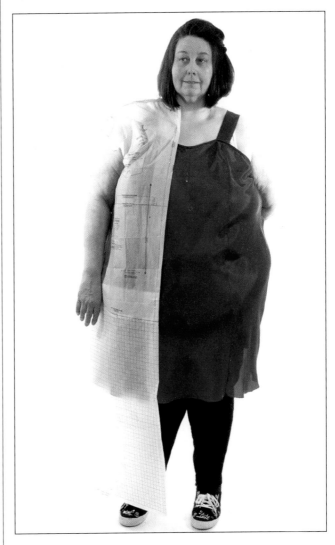

The Back Before

Patty needs about the same amount of width across the back as in the front. The neck seam doesn't reach the base of her neck and her yoke seam curves up in the middle. We will do a **high round back** alteration (page 124).

The Front After Grading

We added 5/8" vertically on the front, the back and the yoke, and 1/2" horizontally on the front and the back through the armhole (page 28). Now we can see that Patty needs more bust width. The tissue meets at the center front in the chest/neck area, but not at the bust.

The pattern does not meet Patty's center back.

Yoke curves up.

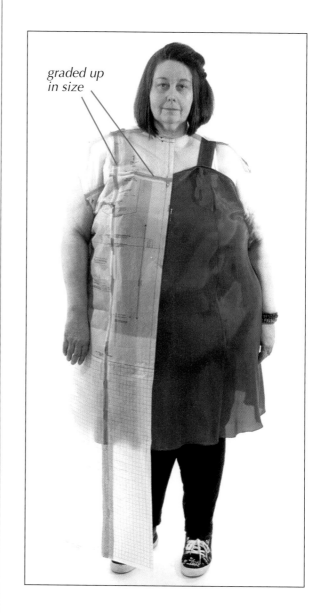

graded up in size

The Side View

Remember that altering the bust also creates more hip room. We will wait to decide how much more hip room is needed until after the bust alteration is completed.

When you do a length grade in the armhole area, you need to lengthen the sleeve cap the same amount or it won't fit the armhole.

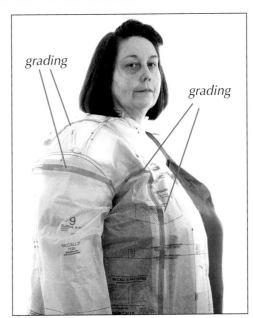

grading

grading

The Front After

In the photo at the top of the next column, you can see the new horizontal bust dart. Width has been added to the side seams primarily at the hips, but some has been added at the underarm as well.

We added a wedge to the underarm of the sleeve to match what we added to the side seams.

The unisex pattern is too wide in the shoulders. We originally cut on the XXL lines but went back to the XL in the shoulders.

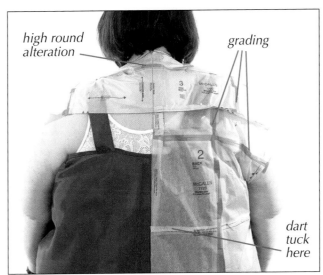

The Back After

After adding 5/8" vertically to the back, the center back swung to the side so we did a dart tuck at the center back tapering to nothing at the side seam just above the waistline. Patty is **very straight in the back and flat in the derriere**. You can also see that her **right shoulder is higher**.

high round alteration

grading

dart tuck here

Pin-fitting in Fabric

Patty tries on the dress and slips on one sleeve. We used two shoulder pads on the left side to visually balance her shoulders.

Patty came for her fabric fitting in a new bra. As a result, the darts were now too low. We re-pinned and marked where each dart point should end because she also is **slightly fuller busted on one side** than the other.

FiT Tip Crinkled rayon has a lot of weight, making it drape very nicely in a dress. However, the weight of the fabric caused it to stretch. When Marta cut out Patty's dress, she made it 2" shorter. The fabric's weight brought the length back to the original pattern length.

The back of the dress looks nice and hangs well. Patty has a pad of "fluff" just below her back neck so we will ease the neckline to the collar in this area to make the neckline hug hers.

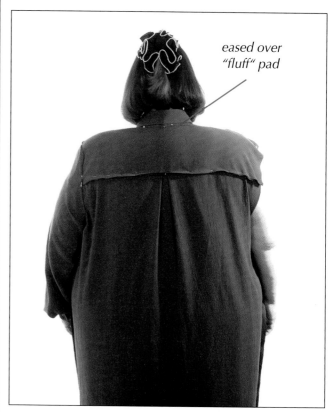

eased over "fluff" pad

We decided to move the armhole seam closer in to her shoulder as it would look better than a dropped shoulder would look on her. This meant we needed to add the same amount to the cap height that we took off at the outer shoulder edge. Since the sleeve was already cut, we simply deepened the sleeve underarm to make the cap a bit less "flat." However, this makes the cap narrower at the top and a little tight across the top of the cap. We let out the sleeve as much as possible.

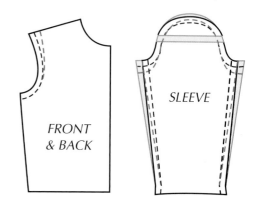

FRONT & BACK

SLEEVE

A Coordinating Vest

Patty tissue-fits a vest to be worn over the dress. We felt that a creative vest would visually break up Patty's width. She is tall and can carry off a "statement" vest very well.

The Front Before

Patty needs a **forward shoulder** adjustment and **more width**.

The Back Before Grading

The back needs width and length, and the center back swings toward the side.

The Vest Front After Grading

She still needs to add width at the bust.

The Vest Front After Bust Alteration

A horizontal dart was added, but it needs to be lowered (pages 142-144). We will cut the vest off at the center front, eliminating the overlap and giving Patty a more slenderizing line. We also lengthened the vest at the center front tapering to the original length at the side seam.

The Back After

We graded her back and front pattern pieces up in length and width. In addition, we added to the side seams, tapering from just a little at the underarm to more at the waistline. The dart tuck at the waist for her flat derriere straightened the back.

dart tuck

grading

Patty's Finished Dress and Vest

CHAPTER 22
Fit Decisions

Sometimes we find a pattern we just love, but it's unlike anything we've ever tried before. Also, there is more than one approach to solving a problem. Our suggestion? Use logic and any idea that comes to your mind and try it. It's only tissue! No ideas are wrong if they work. No ideas are stupid. Be daring and just do it!

Here's a perfect, though quite simple, example of a fit decision.

Gretchen

Gretchen, a Certified Palmer/Pletsch Sewing Instructor and home-school mom, measures herself for size. She is 42¼" at the high bust and 46¾" at the full bust. This makes her a size 20, based on the high bust measurement. She will need a **full bust adjustment**.

Gretchen picked a shell blouse pattern. Everyone needs a shell, and Gretchen thought a cut-on sleeve would be fast. Her dilemma was that her books on fit didn't address bust adjustment for cut-on sleeves.

She tried on the pattern and measured the distance from the blouse center front to hers.

Then, she cut the sleeve off the blouse (page 157), made the alteration (page 146) and taped the sleeve back on.

She gave the blouse a slightly more square shoulder and extended the adjustment to the sleeve edge for more arm width. She also added length to the sleeve—her personal preference.

She didn't like the dart position, so she angled it for a more flattering look. It does look and fit better! Good thinking Gretchen! She had to add a dart extension for this new angle. See page 139.

The 4-Hour Jacket

Gretchen tried on a simple 4-hour jacket pattern tissue. It was tight across the bust. Note the wrinkles in the tissue.

The close-up shows the wrinkles, and that the pattern does not come to her center front.

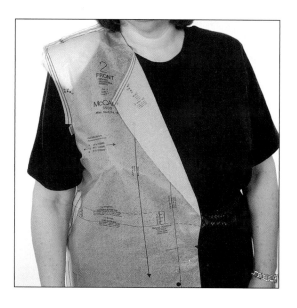

Gretchen did a full bust alteration which gave the pattern a horizontal side dart for a better fit (page 146).

The armhole fits nicely and the jacket center front comes to hers. The new bust dart is quite deep.

Gretchen didn't want a deep side dart, so she used the dart transferring method on pages 136 and 138. She moved half of the width to a neck dart that she created (it will hide under the lapel) and the other half to a vertical dart from the hem. This visually gives her a slimming vertical line. Gretchen is empowered! She is also thankful, as she'd never been able to get good bust fit before taking our workshops. She's learned from experience—the best teacher!

The Cut-on Sleeve Jacket with Gusset

Gretchen tried on the jacket pattern. It is too small across the bust and the lapel gaps.

The wrinkle in the lapel seems deepest at the roll line. Will it be possible to make a lapel tuck deeper there and still keep the pattern flat?? The mystery unravels!

These are normal cut-on-sleeve drape lines.

Because she needed bust width, we cut up the pattern over the bust to the shoulder. Then we cut from that cut at the bust to the edge of the lapel. We pulled the front open and the lapel lapped to nothing at the outer edge. VOILA! More lapping at the roll line just where we needed it, making the lapel fit her chest! Aren't we lucky!

Gretchen wanted super-sized shoulders in this jacket so we squared the shoulders to allow for the larger shoulder pad (page 160).

The facing needed to be altered to match the front. We placed it on top of the front and adjusted it to fit!

The lapel now folds back and no longer gapes.

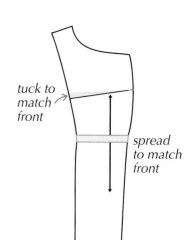

tuck to match front

spread to match front

The pattern is designed with sleeves that extend over the middle of the hand. The wonderful thing about tissue-fitting is that Gretchen can decide now if she likes them that long.

Square the shoulders to create room for extra pad.

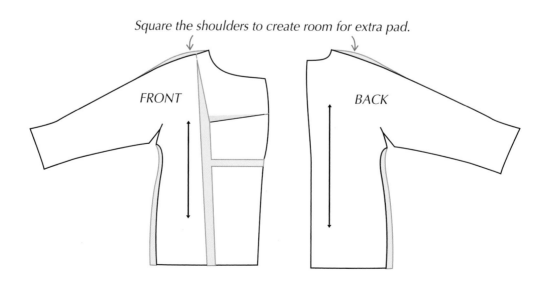

FRONT

BACK

222

Pin-fitting in Fabric

The bust and hip area of the jacket fit great. Remember, a garment with a cut-on sleeve has natural armhole drape.

The back pulls up in the **high hip** area.

We pinned shallower side seams in the high hip area. We still see a small wrinkle. Is it because she needs more width? Or perhaps we added too much for square shoulders.

We can try letting out the hip even more, possibly just on the back piece. Or we could try taking deeper shoulder seams to lift the sides a bit. Fitting-as-you-sew allows you to fine-tune as you go. We ended up doing a little of each!

Gretchen's Finished Jacket

Gretchen and the Cowl Neck Blouse

Gretchen likes challenges. She wants a drapey cowl neck blouse in her wardrobe. She chose one with a cut-on sleeve.

The center front of the blouse is not reaching Gretchen's center front.

NOTE: The neckline is low in the photo because the cowl collar will be sewn to it.

She cut off the sleeve, altered the bust as shown on page 146, and taped the sleeve back into place.

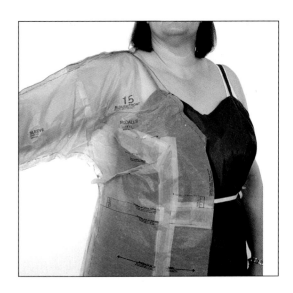

There is a gap in the neckline. It would be best to take care of this now so the cowl will hang nicely.

A tuck usually goes to the armhole, but with a cut-on sleeve we had to pin it to nothing at the bottom edge of the sleeve. It worked since the sleeve was full enough. Yes, it is trial and error and that's OK!! Gretchen will make the same size tuck across the neckline seam of the cowl collar as she made at the blouse neck edge.

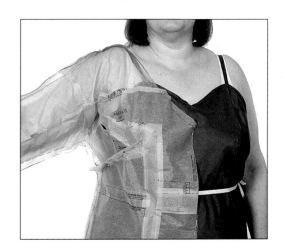

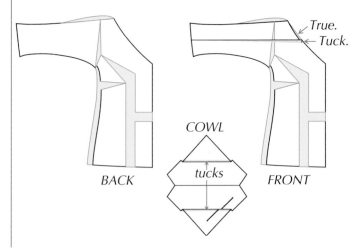

BACK

COWL

True.

Tuck.

tucks

FRONT

224

AND THE COVER JACKET

Denise, a former radiology technician and a volunteer for the cover of this book, measures 32″ in her high bust and 34¾″ in her full bust. Since she is more than 2″ larger in the full bust, we'll put her in a size 8 based on her high bust.

She tries on the tissue with the shoulder pad that will be sewn into the jacket. The tissue doesn't come to her center front in the bust area. Also, the vertical dart extends past her bust apex and the armhole gaps.

We cut the pattern in half at the waist, altered for the **full bust**, and taped the pattern together again. When might you do this? When the hips are small; when the garment is a dress with lots of detail; or, as in this case, when we wanted to leave the vertical dart alone (page 158).

A horizontal dart has been added as well as extra width across the bust. The tissue now fits. The extra width at the waist was not needed so it was removed at the side seams. The armhole fits perfectly.

Since front darts that end at the hip often pucker, and since our silk twill fabric would really show that pucker, we decided the normal way we do the bust alteration would have been fine. We'd then sew the dart all the way to the hem. To show you the options, we took a fresh pattern and altered the front without cutting the bottom off.

We pinned the vertical dart to where it originally ended. It confirmed that we didn't want it to end at that spot. It would certainly pucker in this silk twill fabric. However, before pinning the revised vertical dart, we will transfer the horizontal dart to that area (page 136).

The yellow tissue shows the additional width added to the vertical dart because of the transfer. The horizontal dart is gone.

Denise is a size 8 top and bottom, so she does not need extra fullness in the hip and stomach area that was created by the bust dart alteration.

To get a good hip fit, we pinned the vertical dart until the jacket fit smoothly over Denise's hips.

Pin-fitting in Fabric

Choosing a silk twill for the cover shot was insane! It's a real challenge to sew, but it was the color we wanted for Denise.

We placed two shoulder pads on the right side to balance her **uneven shoulders**.

Denise has a **slightly round back** (page 122) with **one shoulder** being **more rounded** than the other. This pattern has no ease across the back shoulders. Most people are at least a little rounded and need shaping. Without it, you get drag lines like those on Denise's right side. On the left side we scooted the back shoulder in until the drag lines were gone. You can now see a bubble in the shoulder. It will be eased to the front or sewn into a dart.

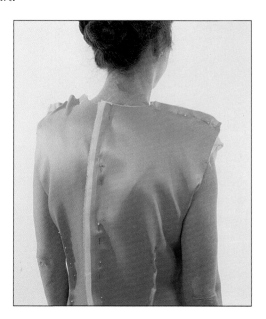

Marta pins darts in both shoulders. Denise has **narrow shoulders** so the new armhole will be marked to set the sleeve correctly.

FIT Tip

The back shoulder darts can be slightly different in width if one shoulder is more rounded than the other.

Denise's suit turned out beautifully, as seen here and on the cover of this book.

227

Dorothy

NO-DART, FITTED CREATIVE VEST

Dorothy, a former nurse and an avid sewer, tissue-fits a vest. She wants to sew a creative vest and have it fit—without darts. She has a **full rib cage** which emulates a full bust, so she'll alter to add darts, then remove them. Trust us—it works!

FIT Tip Not everyone can successfully make a no-dart vest. If you are really full-busted, you need dart shaping or the front will hang out at the lower edge (unless you also have a full tummy).

The Front Before

The armhole gaps. The center front on the tissue is not at Dorothy's center front.

The Back Before

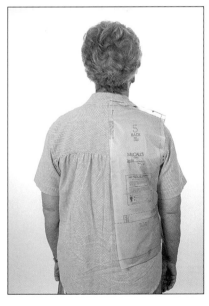

There is a gap in the back armhole. She's **rounded** and needs shoulder ease. The center back swings toward the side at the bottom. Her back is straight below the shoulder blades and she has a **flat derriere**.

The Back After

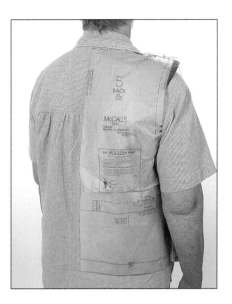

We made a dart tuck above the waist to straighten the back (page 127). We darted the back shoulder then widened it at the outer edge so it would match the front (page 122).

The Front Altered

We've added width and a horizontal bust dart using the alteration from page 146. The armhole no longer gaps.

Getting Rid of the Dart

We transferred the dart to a vertical dart (pages 97 and 136) then removed the width of that dart from the front side seam. This was a good solution for Dorothy's full rib cage.

Janice
FITTING A STRAIGHT SKIRT

Janice is a Certified Palmer/Pletsch Instructor who loves fit challenges. Because she is **small in the waist** and **fuller in the hips and thighs**, an A-line shape is perfect and requires little alteration. However, during a recent workshop, she wanted to fit a straight skirt—much more of a challenge. When we let out the side seams enough to fit her thighs, her straight skirt became an A-line.

After a lot of trial and error using tissue-fit principles, Janice finally arrived at the perfect solution to a great-fitting straight skirt. Simply letting out the side seams didn't work, because she also needed length, but just at the sides. Janice is a size 10 in the waist and 16 in the hips. She first tried a size 16, but didn't like all the fullness in the waist. She switched to a 10, deciding to make the hip/thigh area larger instead of making the waist on a 16 smaller. (No rule is carved in stone!)

Janice tries on the size 10 tissue. This is the fashion skirt from the Palmer/Pletsch basic fit pattern. Because of her full thighs, the center front and back don't reach hers in those areas.

Janice used the fit principle of "the bigger the body bump, the more length and width it needs." She cut the front and back vertically to the waist and horizontally to the sides. She pulled horizontally until the pattern had the width it needed. She gained extra length at the side seam for her full thighs (page 181).

Notice in the photo below that the side seam is not centered over her legs. This is because of her stance. If we made the front larger and the back smaller so the side seam was in the middle of her leg, the skirt proportions would look strange.

Note that we pulled the center back up for her sway back in order to keep the side seam straight and the hem level.

To keep the skirt straight, she had to make the edges of the vertical slit parallel below the hipline. To do that, the side seam was spread horizontally, adding length over her fuller side thighs—just what she needed.

Janice cut the skirt out of wool flannel with 1" "in-case" side seam allowances. She pin-fitted it and it looks PERFECT!!

side seam spread

edges parallel

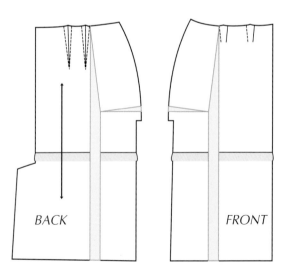

BACK   *FRONT*

The horizontal tuck, done before the thigh alteration, shortened Janice's skirt to her best length.

The back also looks perfect and the skirt is ready to sew.

CHAPTER 23
Make It Flattering

Solutions for a Common Figure Type

Fitting your figure is one thing. Flattering it is another. There are some things you can do to enhance your silhouette. For example, Pati's sister-in-law, Marty, tells us how she made these clothes look better on her.

The Two-Piece Dress

When Marty tried on this two-piece knit outfit she felt "square." To improve the look she tapered the skirt from hip to hem, taking it in at each side seam 2" by the time she reached the hem. Because she has sloping shoulders, shoulder pads were added. She pulled the hem edge of the top through a buckle to create an angle that leads the eye upward toward her face and away from her hips.

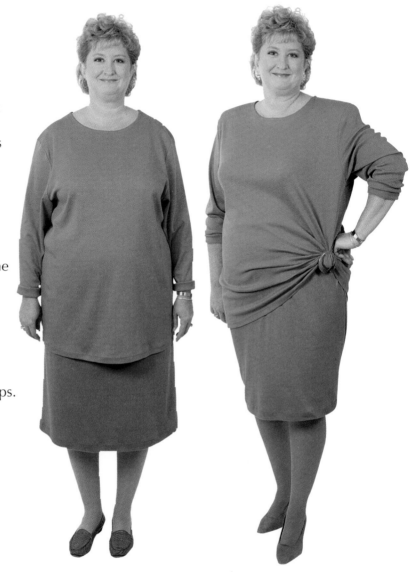

The above photographs are from **Looking Good** (page 254) by Nancy Nix-Rice.

Moved neckline in to make room for shoulder pads.

Dart added for bust fullness.

narrower legs

A Figure-Enhancing Overblouse

For this great overblouse, Marty moved the sides of the neckline in to create room for shoulder pads to balance her sloping shoulders.

She also added a bust dart to fit over and flatter her fuller bust line.

She sewed very narrow legs on the pants for a slimmer look and made them long so they drape fashionably at the ankles.

A Fitted Sundress

Marty needed a sundress to wear on vacation. She had never had one that fit her shoulders and bust. We did a full bust adjustment and sloped the shoulders. We tapered in slightly at the waist so the slight flare at the hem would give her shape the "essence of hourglass."

The rayon has great drape, skimming over her body. The dark color allows her to wear it without a slip—important in a hot climate.

Marty made wider shoulders than normal to cover her bra straps—and she made sure she had a *great*-fitting bra. The wider straps also made her look less triangular.

Camouflaging the Bumps

During a first pin-fitting of this jacket, our friend Marilyn could see body rolls. The soft satin wool she chose tended to cling.

Marilyn let out all the seams through the middle. She looks pounds thinner!

More Illusions of Shape

One of the best tricks to make hips look slimmer is to taper straight skirts at the hem and wear them with a jacket.

If a skirt is as wide at the bottom as your hips, you'll look heavier. If you taper the skirt under the jacket, your hips will seem to be the same width as the hem!

tapered

To taper, turn the skirt inside out and pin both sides in the same amount at the bottom, tapering to the original seamline at the fullest hip area.

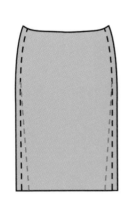

Try it on. If you like it, that is where you sew. Of course, you'll need to undo the hem at the sides and re-hem when finished.

Create the illusion of a waistline, even if you don't have one. Taper the side seams at the waistline just a little. If the garment has shape, YOU will have shape.

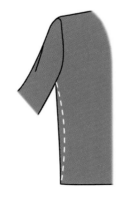

You Don't Like a Detail on a Pattern?

Change it!! We've helped our students make these changes on patterns during our workshops for a more personally flattering fit:

neckline too wide and too low (pages 130 and 131)

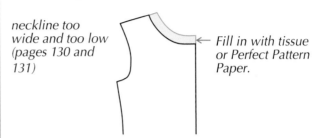

← *Fill in with tissue or Perfect Pattern Paper.*

puckered darts

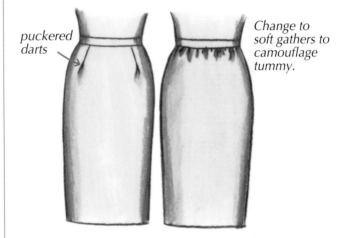

Change to soft gathers to camouflage tummy.

Change patch pockets on the hip of a jacket to more flattering slanted welt pockets.

To keep the cable design in this gorgeous fabric on the entire front edge, Marta deepened the shoulder dart to pull the neck into a "V" shape.

new, deeper dart

233

Designed to Flatter

Pati's Alterations
Yours could be less exaggerated.

Shoulders extended 3/8".

FRONT

BACK

Tapered from hip to hem 1/2".

lengthened 8"

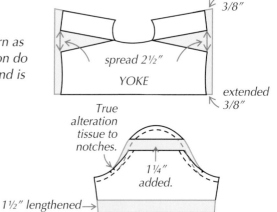

extended 3/8"

spread 2½"

YOKE

extended 3/8"

True alteration tissue to notches.

1¼" added.

1½" lengthened →

SLEEVE

This classic shirtdress was made exactly like the pattern included in McCall's #2718 fit pattern.

Then Pati changed the pattern as shown at right. Which version do you feel has the most style and is the most slimming?

NOTE: Shoulder pads can enhance your figure. See tips on page 172.

CHAPTER 24

Sewing Techniques that Affect Fit

Mistakes Multiply

Accuracy is extremely important in sewing. Mistakes tend to multiply. Take time to make sure you are happy with every step you've done before going onto the next step.

Are both collar points sewn the same?

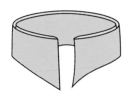

Did the fabric slip, or did one layer grow in length?

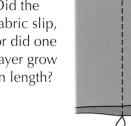

After checking, you may need to unstitch and redo.

Easy Ways to Unstitch

Do not fear ripping. What a wonderful gift to be able to rip when you make a mistake! Imagine not being able to rip. You might never finish a sewing project!

Regular Seams

Cut stitches with a seam ripper every inch on the top side. Pull out the bobbin thread on under side. Remove remaining short threads on the top.

In short seams, you may be able to pull out the bobbin thread and then remove the upper thread in one step.

Or, open the seam and carefully cut the thread with a seam ripper. Pull the seam apart, cut a few more stitches, pull apart, etc.

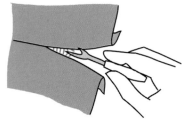

Serged Seams

Smooth out the tail chain where you ended the seam to find the needle thread. It is the shorter thread. Pull on it and the loops will fall off!

On the four-thread seam, pull each needle thread separately.

Fabric Choice

Different fabrics fit differently. Heavy fabrics take up more room on the body, so you might need to let out the seams. Also, they don't drape softly, which visually could add pounds.

drapable fabric   *stiff/heavy fabric*

Some fabrics reveal lumps and bumps. Wrap wool crepe around your hips. Do you see lumps?

Now put a lining fabric under the wool and wrap again. Do the lumps disappear? Lining will usually smooth clingy fabrics over your body and camouflage bumps.

235

Fabric Conversion Charts

Because they are rarely accurate, we don't use them. The best way to buy the correct yardage is to lay your altered pattern on a cutting board and determine the amount needed for 45" and 60" fabric (22½" and 30" respectively when folded in half).

Print Placement

Be careful with large prints. Close-up, Marta's floral blouse looks like any floral blouse, but from a distance, there is a bulls-eye centered over each breast! We had a good laugh over this. See, even the pros aren't perfect!! (P.S. Marta says she did this on purpose to see if anyone would catch it!!!)

Changing Grain to Improve Fit

V-necklines on jackets are bias grain and can stretch. Change the grainline on the facing as shown so it becomes the stabilizer. (McCall's some-times has already adjusted the arrow on the pattern piece for you.)

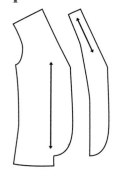

Cut on the Grain

1. Make sure woven fabrics are "on grain." The lengthwise grain is parallel to the selvages (finished edges) and is usually the strongest grainline.

The crosswise grain runs across the fabric from selvage to selvage. It usually has a bit of give.

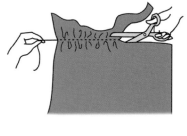

off grain   *on grain*

2. Pull a crosswise thread or tear along the crosswise grain on at least one end of the fabric, so you will know the edge of your fabric is straight.

3. Make sure your fabric is square. Place it on a gridded surface. Fold fabric in half lengthwise, matching selvages, and line up the fold and selvages with the lines on the board.

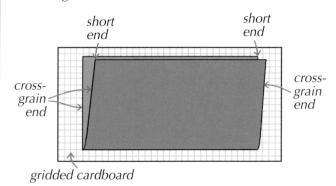

short end   *short end*

cross-grain end   *cross-grain end*

gridded cardboard

4. If the cross grain ends don't line up with the gridlines, pick up the short ends and pull as shown.

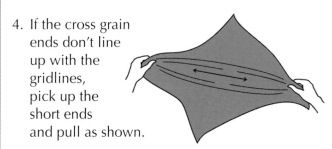

5. Replace on the gridded surface. Both grains should now be along a grid line.

Another method is to square the fabric by steaming it. Pin fabric to a padded pressing table, making sure it is square. (Some people use their beds.) Steam. After cooling and drying, the fabric should remain square. See our book **Dream Sewing Spaces** for how to make a padded pressing board.

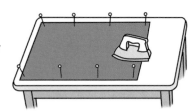

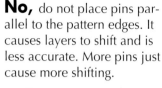

Quick Tip Some permanent-press fabrics are "permanently" off-grain. Do not try to straighten them. Also, denim has a mind of its own and will return to its original position when it relaxes. Avoid stripe and plaid patterns that are printed off grain.

When cutting double, make sure fabric is square, all edges are matched exactly, and there are no wrinkles in pattern or fabric.

Place the pattern on the fabric so that each end of the grain arrow printed on the tissue is equidistant from the selvage or fold.

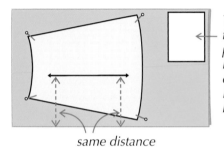

same distance

To make sure fabric is square, place typing paper next to corner edges (or use the lines on a cutting board, page 84).

Quick Tip To find **true bias** in wovens, fold the fabric until the lengthwise grain is parallel to the crosswise grain. The fold line is the "true bias."

true bias

crosswise

lengthwise

Cut with a Few Good Pins

Pati's Favorite Way to Pin

Yes. Pin into cardboard cutting board. Angle pins toward center of pattern so pattern can't move.

No. Don't pin like this. When all pins are at the same angle, the pattern can move.

When cutting, use your fingers as extra pins.

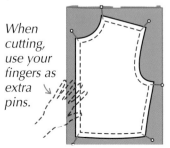

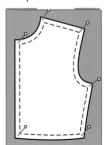

Marta's Favorite Way to Pin

Yes, when pinning fabric and tissue together, just a few pins will do—pointing to the corners of the pattern piece.

No, do not place pins parallel to the pattern edges. It causes layers to shift and is less accurate. More pins just cause more shifting.

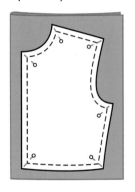

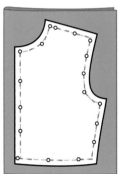

Marking

Mark Often and Accurately

Make 1/4" snips through the center of the notches.

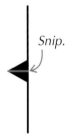

Snip.

The following are places you can snip to save time and improve accuracy:

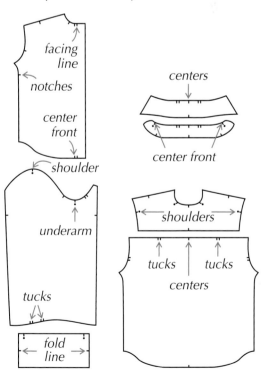

facing line

notches

center front

shoulder

underarm

tucks

fold line

centers

center front

shoulders

tucks *tucks*

centers

Moving Markings

Do you suffer from blouse gaposis at the bust-line? Pati did for years. Susan Pletsch clued her in on the cure for button placement. Try on the garment—the first button marking should always be at the bust level. Mark all other buttonholes from that point. Pati usually spaces them 2"- 3" apart. It's impossible for pattern companies to mark this position accurately for you because of varied figure types. Changing the pattern is okay!

Are your pocket markings too low or too high?

1. Draw a box around them.

2. Cut out the box.

3. Raise or lower the box to a better, more comfortable position for your body.

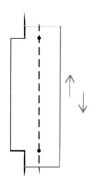

If a welt pocket and dart meet, it's more difficult to sew perfectly.	Lengthen dart to the center of the welt.

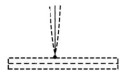   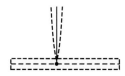

Marking Darts & Tucks the Easy Way

1. **Cut with fabric right sides together** so the seams are ready to pin and sew. Work on a cardboard cutting board. Snip the dart and/or tuck stitching and fold lines.

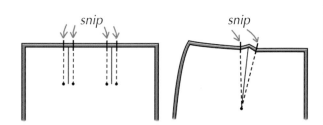

2. Pin through all the layers at the dots on the pattern.

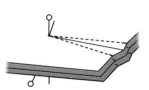

3. Lift all layers of the fabric and put another pin through all layers from the underside where the first pin comes through.

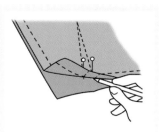

4. Now pull tissue away. Small pin heads will go through the tissue.

 If you are afraid of pins falling out, mark both layers of fabric where pins penetrate the fabric.

Dart Techniques

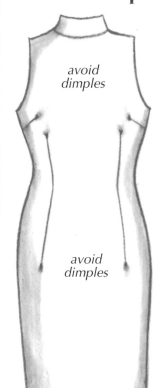

avoid dimples

avoid dimples

Darts, Not Dimples

Dimples at the end of a dart are often due to poor stitching methods. To help guide your dart sewing for a more accurately stitched point, place pins through the stitching lines. Reverse the pin at the end to remind you where to stop stitching.

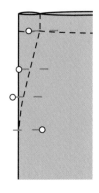

238

Practice sewing darts until you perfect them! Start at the cut edge and stitch toward the point.

1. For a pucker-free dart, sew to 1½" from the point. Change to a short stitch length (1mm).

2. Slowly sew toward the folded edge of the fabric.

3. Stitches should be right on the edge for the last 1/4"-1/2". Once off the edge, stitch in place in the dart allowance about 1" from the point to "tie" the threads.

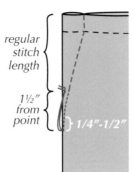

regular stitch length
1½" from point
1/4"-1/2"

Dart Direction

◆ Press vertical darts toward the center.

◆ Press horizontal bust darts upward. This is opposite from most instructions. We do it for a more youthful look. It works especially well on very full-busted figures.

Pressed down, you look "into" the dart. There are then two layers of fabric over the full part of the bust.

Pressed up, the dart is less noticeable. The extra fabric layer is tucked up under the armhole.

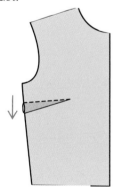
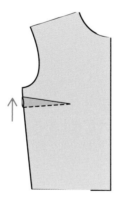

An advantage we mentioned in the dart chapter is that you don't need an extension at the end of the dart when you press it up. This saves time for those needing a bust adjustment. See page 139.

◆ If the dart is slanted and deep, you may need to press it down due to gravity.

You can also trim the dart seam allowance narrower as long as finishing these raw edges isn't a problem.

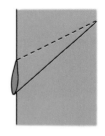

◆ You could press darts flat as shown to balance bulk on either side of the seam. It takes a little more time, but if you are a dress-maker, it could be one of your selling points to your clients.

◆ You may choose to slash a dart down the middle and press it open. Trim seam allowances to 5/8" or less to eliminate bulk.

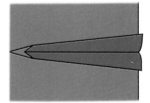

Pressing Darts

1. Press the dart stitches flat first to eliminate puckers and to flatten the fold line.

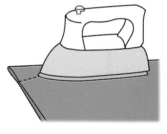

2. Place the dart over the appropriate curve of a ham. Bust darts will be closer to the curved edge and skirt darts will be on the flatter top of the ham. If the fabric is bulky, tuck paper under the fold of the dart to prevent an indentation from showing on the right side of the fabric. Steam. Flatten with a clapper or pounding block.

To GET fit, Marta does isometric pressing. She holds in her stomach while pressing!

239

Gaping V's

V-necklines are bias and can stretch. To make sure they hug your neckline, do the following:

1. After cutting, place your pattern back onto the fabric to see if the V-neckline has stretched.

Shorten to match pattern. Steam to shrink it back.

Fabric bias neckline has grown.

2. Make the neckline in the fabric the same size as the pattern. Steaming with an iron may shrink it back.

3. Pin a stabilizing tape over the seam and sew it to the neck seamline on the wrong side of the fabric. If you are full busted, shorten the tape 1/8" and ease the neckline to the tape.

wrong side

NOTE: If you stitch with the tape on top, the feed dog of your machine will ease the fabric into the tape.

The Big Interfacing Question

We tested the first fusible interfacing in 1968 when Pati worked for the Armo Interfacing Co. We've come a long way since those first "bake-ons."

Our books, **Mother Pletsch's Painless Sewing** and **Easy, Easier, Easiest Tailoring**, give you a lot of information on interfacings. Below are some more recent developments.

- Today, we love the "weft-insertion" fusible interfacings. They mesh with most fabrics.

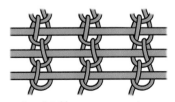

"weft" fiber construction

- Another favorite is a fusible knit that truly won't pucker after washing, even on lightweight silkies.

- Always test your fusible interfacing on a scrap of your fabric first.

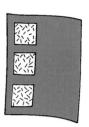

- We recommend fusing to the entire front of a princess jacket so all pieces have the same look. Fuse before seaming.

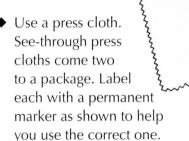

Fusibles - THIS SIDE UP!

Regular Press Cloth - NO FUSIBLES!

- Use a press cloth. See-through press cloths come two to a package. Label each with a permanent marker as shown to help you use the correct one.

Surviving Sleeves

Poorly sewn sleeves are the most common single area that can ruin the look of a beautiful garment. The following pointers will help:

- Set-in sleeves shouldn't be sewn into an open armhole like shirt sleeves are.

- Sewing the underarm seams first and then setting the sleeve into a circle causes the fabric to be much less bulky. The sleeve will hang better.

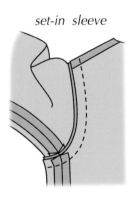

set-in sleeve

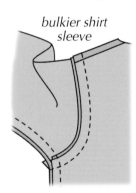

bulkier shirt sleeve

raised cap

- Normally, the seam is pressed toward the sleeve for a slightly raised effect at the cap.

To fill in the ease at the top so it doesn't pucker, sew in a "sleeve head." This is a strip of polyester fleece or bias lambswool that is sewn to the sleeve seam allowance in the upper two-thirds of the sleeve.

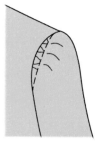
flat cap

◆ For a flatter cap, either press the seam toward the garment and edgestitch on the garment side,

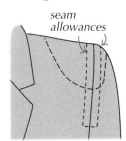
seam allowances

OR, press the upper two-thirds of the sleeve seam open. This works great with a raglan shoulder pad in jackets.

A bit of sleeve trivia: According to McCall's, sleeves are graded 1/4" per size in cap height and 1/2" per size in cap width. This means if you have big upper arms, going up a size won't help much. Learn to alter. See page 169.

Avoid Puckers

You can ease a sleeve cap that is 1" larger than the armhole in any fabric. In some fabrics you can even ease in 2" without puckers. Patterns generally allow 1½" ease in set-in sleeves and 0"-1/2" in shirt sleeves. The higher the cap, the more ease.

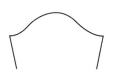

The secret to any sleeve is knowing when and how to cheat! The time to do it is after machine basting the sleeve into the armhole.

Check the outside to see if it is puckered. If it is, try one or more of the following cheats!

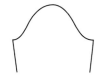

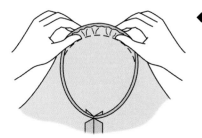

◆ Smooth seam with your thumb and forefinger. Because the basting is loose, you can often smooth out any puckers!

◆ If puckers remain, clip your basting and re-stitch. Sometimes the second time is a charm. Always stitch on the sleeve side and use your fingers to manipulate the ease as you sew.

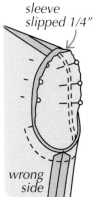
sleeve slipped 1/4"

◆ If you can't get rid of the puckers, remove the stitching in the upper two-thirds of the cap. Slip the cap 1/4" further into the armhole. **Machine baste again at the original 5/8" stitching line of the garment.** If the cap still puckers, slip it another 1/8" and stitch again.

wrong side

◆ When all else fails, place all the fullness at the very top of the sleeve and call it a gathered sleeve!

Quick Tip Marta literally pin-bastes her sleeves into the armhole with lots of pins in the seamline parallel to the edge. She can then try on the sleeve and check how it hangs before machine sewing. The pins are removed as she sews and she uses her fingers to manipulate the ease.

Finishing Sleeves

1. Sew a second row of stitching in the seam allowance 1/4" from the first row. Trim to that stitching. In jackets, trim only to that stitching in the lower third of the armhole. You need the seam allowance in the cap for extra lift.

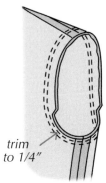
trim to 1/4"

2. Never clip in the armhole curve. Like the crotch curve on pants, it is unnecessary to clip, because it stays in that same curved shape when on your body.

3. Press the cap seam from the inside only, steaming out any ease until cap looks smooth. **Do not press the cap of the sleeve flat from the outside,** unless directed to do so in the guidesheet, or you want a flatter cap (see page 239).

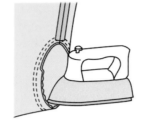

NOTE: If you are going to add a lining, see special tips for sleeves on page 163.

Shirt Collar Shape

Don't choose a one-piece collar over a two-piece for speed. Choose the "look" you want.

A one-piece collar falls open at the neckline, looking somewhat like a convertible collar.

A two-piece stands up, staying closer to the neck.

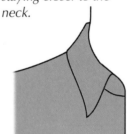

A two-piece has shape built into the seam where the collar and the band are sewn together.

comparing the collars

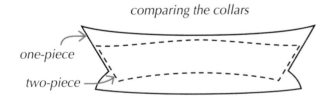

one-piece

two-piece

comparing the bands

one-piece →

two-piece →

Straight Skirts

Vents and Pleats

If you are fitting a skirt and notice the back vent opens,

pull the skirt up at the center back and it will generally close.

Sew your waistband on lower in the back to anchor it. You may need to remove the zipper and sew it lower, too.

Another way to make vents behave is to notice where the center back snips are before hemming.

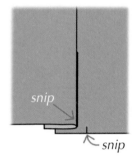

snip

← *snip*

If they are not together, pull the extensions up until the center snips match. Pin.

Then topstitch to anchor.

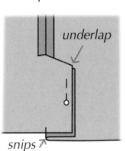

underlap

snips ↗

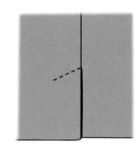

If pleats or trouser tucks spread open,

pull up on the underneath fold until they hang straight.

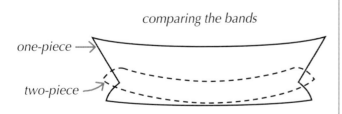

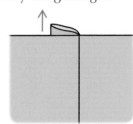

Straight Skirt Tips

- **Don't make them too tight!**

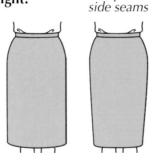

taper side seams

- Taper the side seams 1/2" up to 2" deeper on each side at the hem so you don't look so boxy. You'll look 20 pounds thinner. See page 233.

- Baste pocket openings closed while fitting and sewing your skirt. Remove basting when skirt is finished. Then the pockets won't gap when you wear it.

 Side seam pockets are nice as they help to prevent wrinkling. When you sit, they open up and there is less stress on the fabric where it creases; therefore, you will have fewer wrinkles in the front of your straight skirt.

Sewing Different Shapes Together

Straight to Curved

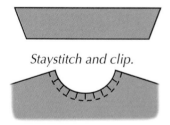

Staystitch and clip.

Then you can pin them together, and stitch a "straight" edge to a straight edge.

Opposite Curves

Staystitch inside the curve and clip.

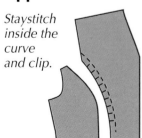

Then you can pin them together and stitch without puckers.

Taut Sewing

This is a must-know technique. To help eliminate puckered seams in any fabric, hold each end "taut" as it goes through the machine. Don't pull. This also helps prevent one layer from becoming longer than the other.

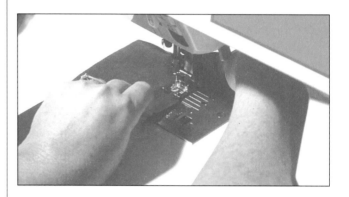

Do NOT Pin in Your Lap!

NEVER pin in your lap. Pinning while handling and lifting the fabric causes the layers to come out uneven.

pinned in lap

ends uneven

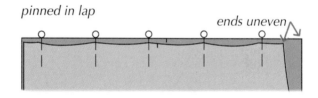

When pinning two long seams together, place the first layer of fabric on a clean, flat cutting surface. Smooth away any wrinkles. Place the second layer on top of the first and match snips, edges and ends. Smooth away any wrinkles. NOW you are ready to pin the layers together.

ends match   *snips match*   *ends match*

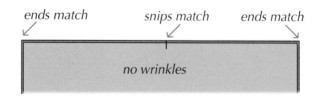

no wrinkles

243

Shoulders

Tip for Sloping Shoulders

Move narrow straps closer to the center back to keep them from falling off your shoulders.

Our Favorite Shoulder Pad Tips

We love shoulder pads. Sometimes they are very thick and other times non-existent; it all depends on the current look in fashion. We don't understand why they are always in men's jackets, but come and go in women's.

◆ We feel jackets should always have padded shoulders to have a beautiful tailored look.

◆ We prefer raglan pads in all sleeve styles as they can become your shoulder. Move them in or out depending on how much wider you want your shoulders. They can extend as much as 3/4" beyond your natural shoulder.

move out

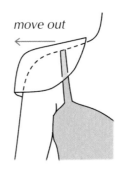

◆ We like the uncovered, layered, molded polyester pad; you can peel out layers to customize the shoulder thickness.

We do this when one shoulder is higher than the other (see page 161). Trim them if they're too wide for your shoulders. Leave them uncovered in lined jackets.

NOTE: To cover pads for unlined garments, fuse knit interfacing to the top and bottom sides and serge the outside edges together. Stretch the knit to fit. Or, try swimsuit lining. It's a knit and is not slippery so pads will stay on your shoulders better.

Shoulder pads balance uneven shoulders, and they also smooth your shoulder line if bra straps make them lumpy. See page 172 for ways a shoulder pad can camouflage a full upper arm.

Filling In Shoulder Hollows

Do you have a hollow upper chest? If you do, your jackets will dimple in that area. Add a layer or two of polyester fleece in the upper chest of your jacket.

1. Cut fleece to fit the pattern up to the neckline. Cut each layer 1/2" smaller than the one below.

2. Place the first layer below the shoulder seamline and out to the armhole edge as shown.

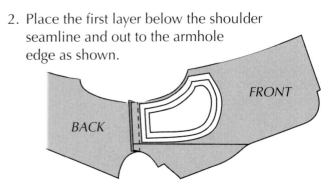

3. Place the second layer at the armhole seamline and 1/2" from the first layer on all other edges.

If your entire shoulder needs padding, lap your pattern pieces at the shoulder. Draw where you want the padding. If you use more than one layer, make each additional layer 1/2" smaller.

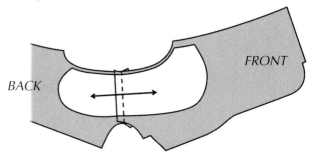

4. By hand, stitch padding layers together and to shoulder and armhole seams.

CHAPTER 25
Designing and Redesigning

Redesigning a pattern to change the style or make it more flattering is quicker than designing from scratch. However, learning flat pattern and draping do empower you to change a pattern. Remember, the pattern is the manuscript and you are the editor.

What is Draping?

Draping is making a piece of fabric into a design on a dress form or a body. Try the following:

1. Cut a square of fabric several inches larger than your front bodice length and width. Draw a line down the center. Draw another line below the upper edge at a distance equaling one quarter of the total length of the piece. These two lines should be perpendicular, with the horizontal line parallel to the floor.

2. Place the fabric on your body so it covers your shoulder seam and the center line is at the center of your body. Pin fabric to your slip or bra straps.

3. Cut on the center line down to the base of your neck.

4. Mark your armhole, shoulder and neckline seam. Trim away excess fabric to those lines or leave a seam allowance.

5. Tie elastic around your waist.

6. Pin darts to fit your shape.

Sandra drapes muslin to create a fitted bodice.

You have just created a fitted bodice front. Do the back the same way. It's fun!

Pattern tissue can be fitted in a similar way. Some call tissue-fitting, "tissue-draping." However, you don't start from scratch!

What is Flat Pattern Making?

Flat pattern making or drafting is designing from a basic sloper instead of draping fabric on a model to create the design.

If you fit the basic dress to you as shown on pages 74-88, you have your own design tools. This is not a book on designing, but the following examples are how you would use your sloper to create new designs or just to make a few changes in a pattern you own.

design desired   *Draw lines on sloper.*

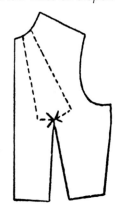

Cut on lines and close original dart.   *final pattern with seam allowances*

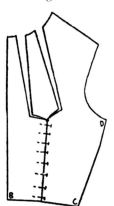
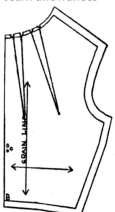

245

Flat Pattern Design Examples

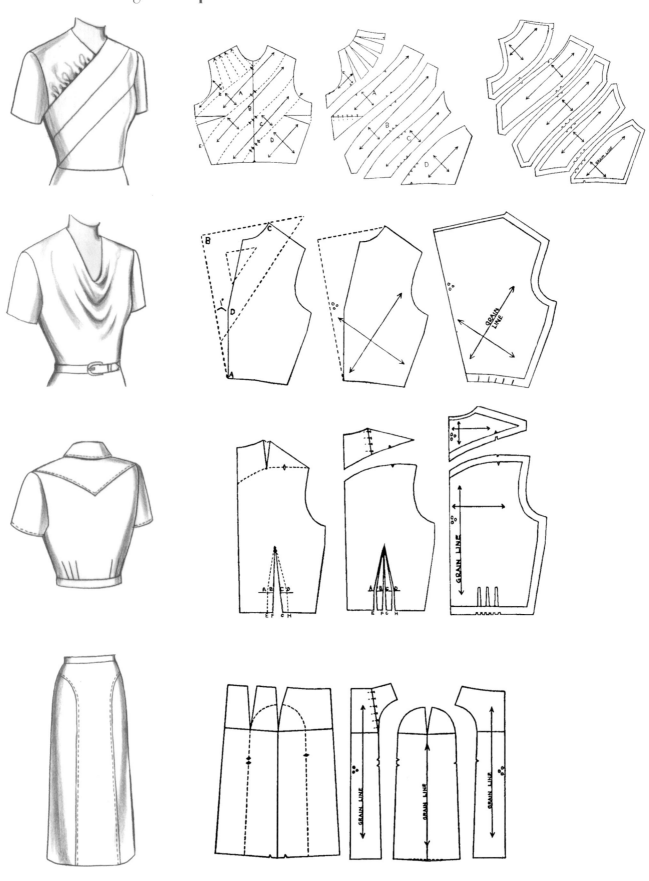

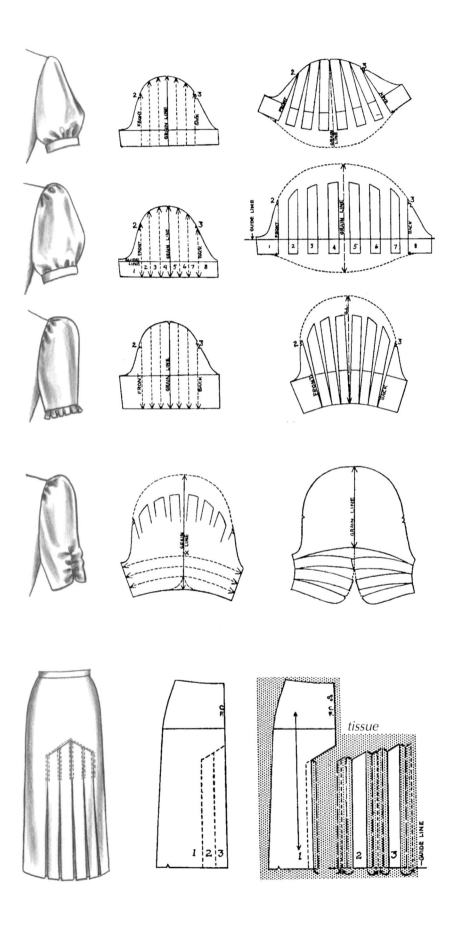

Now go to your favorite fabric store and spend an indulgent hour or so looking through all the 20,000 designs available from the pattern companies. Try to determine how some of your favorite styles were created using a basic sloper. The designs on these pages provide lots of clues.

The designs and pattern-making sequences shown here are from *Modern Pattern Design, The Complete Guide to the Creation of Patterns as a Means of Designing Smart Wearing Apparel* by Harriet Pepin, 1942.

Computer Patterns

The first ever computer pattern was introduced in the early '70s by Dritz. Pati was the Corporate Home Economist for Meier & Frank, a May Co. department store, at the time. She was asked to take the many body measurements required. The measurements were sent to Dritz in New York City and they printed out the pattern on a large printer.

As custom-fit computerized patterns become more widely available, fit issues that you encounter with standard-sized patterns can be minimized. Patterns are drafted to your exact measurements and body characteristics so 90 per cent of the fitting is done for you by a computer.

One of the challenges a sewer faces is obtaining accurate measurements. These accurate measurements are critical to getting a good custom-fit pattern. One company that provides not only custom-fit patterns but also the measuring solution is Unique Patterns Design Ltd.

By using state-of-the-art body scanning technology with the bodyskanner™, Unique scans your body using low-powered lights to get accurate measurements and body information. Using this information, the company drafts patterns from a selection from its catalog for you. Unique takes into consideration all of the issues mentioned in previous chapters such as left and right body differences, posture issues and different body proportions.

One major difference you will find with a pattern that is custom-fit to your measurements is that it may not look like patterns you are used to seeing. For example:

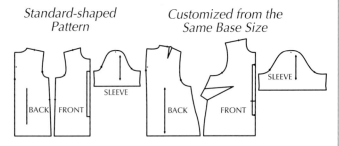

Standard-shaped Pattern   *Customized from the Same Base Size*

In this example you can see that the custom-fit pattern has a shoulder and a bust dart added to accommodate this woman's curves in the shoulder and bust area. This woman has hips that are proportionately larger than her upper body therefore requiring more room in the hip area. The sleeve is also larger to accommodate a full upper arm.

It is important to understand that just because a pattern is custom-fit to your measurements, you can't just sew it up and expect it to be perfect. Since 90 per cent of the fitting is done for you with custom-fit patterns, the remaining 10 per cent is up to you. This means that you can likely skip the tissue-fitting portion of garment construction but it is essential to fabric fit to ensure you're happy with the fit. Fabric differences, style preferences and ease amounts built into the pattern can all affect the results of your garment.

Commercial Patterns

There are nearly 20,000 designs offered by the pattern companies. Each design is fairly inexpensive considering the major companies spend about $40,000 creating and marketing each one. It's quite fast to alter a pattern to fit you once you know what size to buy and how you vary from patterns.

Dress Forms

Dress forms are not essential to sew clothes that fit. A dress form can't tell you how the clothes "feel" on the body.

On the other hand, they are very helpful if you design clothes for yourself. Draping a design on a dress form is fun, but it does take skill and time.

Pati made a dress form cover to fit her and put it on a foam dress form when she was 25 years old. Not many people have a replica of their 25-year-old body. Over the years, she has used it mainly to hang clothes on so steaming a collar roll or pinning a jump hem in a lining would be easier.

The best dress forms are those made on your body. Do-it-yourself kits for body-wrap dress forms are available through notions catalogs.

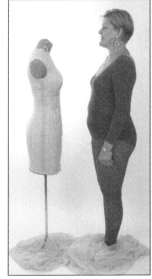

Baby boomer Pati Palmer contemplates the dress form she made to fit her body when she was in her 20s.

Photo styling by Pati's 12-year-old daughter, Melissa Watson.

CHAPTER 26

Pattern Company Basic Bodice Comparison

Now we can really get on our soapbox. We sew with all pattern company's products and we have no trouble fitting any of them. Though ease will change how each design fits, tissue-fitting allows you to see if you like the design ease.

We have heard many sewing authorities talk about how one company fits better than all of the others. The only way that could be is if all bodies were the same. Only then could you analyze patterns to find the best fitting brand.

This posture of creating fear of sewing any of the brands is one of the most negative things that could happen to sewing. Let's take a look and see exactly how different the five major pattern companies are.

We chose the current basic bodice patterns offered by each company and trimmed all seam allowances away; we also folded out all outlets. Where more than one cup-size front was offered, we used the B-cup front tissue.

We chose Vogue as the "control" and compared all other brands to it. We felt this was the easiest, since two other companies are almost identical to Vogue.

Vogue

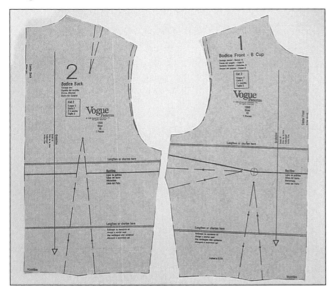

This is the Vogue basic bodice front and back. The extra stitching line on the armhole is for narrow shoulders. We trimmed to the normal shoulder line.

Butterick

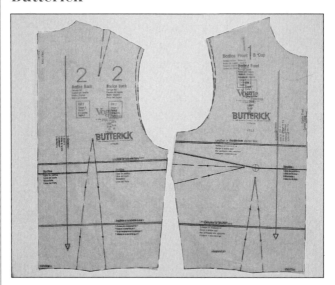

We have placed the Butterick basic on top of Vogue. You can see they are identical. Both brands are owned by The Butterick Company of New York.

McCall's

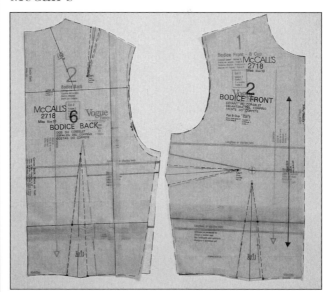

Here McCall's is placed on top of Vogue. The fronts are identical for all practical purposes. If there is an eighth or sixteenth of an inch difference here or there, remember, you could make that amount of error in cutting.

The back looks very different, but look closer. The Vogue vertical dart is deeper. (Do any of us sew darts exactly like the pattern, anyway?)

McCall's (continued)

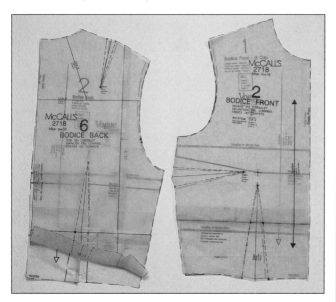

If we narrow the Vogue dart to match the McCall's, the armhole and side seams now match up.

Simplicity

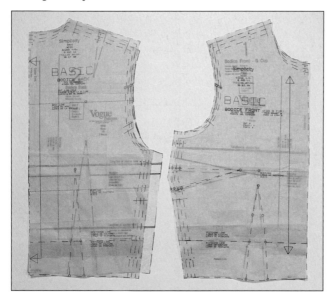

Simplicity has narrowed the back about the same amount as they've widened the front. (It looks like more until you make Vogue's back dart narrower like we did with McCall's.) Simplicity must like the side seam further back, but who's to say where the best place is for a side seam? That in itself won't affect fit.

The back shoulder is slightly more square and longer than Vogue—a minor difference. Simplicity uses ease and Vogue uses a dart in the back shoulder. That might be the reason for some of the difference. The armhole heights would match, as with McCall's, if Vogue's vertical back darts were made the same width.

Burda

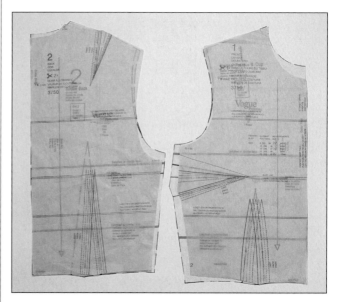

The Burda pattern we are using for comparison came out in 1995 and was Burda's redesigned basic.

The front and back chest areas are identical in shoulder slope and width. If the Vogue back waist dart were reduced, the armhole and side seams would match perfectly just like the McCall's.

The Burda back shoulder is wider, but Burda's shoulder dart is deeper. When darts are sewn, the back shoulder widths would be the same. Burda's horizontal bust dart is slightly deeper and the waist dart slightly shallower. After the front and back waist darts are sewn, the waist width will be similar to Vogue's.

More on Burda

Let's remember we are not comparing apples to apples. American size 10 is 32½" bust or 83cm. Burda's size 10 is 33" bust or 84cm.*

Burda's basic has changed shape three times in recent years. We aren't sure why, but someone said Burda's basic is redesigned to be closer to the current fashion. That's probably why the front neck is a bit lower in the basic pattern. American pattern companies use a consistent basic from which they design all the latest fashion patterns in their lines.

* Burda sizes 10-14 are larger than American sizes in the bust and sizes 16-24 are smaller. See page 27.

Changes in Burda Basic Patterns

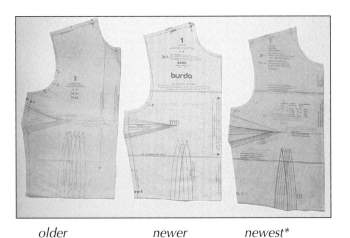

older newer newest*
#3750

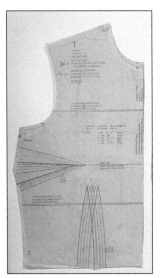

#3750 over the
oldest basic

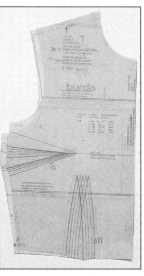

#3750 over the
newer basic

* Under #3750 we placed the green version sold in Europe.
It is exactly the same shape and the same pattern number.

Mail-order Information on McCall's Basic Dress Fit Pattern by Palmer/Pletsch:

All pattern company basics, except McCall's, are available in local fabric stores. You can order McCall's through a fabric store that carries McCall's. If there isn't one in your area, call 800/255-2762 or fax 913/776-0200. Have a credit card ready. Palmer/Pletsch Instructors provide this pattern in fit classes.

Metric Conversions

These numbers are slightly rounded for your convenience.
For complete accuracy, we have printed a metric ruler on the side of this page.

inches	centimeters	inches	centimeters	inches	centimeters
1/8	.3	7	18	29	73.5
1/4	.6	8	20.5	30	76
3/8	1	9	23	31	78.5
1/2	1.3	10	25.5	32	81.5
5/8	1.5	11	28	33	84
3/4	2	12	30.5	34	86.5
7/8	2.2	13	33	35	89
1	2.5	14	35.5	36	91.5
1 1/4	3.2	15	38	37	94
1 1/2	3.8	16	40.5	38	96.5
1 3/4	4.5	17	43	39	99
2	5	18	46	40	102
2 1/2	6.3	19	48.5	41	104
3	7.5	20	51	42	107
3 1/2	9	21	53.5	43	109
4	10	22	56	44	112
4 1/2	11.5	23	58.5	45	115
5	12.5	24	61	46	117
5 1/2	14	25	63.5	47	120
		26	66	48	122
6	15	27	68.5	49	125
		28	71	50	127

metric conversion chart courtesy of the McCall Pattern Company

Metric Ruler

Index

Real People and Their Fit Challenges

LOOK FOR THESE PRODUCTS FROM PALMER/PLETSCH:

Books on Fit, Fashion & Fabric

Our books, written from over 30 years of experience, are filled with color photos and illustrated, easy-to-follow how tos.

Cookbook

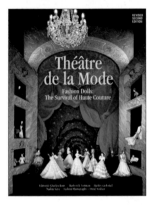

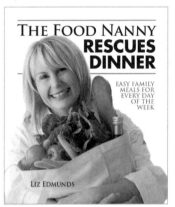

Books For the Home...and Serging

from basics to creative possibilities

*It all started with **Pants for Any Body** over 30 years ago! That book and other "great value" small-format books are still available! ~Pati*

INTERACTIVE DVDs

The styles and techniques in our books are brought to life and expanded on by Marta Alto and Pati Palmer in these DVD videos.

For the Children...

My First Sewing Books and Kits, *by Winky Cherry* Along with a teaching manual and DVD, they offer a complete, thoroughly tested sewing program for children ages 5 to 11.

Patterns

Palmer/Pletsch for McCall's are the McCall Pattern Company's top-selling patterns.

Also look for our *Learn to Sew!* **Teacher-in-an-Envelope**

And don't miss the FREE

FASHION FOR *Real* PEOPLE
ONLINE MAGAZINE

User-Friendly Interfacings
PerfectFuse™

- ◆ Discovered by the pros; thoroughly tested for quality
- ◆ These four distinctly different products cover 90% of interfacing needs
- ◆ Come in convenient 1-yard and 3-yard packages
- ◆ Extra wide for cutting larger pattern pieces
- ◆ Each interfacing has its own separate use, care and how-to instructions
- ◆ All four weights available in charcoal-black and ecru-white

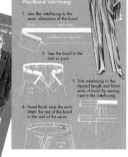

PERFECT SEW NEEDLE THREADER

Now thread both machine and hand needles with ease. On one end of this tool is the specially designed hook that makes threading easy. The other end is an integrated needle inserter for both conventional and serger machine needles.

threading hand needles

threading machine needles

inserting machine needles

PERFECT PATTERN PAPER
two 84" x 48" sheets

PerfectSew™
WASH-AWAY FABRIC STABILIZER

Business & Teaching Tools

SEMINARS FOR TEACHERS

provided on CDs

PALMER/PLETSCH Workshops
Take A Sewing Vacation!

Our "Sewing Vacations" are offered on a variety of topics, including *Pant Fit, Fit, Tailoring, Creative Serging, Ultrasuede, Couture, Sewing Update, Intermediate Sewing, Sewing Camp,* and more. Workshops are held at the Palmer/Pletsch Training Center in Portland, Oregon.

Teacher training sessions available on some topics include: practice teaching sessions, up to 300 digital slides and teaching script; camera-ready workbook handouts, and publicity flyer.

Visit the website for a complete schedule.

For more details on these and other products, workshops, and teacher training, please visit our website:

www.palmerpletsch.com

Palmer/Pletsch Publishing
1801 N.W. Upshur Street, Suite 100, Portland, OR 97209
(503) 274-0687 or fax (503) 274-1377
or 1-800-728-3784 (orders)
info@palmerpletsch.com